A LIFE-CHANGING PHONE

"This is Coroner's Investigator Taylor... was Lucia Elaine Rothwell your moth...

"Wait a minute." My face felt warm, and ... myself with a brochure. Despite all my ... strengthening jogging, I suddenly felt winded. "What do you mean, *was?*"

"Mrs. Mints, we believe we have the body of a woman who may be your mother at the coroner's office, and we need you to come down and make an identification."

I dropped the phone and began screaming. I screamed for five minutes. And in those five minutes my whole life caught up with me.

CATCH MY MOTHER'S KILLER

Paula Mints

Expanding Horizons

Expanding Horizons
An imprint of New Horizon Press
Far Hills, New Jersey

Expanding Horizons books are published by

New Horizon Press
P.O. Box 669
Far Hills, NJ 07931

All Kensington Titles, Imprints, and Distributed Lines are available at special quantity discounts for bulk purchases for sales promotions, premiums, fund-raising, and educational or institutional use. Special book excerpts or customized printings can also be created to fit specific needs. For details, write or phone the office of the Kensington special sales manager: Kensington Publishing Corp., 850 Third Avenue, New York, NY 10022, attn: Special Sales Department, Phone: 1-800-221-2647.

EXPANDING HORIZONS is a trademark of NEW HORIZON PRESS. EXPANDING HORIZONS and the EXPANDING HORIZONS logo are trademarks of NEW HORIZON PRESS and the EXPANDING HORIZONS logo is a registered trademark.

ISBN-13: 978-1-933893-15-0
ISBN-10: 1-933893-15-X

First New Horizon Press Hardcover Printing: 2000
First Expanding Horizons Mass Market Printing: August 2008

10 9 8 7 6 5 4 3 2 1

Printed in the United States of America

For my niece, who has her grandmother's lovely eyes.

Mother died today.
Or perhaps it was yesterday.
I don't know.

Albert Camus
The Outsider

Contents

	Author's Note	ix
	Prologue	1
1	Lost Music	4
2	Collisions	18
3	Moving Around	34
4	Growing Up Mad	52
5	Runaways	65
6	Paula Jean	89
7	Discoveries	123
8	Some Questions	141
9	Patterns	156
10	The Persistence of Memory	161
11	Selective Blindness	182
12	Confrontations and Configurations	200
13	Without Passion or Prejudice	220
14	By Force or Fear	267
15	An Important Day	282
16	The Finale	290
17	Elaine Rothwell, Human Being	309
	Epilogue	328
	Special Update for the Paperback Edition: And After That	330

AUTHOR'S NOTE

This book is based on the experiences of Paula Mints and reflects her perceptions of the past, present and future. The personalities, events, actions and conversations portrayed within the story have been taken from her memories, extensive interviews, research, court documents, letters, personal papers, press accounts and the memories of participants.

In an effort to safeguard the privacy of certain people, she has changed their names and the names of certain places and in some cases, altered otherwise identifying characteristics.

PROLOGUE

I sat at the kitchen table in my comfortable blue bathrobe, sipping strong coffee. My house has one of those areas set aside as both an eating space and extension of the family room and the kitchen. I like it because it is the central room. If you are sitting at the kitchen/dining table, all household life has to pass by you in order to get where it is going. Not much can happen without you being part of it.

The morning newspaper was spread in front of me. Drops of water from my hair, still wet from the shower, kept landing on the newsprint. I told myself to go back and dry it, but I was an inveterate reader and loved scanning the morning paper. Halfway down the page, I browsed through a human interest article in the *San Jose Mercury News*, the kind of story that captures your attention because you cannot help thinking how fortunate you are that it is not happening to you or someone you know.

The body of a slender woman had been discovered yesterday morning on the on-ramp to northbound 880 from North First Street in San Jose. People arriving at work in a nearby First Street building spotted the body through a fence near the parking lot, said Detective Richard Arra. "Homicide detectives sent to the scene couldn't see any visible wounds on the victim," Arra said.

How sad for the family, I thought Then, How horrible for the person who found the body. It was a depressing moment, and the mood lingered as I read the rest of the local section. To break the melancholy, I finished my morning coffee while reading the sports section, then dried my hair and rushed through getting dressed and left for work.

I had all but forgotten the article by afternoon when I received a phone call. It was a business acquaintance from whom I had not heard for a while. Sven Holton was an assistant coroner's investigator for the County of Santa Clara, a sort of apprentice position on his way to becoming an expert body untangler. Sven was from Sweden. The ends of his words had an upward lilt to them, which made everything he said sound like a question.

"How are you, Paula? Long time," he said.

"I'm fine. You're right, it's been a long time. Are you planning a trip?" I was working as a travel agent and was used to people holding brief conversations with me prior to asking for low plane fares. I had gotten into travel agency work at the suggestion of a friend. Before taking the job, I'd worked as a cook on a catering truck, a filer at a medical clinic, a clerk at a glass store, and a wafer inspector in a semiconductor facility. At this point in my lackluster career, working as a travel agent was a definite step up. In fact, to learn more about the travel business I'd begun taking classes a few years before at Foothill Junior College. Once I started back to school I didn't want to quit. At this point I'd finished my associate's degree and was now working towards my undergraduate degree. Motivation comes in all sorts of interesting guises. Sven had been one of my first clients. I'd helped him with an emergency ticket to Stockholm, and we'd become acquaintances of the sort that every couple of months he'd call to update me on life in the coroner's office.

"No, no," Sven said strangely, and we shared one of those awkward silences only possible over telephones.

Sven cleared his throat. "Paula, tell me. What is your mother's name?'

"Excuse me?" I put down the brochure I was holding. "What do you mean?" I looked around the room at my officemates absorbed in their own work at their own desks. I felt my face begin to redden. Sven and I were definitely not at the point in our acquaintanceship where I felt comfortable enough to offer confidences about my personal life.

"When was the last time you saw your mother?"

"Sven, why are you asking this?" I began restlessly moving items around on my desk. *What could he have found out?* I wondered.

"Just a minute." Sven put me on hold. Muzak drifted through the receiver at me. I put my free hand to my throat and waited.

"Paula Mints?" A voice I didn't recognize came on the line.

"Yes. Who is this?"

"Were you formerly Paula Jean Rothwell?"

"Formerly and still reigning champion. Who is this, please?" My left leg began shaking. I put my free hand on my knee to calm it.

"This is Coroner's Investigator Taylor Minor. Mrs. Mints, was Lucia Elaine Rothwell your mother?"

"Wait a minute." My face felt warm, and I began fanning myself with a brochure. Despite all my lung-strengthening jogging, I suddenly felt winded. "What do you mean, *was*?"

"Mrs. Mints, we believe we have the body of a woman who may be your mother at the Coroner's Office, and we need you to come down and make an identification."

I dropped the phone and began screaming. I screamed for five minutes. And in those five minutes my whole life caught up with me.

CHAPTER 1

Lost Music

My mother never sang when she was crazy. Music only came into her when her mind was quiet and she could clearly hear her own voice. Mother sang from the time she was a little girl. Even when she was a teenager and the madness first hit her, she kept singing. As time passed, voices and visions began to control her thoughts and actions. My mother never described her visions to me, so I can't tell you exactly what she saw. I suffer from classic migraines and that's the closest I've ever come to losing control over what I see or perceive. I can't control the aura that signals a migraine headache, just as my mother couldn't control the hallucinations that signaled the deterioration of her sanity.

At first, my mother probably used her beautiful singing voice to fight off the demons. I'm guessing that was the time when singing quieted them but gradually they took over her reality. Finally though, the noise and apparitions inside her head crowded everything else out. I suppose that's why after a while she sang only when the voices were silent. Then she must have wanted to fill her head up with happy sounds of her own making. That's what music was to my mother: the sounds of joy and normality bubbling over inside her head and out of her mouth. Sometimes being normal or average is the best gift that life offers.

Mother was a southerner by birth who grew up in a huge rambling house in Tennessee. My southern grandparents' old house was higher than the sky, surrounded by tall green trees, all of it covered with air that sat heavily on the top of your head. "This is the place to be a kid in," I whispered to my little brother during the only time we ever visited there. It was just the kind of place where you could run barefoot without anyone caring. I was eight years old the summer we drove across the country to visit my grandparents, and it was a kid's paradise to me. Even though I only visited my grandparents' farm that once, the memory clung, until I feared that the dose of reality revisiting it would provide, would also wipe those memories away.

All memories have two sides to them: the side you want to remember and the side you want to forget. Seems a simple concept, but it's not. The more choosing you do and memories you rewrite, the less you understand how they define you. I expect that what you choose to forget is powerful, having as it does the ability to alter your happy perceptions of the past.

The truth is that my mother's childhood in Tennessee was different from my one visit.

Religion was very important to my mother's parents, who believed God granted everyone at least one special gift. They also believed that any deviation from a normal personality was punishment for some unrepented sin. My mother was born in 1927, her fate in the hands of a hillbilly mother named Mildred, and a solemn, ill-humored, and well-to-do father named Lucian.

My grandmother grew up in a one-room cabin in the hills near the Tennessee River. She didn't get an education past the sixth grade, but she did spend her childhood surrounded by colorful quilts, folklore, superstitions, and a still behind the house that produced fine, smooth Tennessee whiskey. Mildred ran free and barefoot until she was fifteen years old, when she met and married my grandfather, an older man of twenty-five. Lucian was an only child. His parents had died earlier that year, forcing him to drop out of college but leaving him a landowner and a man of comfortable means.

He saw Mildred from a distance at the county fair and watched her running with her friends, barefoot in the twilight, long dark hair flying behind her, playing with the younger children. Lucian imagined Mildred to be a wonderful, free-spirited creature, he said later, and he longed to tame her.

My grandfather-to-be approached his intended's father, crumpled hat in hands, twisted and sweaty as he turned it round and round, and asked to come courting. Every other evening he came and sat on the porch with his beloved. They spent long silent evenings watching fireflies while he worked up the courage to ask for her hand in marriage. He was shy and awkward. She was fidgety and felt trapped on the porch with the silent stranger when she wanted to be running barefoot through the green hills. Still, Mildred knew that marriage would give her her own house, and the thought appealed to her.

Lucian moved his new bride into his farmhouse. Mildred found herself removed from her one-room cabin in the deep, sensual green of the hills and plunked down in a fifteen-room house with more furniture needing dusting on a regular basis than she had seen in her life.

The house was set back on a shady street in a country neighborhood where there never seemed to be enough green overhang to fight off the summer heat, and the wearing of shoes was required. Plant more trees, she urged her bridegroom, and he did.

Lucian was a somber, naturally disapproving young man. His solemn ways slowly peeled away the exuberance from Mildred's personality. After a year of marriage, her smile had receded into a grim straight line, her years of laughter soon forgotten. The young couple began having children at the rate of one every other year, until the count stretched to sixteen. Five of the babies died in infancy, leaving an ample-sized brood of eleven: five girls and six boys. My mother was somewhere in the middle of the gang.

They named my mother Lucia Elaine; Lucia for her father and Elaine after a several-generations-removed aunt. My mother hated the name Lucia and wouldn't answer to it. Sometimes her brothers would tease her by calling her Lucia. When they did, my mother would cry until her older sister, Dot, came to her rescue. Anyway, for the rest of her life everyone called her Elaine, and after she died I found myself correcting people when they referred to her as Lucia. Refusing to let people call her Lucia was one way that I could still protect her.

My grandfather's rules for rearing children were absolute. He believed in order, discipline, religion, and silence. Any break with order and discipline brought out the strap. Besides children, he also raised hogs and watermelons. Though Lucian might not have talked much to his family, he could be heard in the evenings quoting poetry to his favorite hogs. More specifically, he read to the ones fat enough to slaughter.

My mother was the runt of the litter of children, being tiny, always shorter than her brothers and sisters, and skinny: a quiet, plain child with thin brown hair and huge blue eyes. She loved to run barefoot through the orchard with her long pigtails sailing behind her and the dust from the ground coating her legs. She would call out as she ran, "I'm flying!" From the beginning she both loved and did well in school. She wasn't brilliant but she was diligent, and she especially loved the way numbers fit together neatly. With mathematics, my mother believed, you got a game that, if you used the correct formula, had a solution. She didn't stand out in school, but she was thought of by her teachers as clean, polite, and correct. She sat quietly at her desk and always had the answer when the teacher called on her. When you think about bits and pieces of our lives that go together to create the whole people we become, there are worse ways to be remembered than as quiet and studious.

After an even-tempered early childhood, when she was about thirteen years old Mother suddenly began behaving strangely. Sometimes she wandered the house at night, interrupted the silence of dinnertime with bursts of laughter, carried on one-sided conversations, and gave my grandfather ample reason to use his leather strap on her. She also began believing that people were plotting against and stealing from her.

Despite this, Elaine still did well in school. And her singing voice was so fine that when she was sixteen years old she was invited to sing with a gospel choir. The choir toured the country for a month, and she went with them. Her parents were proud. They were pleased to see their quiet and somewhat strange daughter evidence so fine a talent and do something to make herself stand out from her brothers and sisters.

If you squint, you can see my mother now, just a frail little thing with light brown hair and glasses, standing in the middle row of the choir, surrounded by taller and more confident adults, but singing out with her clear beautiful soprano. Thinking about it, I believe that if she'd stayed with that gospel group instead of returning home to her parents' farm, her life may have gone in a completely different direction. She could have spent her life involved with music that she loved. At least then, even crazy, she would have been appreciated. She would have had applause to divert her attention from insanity. I can relate to what attracting attention can do for a person. All my life I've craved a great big loudness around me and despaired of the quiet. During my childhood I found out too much thinking gets you into a heap of trouble, and solitude gives you an empty room in which to do nothing but cogitate.

When she was sixteen, the same year she was in the choir, my mother also spent a lot of time locked in the basement repenting her sins of emotion and recovering from her father's stern, swift, strap-laden punishments. Her parents, frightened by their daughter's strange behavior and hysteria, dragged her from doctor to doctor until they found an answer. Obviously, this was no easily understood nervous breakdown, no girlish fit of pique or the vapors. Finally, when she was seventeen, she was diagnosed as schizophrenic. In literature, southern attics are filled with the ghosts of crazy relatives both real and imagined, but in reality there is a perceived taint that insanity touches the entire family. My mother was a genteel schizophrenic, crazy for years in a quiet way that could be suppressed with medication. True to his religious beliefs, Lucian, her father, deemed his daughter's diagnosis a retribution of some obscure sort for some unrecognized sin and suffered the indignity of it in silence, which was his approach to most things.

Meanwhile, Lucian profited from his pigs, and since he believed it was a father's duty to educate his children, as each child was ready to attend college he sent them off to learn a profession. Despite her sometimes tortured thoughts, my mother, heavily medicated by that time but still performing well in school, went to the University of Tennessee.

My mother's memories of her family must have been bittersweet, with a you-can't-go-home-again quality to them. Despite whatever painful remembrances my mother kept to herself, to the end of her life she loved the South, Tennessee, and her family. She always thought of her parents' farm as home. My mother had the virtue of forgiveness, though in lucid moments she forgot nothing.

During college, Elaine was a quiet and intense student. She didn't date much, but when she did her dates found her intelligent and possessed of an unexpectedly quick sense of humor. Elaine wasn't one to tell a joke just for the sake of getting a laugh—her humor was more subtle than that. She always noted the absurd side of life and was willing to laugh at herself. She captivated those around her with her infectious laugh, which had an undeniably sexy, throaty quality to it. Mostly though, she kept to herself. Since she didn't go out very often, it wasn't until she began her first year of teaching that she met my father. They were both around twenty-five years old, working as teachers, registered Democrats, taking graduate courses at San Jose State University, and fond of Bob Hope movies. On the basis of these few similarities, they began having lunch together every day.

If a passionate romance blossomed between my parents when they began dating, certainly there was no evidence of it by the time I came on the scene. My father, never one to confide, has on occasion mentioned that he liked my mother's laugh. Her laugh drew his attention to her in class, along with her quick, intelligent mind. Once she attracted his attention, he noticed her beautiful blue eyes. Mother was also a good listener. Since my father loves conversation and especially enjoys telling humorous tales about his past, my mother's ability to enjoy a good story was an added attraction. Unlike my mother, my father is a teller of stories and a creator of his own oral history. I take after him in that regard.

My father has always told anecdotes about his childhood. It seems he remembers every detail of his growing up and practically every detail of his life from then on. It's only his life with my mother that he's chosen to forget, and I suppose I can't blame him. Father says he got his great memory from growing up poor during the Depression, when every scrap of information might be worth something, sometime. His own father abandoned the family when my father and his twin brother were born, leaving my grandmother to raise four children on her own: her older son and daughter and my father and his twin brother. Grandmother managed her brood by raising her daughter, Betty, to be an obedient and responsible child, and letting her three sons run wild. Unusual for her era, my grandmother got a divorce and married again, but her new husband was an alcoholic. According to my father, one day he just up and died of something to do with his liver, though my grandmother was more than capable of whacking him over the head with a cast-iron skillet. My grandmother, Lillian, packed up her family and moved from Illinois to Los Angeles, California. My father says that in California they were poor, which Lillian hated. She hated being poor so much that she remarried once more and moved back to Illinois with her new husband, leaving her children in California with relatives.

My father refers to these as "the castor oil years". The children were in the care of an aunt who believed in administering castor oil for health reasons and also as punishment. The aunt was very health conscious, and dutifully boiled the germs out of everything from water to milk. As a result, to this day my father hates milk. When my father and his twin were fifteen and his sister Betty was seventeen, Lillian moved back to California. Her third husband had recently died, leaving her a bit more financially stable. During her California mourning period, she met and married a new man. Lillian was a short, well-groomed, extremely feminine woman. She accomplished everything she set out to do with brisk competence. Her heel-clicking little walk sounded a tap dance whenever she entered or left a room. Men found her attractive: they pursued and obsessed over her. She was never without romantic choices, though she seemed to choose men who drank too much. Her husbands were always recovering from periods of heavy drinking, well on the way to destroying their livers.

After her fourth marriage, Lillian reunited her family and moved everyone to San Jose, California. My father and his twin did not like their new stepfather, who was a violent alcoholic given to pinching noses until they bled and slapping the teenage brothers on the backs of their heads. The twins retaliated by stealing money from his wallet and putting salt in his cereal. For a year they put a strain on their mother's new marriage. They were a tough pair, short of height at five feet, four inches each, but athletic and very intelligent.

The twins were known as the family troublemakers. My father especially was viewed by my grandmother as too independent for her tastes. Whereas his brothers and sister, and even his twin, regularly sent money home to their mother, my father refused. Though his siblings discussed all their personal decisions with their mother, my father did not. Grandmother was the family matriarch. All family activity revolved around her and my father's refusal to bend to her will rankled until she died. As for my father, it took my mother's breakdown to bring him in line and back into the family fold.

One day shortly after the twins turned sixteen they came home from school and found the house empty. No furniture, no pets, no family, just a note on the door letting them know that the family had moved. The note, in Lillian's neat handwriting, wished them luck finishing high school and did not provide a forwarding address.

At sixteen years old, my father was temporarily homeless. He was the lucky twin (being athletically talented), and the high school wrestling coach, who wanted him to join his team, took him in. My uncle got temporary shelter with a friend's family. Other than his twin, my father didn't see the rest of his family again for ten years.

Pictures of my father from this time show a compact, muscular, and good-looking teenage boy. My father was the best wrestler on the squad and even made state champion his senior year. I don't know what would have happened to him if he hadn't been so athletically inclined. Luckily though, he was the coach's favorite on the squad, so he lived for two years with his coach and his wife, sleeping in the spare bedroom. Father never discusses this time in his life other than to talk about the trouble he continued to get into at school. After graduating from high school, he never saw his coach or his coach's family again. My father has always believed that too much gratitude will eventually make you feel ill.

Not long after they had been separated, Father's twin brother dropped out of school and spent his time hanging out with his friends until he joined the merchant marines. Except for my father's relationship with his wrestling coach, neither of the twins was popular with their high school teachers, who viewed them as poor students and troublemakers. My father and his twin took pride in giving their teachers a difficult time, which is ironic when you consider that my father earned a teaching certificate and taught school for a time.

The incident that prompted my father's twin brother to drop out of high school happened in the library. My father had cut class and was hiding out amongst the stacks of books, killing time. The librarian, a tall, thin, plain single woman with the misfortune of looking like a stereotypical librarian, came up behind my father as he knelt between the stacks and began kicking him in the rear end while shrieking, "Rothwell. I know you Rothwell brothers. You are bad, bad boys. Go to class."

My father turned to her, grabbed her foot, and said, "Madam, mount your broomstick and fly away." Immediately realizing that he should not have spoken, my father fled the library. He didn't know that his twin brother was sitting at a table, quietly studying, on the other side of the library. To be fair, I do not think that his behavior would have changed if he had known. Being identical twins, they were quite used to taking the blame for one another. When, at the librarian's urging, the principal arrived to dispense discipline, they found my father's twin at his studies. My uncle was expelled, and my father went on to graduate after an undistinguished high school academic career. He joined the navy directly after graduation, enrolling in college at the navy's expense when his tour of duty was over.

Truthfully, I've always been more comfortable with the war between my parents than any peace there might have been, let alone any romance. It is very difficult to imagine one's parents falling in love. The most my mind will allow me to ponder over is that they probably made a very nice couple. Both were short (under five-foot-four-inches), athletically slim (my father who continued wrestling was California State Wrestling Champion when he was in college), and very intelligent people.

My father says my mother was friendly and feminine. She enjoyed going to the beach, out to dinner, and to the movies: the type of woman who would make a pleasant, intelligent companion with a few surprises thrown in for spice. She continued to laugh at his stories and was very affectionate, liking to hold hands often. This may not sound like the passionate declaration of a young man in love, but my father is too private a person to let the secrets of his romance with my mother out for public view.

Neither of my parents were makers of abrupt decisions, so they dated for three years before they became engaged in 1955. If my father noticed any odd behavior on my mother's part before they married, he has never mentioned it. Perhaps if they'd lived together before getting married my mother's true mental condition would have been more evident. However, in the 1950s people like my parents didn't consider living together a viable choice. Certainly no one in my mother's family thought to discuss my mother's past emotional breakdowns with my father. Probably they wanted her to have a chance at a happy, normal life, and probably Father wouldn't have understood anyway. Since my mother's condition had been stable for several years, everyone held a wait-and-see attitude about her mental state. Before they were married my mother explained her condition to her future husband. She told him she'd suffered breakdowns in the past, but she was fine now. It's safe to assume that my father didn't really understand what my mother meant by *breakdown*.

After the wedding my parents put off having children for a few years in favor of working hard and saving money.

So, instead of trying to make a career of singing professionally, my mother tucked her dream into her private never-to-be-mentioned memory box and had decided on college and getting married. She was one of those ethereal, thoughtful types, given to introspection and analysis. When she was young she never went anywhere without a book. The older she got, the less literature comforted her, and the less music distracted her.

My mother was a disaster at housewifery. She was meant for music and intellectual pursuits and ended up badly scrubbing pans and wistfully sweeping the kitchen floor with a book in one hand. In my mother's kitchen, if you opened a cabinet, a box of cereal was likely to fall on your head. This may be the reason I have a fear of falling objects.

During the early years of their marriage when both of my parents were teachers, my mother taught high school mathematics. She loved teaching. She was a natural, and very good, teacher. The quiet, self-effacing attitude she presented to the world most of my growing-up years wasn't present in the classroom. Of course, schizophrenia hadn't overtaken her completely at that point and she generally acted like everyone else. Enough like everyone else that, according to my father, the boys in my mother's classes tended to develop crushes on her. They liked that she was feminine. They liked that she was kind. They liked her musical voice and cheerful laugh. And they loved her beautiful blue eyes. Boys in my mother's classes did corny things like bringing her apples and cleaning the chalkboard for her after class. The students in my mother's math classes did well and did not hate math one bit. Despite her love of teaching, my mother fully expected to give it up as soon as she and my father were financially set up to live on one income and raise a family.

My father was a different sort of teacher from my mother. He was the type that children both dreaded and loved. They loved him for his funny stories and dreaded him because he was strict. While my mother was pregnant my father was teaching in a one-room schoolhouse in Morgan Hill, California. He had one student in each grade, from first grade through sixth grade. One day he came back from recess a few minutes before the class was to return and found that one of his students had written "I hat Mr. Rothwell" all over the chalkboard. With only six students, finding the poor speller was easy. My father had the perpetrator erase the boards and then write the same sentence one hundred times, spelling *hate* correctly.

My parents' marriage was uneventful until my mother became pregnant. Out of fear of harming her unborn baby, Mother stopped taking her medications. Then, when she was five months pregnant, she had a breakdown. She became afraid that my father had secret plans to take me away from her after I was born.

My birth was amazingly uncomplicated for a breech delivery. I backed into the world exactly on time. Probably life in an insane womb was less than placid. Separation anxiety has not played a large part in my personality. By the time I was born I was trained to accept upheaval as the natural course.

The status quo was more difficult for a woman to ward off in those days; so Mother put away her studies a few years after she had me, packed up her teaching degree, and only sang to the furniture after that. She never mentioned whether she regretted giving up either singing or intellectual pursuits to become a housewife and a mother.

CHAPTER 2

Collisions

My parents named me Paula after no one in particular and for no special reason other than the fact that my father saw the name in a book he was reading and liked it. I wasn't planned for, and I wasn't a surprise. Children were what my parents expected to have, much as they assumed the eventuality of a mortgage, marital arguments, and visits to the dentist. When my mother filled out my birth certificate, she tried to change my name to Patricia after one of her sisters, but my father caught her just in time. I always wonder if I'd grown up as Patti, might I have lived an entirely different life? Both my parents loved me very much. My brother, Michael Alan, was born five years later, and they loved him too, but by that time love in our family had begun to take effort.

All my life I was Paula Jean when my parents or anyone in my family was angry with me and plain old Paula at all other times. I learned early to listen for the distinction.

I never trust anyone with my childhood all at once. Instead, I dole it out in increments, small servings of me designed to find out slowly who will stick around and who won't after they know the whole truth. My family is a secretive bunch—small truths are never freely offered but must be forced from us. Even now my father tells no one his true age, and my brother likes to keep his whereabouts private.

Most of my childhood is a memory-free zone. This does not mean that I have no memories, but they are more like dreams, easily forgotten upon waking. I go to my father for confirmation of what I remember, and he listens, looks downs at the ground, and either nods or lies. Now that I am all grown up and my father is more comfortable with what remains behind us, he is sometimes willing to offer up a memory or two of our life as a family, though he's always willing to tell stories of his own youth. He covers these memories of our life together over with recriminations against my mother, her family, and the happy life they robbed him of. Still, he is my point of reference and so I listen carefully to all he says. I unwrap my father's recollections of my childhood and teenage years, ooh and ah over the experiences, and my father leaves happy to have done me a service.

This isn't to imply that my early childhood is a complete blank. I remember when my mother used to laugh all the time. When she was sane my mother had a soft and happy laugh. Her hair bounced when she laughed, and her smile reached right up into her eyes.

When I was very little, still a baby really, my mother always tucked me into bed after my bath. She brushed my hair off my forehead and ran her hand down the side of my face. "Your hair is always in your eyes, Paula," she said as she smiled down at me. I thought she had the prettiest eyes in the world, and I wanted mine to be just like hers.

My mother would come to me when I had nightmares and sit beside the bed holding my hand in the darkness. She carefully saved my fallen teeth for the tooth fairy, baked chocolate chip cookies with me and read stories to me at bedtime.

During my early childhood, when my parents were high school teachers in Morgan Hill, money was tight during the summers when school was closed. My father always took a summer job working in a local cannery, while my mother stayed home with me. Every morning my mother dropped Father off at the cannery and we had the rest of the day to ourselves.

The summer I was three years old my mother decided we needed a new car. For two weeks, starting from the instant we dropped my father off at work until it was time to pick him up again, we answered newspaper advertisements and visited car lots. Each day we had a picnic lunch. After lunch we played our version of hide-and-seek where I always hid and she sought.

"Paula," she'd call out while she pretended to look for me, "where are you hiding? Come out now, Paula. You have your poor mama worried to death."

I would sneak up behind her and yell boo.

"Paula," she'd say, "why you little stinker. Where were you hiding, Child?" And she'd tickle me until we laughed so hard that we both fell down.

On Friday of our second week of car shopping we found a car that my mother deemed both affordable and reliable. Mother traded in our old car and signed papers while I fidgeted. I sat next to her in the salesman's office, practicing holding my legs out in front of me until they ached. Every now and then my mother would pat me on the knee.

"Daddy will be surprised," I said.

"Yes, he will, honey," my mother replied.

"He'll think we were smart, right?" I asked.

"Yes, Paula, your father will be very happy."

We picked my father up from work that day in our new car. My father walked around the car for a long time. His forehead was crinkled, and he tapped his mouth with an index finger and hummed while he walked.

"Elaine," he said, "what were you thinking? We can't afford a new car. I don't know what you were thinking. If you mentioned to me what you were up to I would have told you that we couldn't afford a new car." My father stood looking at my mother, tapping his index finger against his mouth.

"Bill," my mother said, "this is a used car that happens to be in better shape than the one I traded in. I'm getting tired of having the darned thing stall on me every time I come to a stop sign. Besides, after trading in the old car this one only cost five hundred dollars. I've thought it through—we can afford it."

My father stood in front of my mother and put his hands on her shoulders. He gave her a little shake. "Elaine," he repeated, "we cannot afford a new car." Then Father smiled. We got into the car and my father drove back to the dealership. After much arguing he convinced the salesman to give us back our old car.

My parents returned to their teaching jobs after Labor Day, and I was turned over to a baby-sitter. During the summer we'd moved from Morgan Hill to San Jose. My mother's last complete breakdown had occurred before I was born. We were poor and money was tight, but I remember those summers as the happiest of my childhood.

Each day my father would bring me to my baby-sitter, Helga's, house. Each night he picked me up from Helga's freshly bathed and in pajamas, having been fed my dinner and readied for bed. After three months of this schedule my mother went through a bad spell and would not let my father take me to the baby-sitter. Helga came to our house instead. Usually Helga stayed until my father came home from work, but one day she went home early in the afternoon. Left to myself, I did what any small child would do and explored. I found an empty can of food in the garbage which I decided to play with. I fell on the sharp edge of the can, which cut through my cheek. I sat crying until my father came home. My mother, on heavy medication at the time, slept through my tears.

Father took me to the hospital. My clothes, my face, and my hands were covered with blood, so the nurses undressed me figuring to send me home in a tiny hospital gown. When they took off my T-shirt they discovered that my back was covered with welts, bruises, and slashes. The marks continued down the backs of my legs.

The doctor's first instinct was to take me away from my parents and put me into foster care. My father persuaded the doctor to let me come home. From that point on Father never trusted another baby-sitter.

In all pictures of myself from that time I am smiling and happy, a tribute to what children can overcome by virtue of their tiny stores of resilience. But the truth is that even now I expect to be hurt instead of made happy, and I silently accept whatever pain comes my way without crying out.

Even though my father refused to secure the services of another baby-sitter, he also refused to either ask his family for help or look for alternate means of daycare. My father possesses a seemingly aggressive personality that crumbles in the face of confrontation. It was left to my mother to pull herself together long enough to find me safe daycare. Prompted by her love for me she began looking for a nursery school. She chose BoPeep Nursery School in Salinas for its good reputation. The proprietress was a formidable lady named Maggie Upton. Together, she and her husband George ran a tight daycare ship.

When my mother telephoned the school, Mrs. Upton told her that BoPeep was full and they couldn't accept me. Mother, convinced that Mrs. Upton would not be able to refuse me once she was face to face with my small self, bundled me up and drove us from San Jose to Salinas.

At first Mrs. Upton proved as strong-minded in person as she was on the phone. The school was full. She would accept no more pupils. Finally my mother gave up logical means of persuasion and, fixing her blue eyes on Mrs. Upton's face, said, "Please take my little girl. She's been abused by her baby-sitter and I've nowhere to leave her while I work." And with that I became a pupil at BoPeep Nursery School.

I spent three months at BoPeep. Every day my father woke me up, helped me get dressed, drove me to school, and handed me over to Mrs. Upton. Every evening he picked me up. For the first month I would not play with the other children. If they were outside playing on the swings and slides, I hid inside. If the other children were inside playing blocks or napping, I hid outside behind the bushes. Just about the time I began playing with the other children, my mother decided she wanted me with her and took me out of nursery school.

In the periods my mother was psychotic, our house became a loud place filled with screaming and accusations. During my parents' all-night fights, my mother would get me out of bed and keep me up with them.

"What's the matter?" she said to my father. "Don't you want your daughter to know how evil men can be? Look at him," she said to me. "He's had me—now he wants to kill me. All night his girlfriends come, they park in the driveway and honk for him to come outside. He screws them in their cars, right in our driveway. Do you understand, Paula

Jean? Those women call night and day. They call me to tell me they are outside."

"Put her to bed, Elaine. You're imagining this. There are no other women," my father said while he tried to pick me up. My mother grabbed my arm, and they played tug of war with me.

Odd as it seems, I often drifted off to sleep during their fights, and my mother shook me awake while my father screamed at her to put me back to bed.

"See," she said, "he's the crazy one. He wants to kill me."

Sometimes there were quiet times, nights with bed-time stories and my teddy bear, days sitting on a kitchen chair listening to my mother sing. These were the best times I remember with my mother. I envied the ability she had to make you want to listen to her. I imagine that her singing voice must have been one of the reasons my father fell in love with my mother. Her voice was like soft velvet. You wanted to rub yourself all over with the sound of it. She loved romantic songs the most and never sang country-western or pop tunes. But give her a Frank Sinatra standard and she would grab hold of the lyrics and not let go. That last note would just hang out there in the air until it seemed to become part of the movement of the room, finally fading away just as time will do. Even her speaking voice was musical in tone. One of my earliest memories is of my mother singing me to sleep. I could never stay mad when my mother sang. I inherited my mother's singing voice, but I keep it to myself. It is one of my secrets, revealed in the shower and when I'm driving alone in my car. I sing when I'm sad and when I'm happy, but never when I'm scared, which makes me more like my mother than I thought.

My mother's life is divided, at least for me, into the sane and insane. I grew up practicing various reactions de-pending upon which period we were in. Somehow I was more comfortable with the emotional times. Perhaps because during the calmness I was always waiting for the storm. Even today I am more comfortable with upheaval, which to me is perfectly understandable. I appreciated my mother when I had nightmares and she held my hand in the darkness. I appreciated her when I was sick and she sat beside my bed all night long. I remember her singing "Moon River" while she washed the dishes after dinner— and still laugh over her football-textured meatloaf.

Among my most cherished memories are those of my mother picking pretty dresses for me to wear, bandaging my skinned knees and reading to me from her favorite books. Together we survived the ordeal of picking out school clothes and visiting the dentist.

Despite the calm intervals I still never felt at ease. My father grew fearful of leaving me alone with my mother during the daytime after school. The only options for my care were baby-sitting, his family whom he kept in the dark as to his situation at home, or making do. Making do won.

By now my mother believed people were plotting against her. She stopped sleeping at night and began chain smoking. Sometimes she would have three cigarettes burning at the same time, all fighting for space in the same small ashtray. Eventually my mother's delusions forced her to stop teaching completely. She had gone back part-time, as a substitute teacher. With her mind now unoccupied she had plenty of time for her visions to take over. Finally, my father called her parents for help, and my mother's sister Dot came out from Tennessee. Together Dot and Father persuaded my mother to check into the hospital. It took a month for my mother's mental state to stabilize to the point where she was allowed to come home. My father finally realized that my mother's problems were more severe than a case of nerves.

After she returned from the hospital, she wasn't the

same. Each morning my father helped me get dressed, packed a lunch for me, handed me a doll, and told me to run away and hide from my mother all day. "Never let her catch you," he said, "and if you need to go to the bathroom go to the neighbors." Sometimes my mother chased me while I ran.

Often I spent time with Mrs. Gonzales, who lived across the street. She sat me on a chair next to her own daughter and let us watch while she made tortillas, explaining each step in the process as she rolled the dough in her hands, patted it flat, and heated it up in the pan. Some days she gave us a soft, warm, freshly made tortilla to eat. Mrs. Gonzales was round and short. She smiled a lot and didn't talk much. On hot days I sat on a stool in her kitchen while she cooked, feeling little trails of sweat drip down my face.

"You're so thin and too pale," she always said and gave me hugs and fresh tortillas to eat.

Late at night tucked into my bed, I whispered to my dolls, "I'm Mrs. Gonzales's daughter, and someday she'll come and take me home for good."

But other, rare times I was still glad I was my mother's daughter. Like when she taught me to curl my hair or listened so intently, comforting me when I came home crying because of some small, though to me, severe slight I'd received from a playmate.

Even today, I keep my childhood recollections in piles separated by my mother's moments of sanity versus bouts of insanity.

One day I came home from Mrs. Gonzales's house to check for my father's car and found my mother being dragged screaming into an ambulance, while the whole block watched. All around me our neighbors stood, muttering "Poor child," and "How he puts up with this, the man must be a saint." I looked up at them leaning towards each other, hands over their mouths, shaking their heads and talking as they watched my mother being wrapped in a straitjacket: watched as my mother arched her back and fought. I had a clear view of the bottoms of our neighbors' chins wiggling with conversation. My father stood on our porch. Mrs. Gonzales pulled me towards her stomach and put her hands over my eyes. I went to stay with family friends while my mother rested. While I was gone Mrs. Gonzales moved, and I never saw her again.

This time the hospitalization lasted six months. After that, my mother came home much calmer through the magic of medication and electroshock therapy, and life returned to normal, except that my mother never taught school again. She did go into the hospital a year later, but this was because of my brother being born.

We attempted a normal family life the way other people try on clothes: slipping everydayness on to see if it fit. This is the childhood I show off for my friends when we play re-member-when games. The childhood of milk and cookies, hide-and-seek, and mommies who read bedtime stories and smelled like flowers.

We went on a family vacation. We went out to dinner and played miniature golf. My parents taught me to play chess, first the pawns, then the other pieces. I learned how to read word instead of picture books. My father decided that teaching did not pay enough to support a family and got a job working for the Social Security Administration. Now he carried a briefcase to work every day. Father looked around and decided that something was missing from our family life, and we bought pets. He considered something exotic, but decided upon the American variety of pets, namely a dog and cat. I loved them both.

The cat was a natural hunter of birds. I believe that even if she had been a sedate house tabby she would have found some reason to wander, assaulting anything with wings. As it was, my father decreed that any pet of ours had to live outside, and so I had to go outside to visit our animals. Free to hunt, the cat, who was a lovely Siamese whom my father named Jasmine, became more feral. Each day I poured cat food into her bowl while she disdainfully flicked her tail and kept her eye out for birds. Though Jasmine was an undaunted huntress, she usually did no harm. She did, however, develop impressive stalking techniques.

Once I was sitting and talking in our garage with another little girl unaware that my mother was standing nearby on the top step of the back porch. While we sat cross-legged on the floor watching the cat with her newborn kittens, my friend remarked that I had pretty blue eyes. In my most grownup voice, I responded, "I got them from my mother. They're our most attractive feature." I looked up to see my mother smiling lovingly at me. She smiled all through that evening.

One Tuesday I came home from playing with my friends and found a group of wounded birds hopping around the back yard. Apparently Jasmine had surprised them while feeding and managed (at long last) to do some damage. Unfortunately she lost interest during the process, didn't finish the job, and left the injured birds to their own devices. My ardent sympathy aroused, I became a rescuer of birds.

Inside the house I heard my parents arguing. My mother, who had become disenchanted with the cat, was saying, "See, Bill, you see. Now what do we do?"

My father, who believed cats (especially outdoor cats) would be cats, replied, "Christ, Elaine, she's only a cat. She's doing what cats do."

"Well, what will we do with the poor birds? Can you answer that?"

"Nothing. They'll hop off on their own."

I looked at the little birds hopping around the backyard and imagined Jasmine crouched somewhere preparing another attack. My parents carried their argument into their bedroom. I went into the house and got the new box of Popsicles out of the refrigerator and poured hot water on them until the sticky sweet stuff melted away. Then I took a box of bandages from the bathroom. I believed the bandages were rightfully mine. After all, I was always the one with the skinned knees and scraped elbows.

In the backyard I caught the birds one by one, attached the splints made from Popsicle sticks and bandages to their legs, and set them free. The birds didn't appreciate my attention to their wounds. They pecked at my hands and squawked as I worked. Finally they limped off, dragging their injured legs which were now artificially stiffened by my doctoring efforts. When my father discovered the birds he asked what the splints were for. I told him, "So the birds' legs will heal, and then I'll remove the splints and they'll all fly off." Later my father and mother put the fledglings in a box and took them away, disbanding my little bird hospital.

Like our cat, our dog, Otto, had a tendency to wander. Otto was an enormous boxer with a misshapen face, being long-jawed instead of flat. Otto paced the backyard barking at passersby, terrorized visitors by standing behind the sliding glass doors and growling, and once a month leapt over our fence and disappeared for a week or two.

Neighbors and friends would spot Otto across town assaulting female dogs, destroying gardens, and running from city pound trucks. He always dragged himself home from his escapades tired, thinner, but quiet and well-behaved for at least a week. My mother, who was rather fond of Otto, defended him against officials from the city pound who came to our house on a regular basis.

After a while Mother again decided she no longer

needed medication or psychiatrist visits and stopped
both. Not long after that she put my dolls away because
she was afraid they would hurt me. She became paranoid about my safety and wouldn't let me leave the
house to go to school, and no one was allowed near my
brother. Once, I picked him up to quiet his crying and
sat on the floor with him in my lap. My mother discovered us and became upset. She picked up my brother
and carefully checked him over. She imagined she saw
a bruise on his arm and began yelling at me, "What did
you do, Paula Jean? What did you do?" Finally she put
my brother in his crib and locked me in the closet for
the afternoon. My father found me when he came home
from work, curled up on one of his coats.

Another day when my father was at work, my mother
packed up my brother and me and ran away from home.
She called my father each night from a succession of
motels, making it quite easy for him to track her route
home to her family in Tennessee.

We were driving through Texas when a police car signaled for us to pull over. We were taken to the police station to wait for my father to fly out and drive us home.
One of the police officers took pity and brought Mother,
Michael and me to his house for the night. I was disappointed, because I thought I was going to get to go to jail.
The officer lived in the countryside in a small white house
that was set back from the road. The kitchen was warm
and smelled of fresh bread, and the officer's wife was
plump, smiled a lot, and pinched my cheeks way too
much. The officer and his wife were childless. During the
evening the wife kept picking up my brother, shaking him
and making gushing noises, while my mother watched,
making a knot of her hands in her lap. My brother,
mother, and I slept in the spare bedroom. In the middle
of the night I snuck out of bed and listened to the officer

and his wife talk; they spoke in whispers, making shushing sounds to themselves. "Be quiet. They'll hear you," they said, and "Poor things, poor little children." After my father brought us home, my parents fought constantly. My mother paced the house at night and accused people, beginning with my father, of trying to drive her crazy. The neighbors began crossing the road when they saw her coming, and store clerks groaned when she appeared at their counters. My mother's favorite sister, my aunt Dot, came to visit from Tennessee once again to try to help.

Dot, tall, red-haired and green-eyed, was a forty-year old ex-army nurse. She was getting married for the first time in thirty days but swore to my father that she would stay with us as long as necessary. Dot and Mom's older sister Gayle had always been protective of my mother. Dot even took blame upon herself as a child so my mother would not be beaten, and was sometimes the only one to whom my mother would listen. While she stayed with us, she took me for walks, out for ice cream, and rescued my dolls from their hiding place. At night Aunt Dot tucked me in, then sat by my bed and told me stories about her childhood. She told me that when she was a little girl, she ran barefoot through the orchard, swam in the Tennessee River, and that she laughed all the time and never cried.

At my mother's insistence Aunt Dot flew home to Tennessee and got married. She and her new husband went to New York on their honeymoon. One night her new husband took a shower while Dot lay on the hotel bed reading. He came out of the shower and she was lying on the bed peaceful as can be, but dead. She died of an aneurysm. Her mind exploded on the inside, instead of the outside like my mother's.

When my grandfather phoned to give my mother the news of Aunt Dot's death, Mother began screaming and would not stop. My father had to pry the phone out of her hands and drag her off to the bedroom. I crawled into my brother's crib and slept with him until my father found me. My brother and I lived in a world of disappearing people where no one could be trusted to stick around, and when they did it was usually worse than if they'd left.

One morning after my father left for work, my mother, looking agitated, locked the door and put a kitchen chair under the knob. She stood at the door for a long time laughing and smoking one cigarette after another. She used the palm of her hand to catch cigarette ashes and ground out the butts against the door.

"He'll see now," she said. "I'm in charge now. He'll see now and all his women too. He'll see now." My mother paced and smoked, talking to herself. Every now and then she'd stop and slap at her head. "Leave me alone," she said. When I tried to leave the room she said, "Stop. This is the room today. Don't you leave this room. This is where we stay today."

My father had forgotten his briefcase and returned home an hour later to discover himself locked out of the house. He went around to the back yard and began banging on the sliding glass doors. My mother screamed, and I screamed with her. "Mommy, Mommy," I cried, my hands over my ears. My brother began crying, and I crawled over to him. Outside the house my father pounded on the glass door, while my mother yelled for him to go away. "He's trying to kill me," she yelled. "He'll kill me."

My mother picked up my brother, and taking my hand brought us into the bathroom, locking the door behind her. She squatted inside the bathtub crouching over my brother. I could hear my father yelling and slamming the glass doors with our backyard lawn furniture.

Father broke through the glass with a lawn chair and

pounded on the bathroom door, demanding to be let in. My mother crouched over my brother protectively. She said, "No, Paula. Your father will kill me. Don't let him in. Don't do it. He'll kill me."

I unlocked the door, and my father opened it so forcefully that I was slammed back into the wall. He was covered with blood from coming in through the broken glass doors. Little bits of spit came from the corners of his mouth, which was an ugly shape as he yelled, "Elaine, Elaine."

My father grabbed my mother by the neck and shook her. He hit her on the back and began kicking her. He kicked her until she passed out. Then he picked up my baby brother and left the room. I stood behind the door watching my mother, who lay in the bathtub for a long time. I thought she was dead. I had let my father into the bathroom and he'd killed her. I watched my mother for any movement, waited for her eyes to open. I touched her face, pinched her arm and then lay down on the bathroom floor, curled up in a ball, and sucked my thumb until my father came to get me.

CHAPTER 3

Moving Around

My father took my mother out of the bathroom and settled her on the couch. Then he put my brother and me in my bedroom until the ambulance came. Looking down at the floor as he spoke, he told us, "I want you to stay put until I come to get you." His hair hung over his forehead, and his jacket pocket was torn. In my room my brother went almost instantly to sleep, and I curled up on my bed staring at the wall. Through my closed door I heard the doorbell and my father's muffled voice, then footsteps as the paramedics from Agnews State Mental Hospital walked through our house with my father showing them the way. I heard my mother protesting and moaning and then more footsteps as they took her from our house. After that there was a long silence during which I could only hear the beat of my pounding heart. Then I heard my father crying. His crying had a muffled sound, as if he was holding something over his mouth. The sound of it continued for a long time while my brother slept and I lay curled up on my bed staring at the wall.

After my mother was taken away, everything happened in a rush. "You're going to stay with my sister for a while," my father said. "Just a while," he kept repeating. He didn't even take time to pack our suitcases; he just rushed us out to the car as if something evil was chasing after us, as if the house itself was a force too powerful to be dealt with. There were evil spirits dwelling in our house all right, but they were the kind that followed you wherever you went. The faster you ran away from that kind of haunting the more it stuck with you. My father's only thought was to get away, and I suppose if he could have kept running, he would have. After that day my father's mouth learned how to smile in a grim, humorless fashion. His new smile was painful to look at, being unnaturally straight with tight lips that sometimes became white with the strain.

"When are we coming home again, Daddy?" I asked.

"Soon," he said and ran a hand through his hair.

"What about Otto and Jasmine?" I asked, remembering our dog and cat. "They can't go with you," my father said with his new grim smile.

"Why not?" I persisted. All my child's intensity focused now on my pets. It's much easier to worry about pets than people; pets have personalities that you can count on, and they're always happy to see you.

"They can't go. We'll be coming home soon. They have to stay and take care of the house," my father, with his grim smile, repeated. I stopped asking questions then and curled up in a ball on the back seat of the car. As far as I was concerned, my mother had abandoned me, and I refused to turn around and look out the back window of our car to see my old neighborhood fade away, maybe never to return.

One thing I remember clearly from that drive to my Aunt Betty's was how my father's hair stood straight up in the air after the third or fourth time he ran his fingers through it. It stood up in spikes, partly because his fingers ran through it in an upward motion, but mostly because of the gel he used to hold his style in place. When he was dressed up in his suit for work, even a strong wind wouldn't disturb the careful positioning and styling of his hair, so its current misbehavior caught and kept my attention. I watched his hair most of the way to my Aunt Betty's house. I held onto the vague promise of *soon* for quite a while after that.

It seemed as if we drove a long time until we got to my aunt's house, but I was figuring time in child's hours, which can go on and on. Everything seems to take forever when you're a kid. The time it takes to drive ten miles may as well be the time it takes to cross a continent. When you're grown up you only get that type of stretched-out time when you're scared or sad, and then time stretches out horizontally. You think the sadness will never pass and that nothing will be right again. For kids it's like that all the time, so that ten-mile drive to my aunt's house felt like an eternity.

I didn't want to get out of the car when we arrived. At first I had to be coaxed and then threatened with punishment. Neither method proved persuasive, and my father's remaining patience was beginning to give way when my aunt came out and smiled through the window of the car. "I have cookies and hot chocolate ready for you," she called. By that time I was starved, so I got right out. My brother was too young for hot chocolate, so he got a bottle. My father left while I was eating my cookies. As he passed me in the kitchen, he patted me on the head, but he didn't look at me.

Aunt Betty was my father's older sister. She was married

to a quiet man named John. They had three daughters, Jill, Sara, and Beth. Life at my aunt's house was like one of those half-hour television family shows where everyone likes each other and no problems are serious enough to avoid a quick resolution. At least it seemed perfect to me at the time, though I had no valid comparison. At my aunt's house little children didn't have nightmares and family rules were the easily understandable kind, such as eat your vegetables and brush your teeth.

For a while, everything was fine. I believed that I was part of their family and wanted to stay with them always. I began calling my Aunt Betty Mommy. I followed her everywhere. My brother and I lived with my aunt's family for two months during which I picked up the habit of purposefully listening to adult conversations. Eavesdropping is a useful skill when you are a young child and don't know what will happen to you next. I hid in closets and behind doors and heard the adults talk about me. "She'll have to be watched for signs," they said. "We have to keep an eye on her," they said. I kept a close ear on all conversations after that. So, I knew before they told me that there was talk of me going to live somewhere else. I tried to pretend that I didn't have to leave, but one day I came home from playing in the neighborhood sprinklers to find my father waiting and my suitcase packed. I was going to my father's mother's house, while my brother got to stay with Aunt Betty.

By then, Lillian had divorced the evil stepfather my father remembered, the one who had abandoned him and his twin. She was now married to a property-owning man named Lloyd. My new grandfather was an alcoholic, a fact he tried and failed to hide from my grandmother. Lloyd was tall, quiet, and very gentle. He read to me in the evenings, and asked me to call him Papa. He owned three duplexes, two apartment buildings, ten houses, and a junk yard. Papa spent most of his time tooling around in his junk yard hammering used license plates onto a fence and drinking from bottles of vodka that he kept hidden inside rusted cars. Despite the fact that she scared the hell out of him, Papa loved my grandmother very much.

Grandmother ran a strict household. She wasn't one to show an excess of emotion, but she did take her responsibilities seriously. On my very first day with her, before bringing me entirely into her house, she had me stand in the entryway while she informed me that the household rules were: neatness, promptness, courtesy, good table manners, and no displays of excess emotion. Grandmother Lillian believed that a person should always remain calm, and I was anything but a calm child. She believed in formality and insisted I call her Grandmother: this was no granny-in-a-rocking-chair type of homey gramma. Her name always felt huge in my mouth when I said it, stern and full of dignity. I may have been a child desperately in need of hugs, but Grandmother chose to fill that void by teaching me to appreciate competence. For two years I worked hard at impressing her. Not only did this give me something to do, it was also a largely unachievable goal. Grandmother did not bestow her approval easily, and I had a knack of getting on her nerves. Like my father before me, I was much too independent a child for her tastes.

Grandmother took me everywhere with her. Thanks to my latest grandfather, she was a woman of means at last: a property owner. I rode with her each month in her Rambler station wagon all around San Jose as she collected rents. She made me sit in the back seat. She kept a little tin box on the seat next to her to receive the rent money she collected.

Years later I realized that Grandmother's renters must

have been very poor. The houses we visited had unkempt yards, very little furniture, and the corners of everyone's mouths turned down instead of up. Grandmother often didn't collect rent from the poorest people, and instead, brought them groceries. "Just some extra things," she told me. "Just some things I don't need cluttering up my cupboard." In her house I lived in a room filled with antiques, most of which I was not allowed to touch. I often snuck into her bedroom when she wasn't around and examined the delicate things on her dresser, the lacy doilies and elegant bottles of perfume: things I had difficulty equating with my grandmother, who dictated straight edges for the linen napkins I folded at dinnertime and believed all clothing should be sensible.

People patted me on the head too much, pinched my cheeks, and said, "Poor little thing" a lot. I was truly tired of being a poor little thing and set out to prove that I wasn't. When this didn't work I spent my free time alone, either reading or traveling around in my imagination. If I learned one thing from my childhood, it's that no one can take what's deep down inside you, all your secrets. People think they know you, believe you've given something true of yourself, but all they really have is an image. If you keep the rest close, no one can really hurt you.

One of my grandmother's rental houses was a tiny one-bedroom house located next door to where she lived with my step-grandfather. A succession of single mothers rented this house from my grandmother at a substantially reduced rent from what they would have paid to anyone else. I always made friends with the children of these women and so spent most of my time next door playing paper dolls and hide-and-seek. The highlight of my week was when my father came to visit. Once a week he came with presents, such as new coloring books or paper dolls, and every weekend my father took

my brother and me to our old home for a visit. The first
time we went home, I ran straight to the bathroom to
check for blood and to the patio door to look for broken
glass, but everything was repaired and clean.

The first pet I always wanted to see was Jasmine, and
then, if Otto wasn't out gallivanting, I played with him.
One weekend my father brought us home to a petless
house. I asked him where Jasmine and Otto were, and he
told me that someone had poisoned them. They were
dead. I put my hands over my ears and cried, "I won't believe you! I won't believe you!" until my father picked me
up and carried me to my bed. There is just so much of
loved ones leaving that a child can take. Years later I
found out that my father, believing that he couldn't
properly care for them, had taken both the dog and cat
to the pound. Although I learned this when I was grown
and on my own, the knowledge still stung and felt like
betrayal. It's always difficult to face the reality of your
parents' humanity, especially when it's tied up with their
inability to cope. A few broken dreams of your own, however, will knock that nagging tendency to be judgmental
right out of you.

My life settled into a pattern of visits from my father
and stern affection from my grandmother. In my adult-
decorated bedroom filled with antiques and other
untouchable items, the four-poster bed was dark oak, and
the dresser had a huge, ornate mirror. My grandmother
kept a silver-handled brush, comb and hand mirror set
on the dresser. Each night after my grandmother tucked
me into bed, I quietly got up, turned on the light next
to the dresser, and pretended I was a grown-up woman
safe in my own home. I combed and brushed my hair
with the silver-handled brush and comb. I looked in
the silver-handled mirror and imagined what life would
be like someday when I was a grown-up safe in my

own home. I wanted to be far away, but I couldn't have described where "far away" was, or what it would look like. My room also had a bookshelf filled with books by D.H. Lawrence, the complete works of Shakespeare, and Jane Austen. I couldn't even read the titles of those books when I first arrived, but I knew I wanted to read them all the way through, from cover to cover, someday. I was a reader-to-be from the first time I saw a book, and I wanted to read all the important ones. My humble goal was to learn everything in the world worth knowing by the time I grew up. By this time I was a serious young girl with long brown hair and huge blue eyes. Whenever anyone told me that I had eyes like my mother's, I ran away and hid from them.

My grandmother never made me feel unwelcome, nor did she treat me as a duty she was bound to fulfill. She did, however, make certain that I was aware of the eventuality of going home to my parents "someday," as she put it. My grandmother took me to my aunt's house several times a week to see my brother so that we would have brother-sister time. Grandmother nursed me through chicken pox and gave me gloves to wear so that I would not scratch when it itched. She let me work crossword puzzles with her and went to school to defend me when I, truly my father's daughter, got in trouble with my teachers. Every night she tucked me in, kissed me on the forehead, and said, "Good night, Paula. You have a happy dream or two to see you through the night." Despite her nightly admonitions regarding happy dreams, sleep sometimes eluded me as I remembered bedtimes at my own home disrupted by moaning, crying and parents' fighting.

By then, I had not seen my mother for two years. My mother spent those years in the mental hospital overly medicated and receiving shock therapy. Once every week or so the doctors took my mother into a room, restrained her, put a piece of rubber into her mouth so that she did not bite off her tongue, and shot electricity into her body. While the electricity shot through her she arched her back and strained against the straps holding her down. When the doctors and nurses took her down from the table she was shaky and blank-faced. As time passed, her thin brown hair grew thinner. She became very quiet and docile and learned to walk with her head down and never to look anyone directly in the eye. After this, my mother was an expert eye-averter.

My father denies approving my mother's electroshock therapy. He blames the hospital or the nurses or the doctors for putting her through the pain and humiliation of being stripped of her dignity, but he felt helpless too. Once upon a time he had married a woman who laughed a lot, loved the beach, taught high school mathematics, and complimented his impulsive nature with her own cheerful, calm one. After shock therapy, her personality was bland, and she avoided even simple addition and subtraction. Though he says he doesn't remember it, Father had approved her therapy, hoping to cure her and gain a normal family life. Instead, we all lost her. The truth is that we would have lost her anyway.

My life had been so filled with upheaval that at my grandmother's house I needed to invent a place where I could control events and make up some happy ones. I began creating a fantasy life that lifted me up and away from reality. In my make-believe world I lived alone in a cottage and took care of myself. Once I perfected my imaginary world, I took it public. I told everyone at school that my mother was dead and made up outrageous stories about being adopted by a tribe of horses or extremely rich people. To me, there didn't seem to be much difference between these two fantasies. I didn't think I knew any rich people and I knew I couldn't really transform myself into a horse. Sometimes the easiest fantasies are the ones you know won't come true. My stories were entertaining, but not believable in the barest sense. As for my mother, I never asked to see her and did not want her to come home. I wanted to be like other people. I imagined that being like other people was the best thing in the world. I already knew that my family was different from everyone else's, though mostly I compared mine with the families I read about in books. It was around this time that I began writing stories, though I didn't show them to anyone. First I wrote my stories down and then I told them to anyone who would listen. I had begun creating my own oral history.

My mother came home from the hospital the year I began writing. My father, deciding that San Jose held too many bad memories, bought a house in Hayward, California and reunited his family of strangers. My mother was now thin and pale, and she didn't have much hair. If this stranger really was my mother, I hoped I would not grow up to look like her. She was also even quieter than before, and didn't smile much. Probably years of being clinically observed didn't leave her much to smile about. All I knew was that this wasn't someone I remembered, and even though everyone said this was my mother that didn't necessarily make it so.

I wonder now that I am an adult, and considered mature and reasonable, if my mother and I would have had more of a chance to relate to each other if my father had taken me to visit her in the hospital. It wouldn't have been pretty visiting her in the state psychiatric ward, but I might have accepted her more readily when she came home. As for my brother, he left a happy, well-adjusted childhood with my aunt's family to come home to an angry and frightened group of strangers.

One night shortly after we moved into our new house

my mother came into my room after I had gone to bed. She sat on the edge of my bed and stroked my face. I noticed that her hands were small and graceful, like I remembered. I tried not to pull away from her touch, but her nearness made me nervous. I turned my face away.

"Paula," she said, "I want you to know that no matter what has happened to me, no matter how long I was away, you've been on my mind every minute. You are always on my mind." She turned my face so that I was looking at her again. "Always," she said. "I never forgot you." Then she left my room, walking quietly with her arms wrapped around her waist.

She had been away such a long time, for all I knew she could have been a ghost. I felt that my real mother had abandoned me. I didn't know who this person, claiming to be my mother, was. Now she soundlessly entered and exited rooms. She just seemed to appear. I looked up and she was staring at me. I suppose she'd learned while she was in the hospital that it was better not to be noticed. Less can happen to you when you are invisible. I never wanted to be someone that no one noticed. When I entered a room I always wanted people to look up immediately. Indeed, I wanted them to be aware of me before I came into the room.

After a while it was obvious that my mother had not come home from the hospital cured. Maybe she'd given up the possibility of being normal, of being like other people. In any case, after watching her slide quietly around our house for a while, I decided that she really was a ghost. Like so many young girls, I had become capable of strong and ruthless judgments about my mother.

With both of his children clamoring for his attention and his wife obviously unwell and turning into an emotional recluse, my father searched for a way to make us a normal family. This was not easy, as his life was filled up with the daily tasks of taking my mother to her psychiatrist appointments, making certain she took medication, and making my brother and me feel that we were members of a normal family. Eventually he decided that a nice family vacation was what we all needed to re-bond. I wanted to go to Disneyland, but my mother wanted her children to get to know her family. So one morning we all piled in the car and began driving across country to Tennessee.

My mother was right. I have wonderful memories of that summer when we visited my southern grandparents. To me it was a world closer to the one I read about in books than anything I had known as a child. For the two years I lived with Grandmother Lillian, she had provided me with strict stability. She tried to give me a calm place to ride out the storm. I didn't trust stability at that point. I wanted magic.

The moment I stepped out of my parents' car and looked up at the farmhouse, I became Dorothy from *The Wizard of Oz*. All I needed was a tornado to sweep me up and dump me off somewhere adventurous.

We arrived at Grandma's and Grandpa's early in the day, and soon relatives began to come for the big midday meal. Dinner in a southern farmer's household is a filling event. The dining room table groaned under offerings of ham, turkey, creamed corn, mashed potatoes, gravy, cornbread, and fresh vegetables. My grandfather produced his prized watermelons for dessert. My mother's brothers and sisters and their wives, husbands, and children sat around the table, all talking at once in slow cadence. A southerner can be talking about the weather and unspoken in every drawn-out vowel is an invitation to set awhile on the porch.

Besides the great welcoming house there were apple orchards to run through, barns to explore, animals to play with, and close by, the Tennessee River in which to swim. The house itself was filled with secret places to explore. There were the parlor, the warm kitchen that led onto the screened back porch, and an enormous dormitory on the third floor where my mother's four brothers had slept. Once you were in the dormitory you could pull down the ladder and climb to the attic, and from that great height you commanded a view of the very tops of the tall trees and my grandparents' entire farm. Best of all, the big bathroom on the second floor held an enormous claw-foot bathtub, perfect for the long steamy baths I loved even as a child. My grandparents' farm matched every daydream I'd ever had after reading an especially good book. Here, I could become any character and play all the roles I'd imagined myself in. Here also, my mother had spent her girlhood, climbing trees and having the same adventures I now anticipated.

That summer I divided my days between exploring, climbing the trees in search of green apples, hanging from a tire swing over the Tennessee River, and reading books in the dormitory. I prized my skinned knees and scrubbed my tanned skin to gleaming as I soaked each evening in the claw-foot bathtub. My brother and I found the tree house my uncles had built and hid there in the late afternoons supplied with lemonade and cookies, dividing the green apples from our latest haul. We swung upside down from the branches of trees and threw rotten apples at passing cars, fading into the orchard when drivers spotted us. It was just like being inside one of the books I loved to read. You know the sort of book I mean, where summers are filled with children running, playing, laughing, and having adventures.

After evening supper, a casual meal made up of leftovers from dinner, my brother and I invented games outside until darkness and adult restrictions forced us into the house. Once inside we played checkers, watched television, and annoyed the adults until they sent us to the bed that my brother and I shared. Tucked safely under the covers, I stacked pillows between us to create a makeshift dam so the little river created by my brother's bed-wetting habit would have less of a chance of reaching me, clicked on a flashlight, and read aloud to him until our eyes dimmed and our heads dropped onto our soft, feathery pillows.

Accustomed as we were to stealthy departures, at the end of our vacation we left very early one morning while it was still dark. My father carried my brother out to the car still asleep, and my grandmother handed bag lunches to us through the car window. I watched out of the back window as we drove away, trying to see the house in the dark and imagining my grandmother waving goodbye.

From that summer vacation with my southern grandparents I developed my opinions of what a happy extended family should be, and from there decided exactly what was wrong with mine. Since we were never invited back to visit, I also developed one more grudge to nurture against my mother, since never returning, of course, was her fault. Whatever memories I might have forgotten about that summer in Tennessee didn't matter to me for years. That which survived intact within my imagination got bigger and cleaner until it loomed over the rest of my chaotic home life, daring comparisons. That summer existed like a bookmark in my memory, saving a place that read: *Here I was happy for a while.*

By the time we got home from our trip, my mother was worse. At night she made long lists of the items people had stolen from her. When I began playing the flute, she added it to her list. She thought the mailman was stealing her thoughts and hid in the bathroom when she saw him coming up the sidewalk. After he was safely around the corner, she checked the mail for transistors.

"I hate you," I told her with regularity. "You're disgusting. You're crazy. I wish you were dead," I said first thing in the morning and before bed at night. But she just turned her face towards me and looked at me with blank eyes. I don't know if she internalized these childish cruelties or understood them for what they were, immaturity. The quieter she was, the angrier I got. With time, as she became more and more deranged, the habit of hating her settled in and became a pattern, leaving little room for my memories of her laughing, playing with me, and reading me stories before bedtime.

Mother read her lists of stolen items to us at dinner. Depending on how she was feeling, dinner wavered between inedible and unhealthy. Chicken was often served raw and beef so well done that it was rendered ashes. Sanity was hard work for my mother now. Every task she began was left unfinished: the vacuum might be found in the bathroom, or the kitchen faucet left running until the sink overflowed. In my mother's case even normal forgetfulness such as not buying milk at the store when we were out of it at home brought about a judgment of her mental state. People lose patience with someone who's lost their mind. As if a mind, once mislaid, can be relocated and reinstalled with little effort. And if you are the child of someone who is crazy, it sits on you all the time, until your shoulders dip under the weight. Yet despite my mother's illness, the side of her that loved to teach refused to die. In her lucid periods she made certain my brother and I read one classic book every two weeks during the summer, and made time to sit and discuss the characters, plot, and meaning of each one. During those moments the mother and person she could have been lit our imagination.

My mother did not fit any pattern other than the one of her own making. She was, most often, a woman trying to hold on to her sanity in an impatient world, within an often hostile family. My mother's reputation preceded her into every family gathering. People were extra-solicitous. My grandmother and Aunt Betty whispered together, and I thought they probably whispered about me too. My three cousins were blond, good in school, and no trouble to anyone. My brother and I were dark, moody, unreasonably angry, and resentful. *The hell with them*, I thought.

My brother, Michael, was growing into the type of kid who could slide right into the back of your mind and before you knew it you'd forget he was in the room. It was a real talent he had, this ability to escape. When he was in the first grade, he began wandering off without telling us where he was going. Strange men and women were always bringing my brother home from across the neighborhood. Still, he and I were allies of a sort.

Michael liked to make people angry. When he got other kids mad enough to try and hurt him he would run to find me and together we would fight the enemy off, pelting them with rocks or mud, whatever was handy. For a while my brother and I ran a little business. I charged a quarter for the neighborhood kids to come watch my brother drink mud. All the kids thought this was creepy, and my brother and I made money until everyone grew bored. After our mud-drinking business went bust, my brother began mowing lawns. He stashed the money somewhere in his room. The kid was full of secrets.

A month after my thirteenth birthday, my desperation from living in a tumultuous household overwhelmed me. I turned myself into the authorities at Juvenile Hall and asked to be placed in a foster home. I knew that I deserved a better life than the one I had. To me, a better life meant a different family. I made the decision to telephone Juvenile Hall quickly, giving myself no time to think it over. In decision-making I take after my father.

He tends to act on decisions almost simultaneously upon making them. With my father and me you often can't tell the difference between the decision process and the act, until it becomes quite a chicken and an egg conundrum. Most of my worst mistakes have come about because of my tendency to think and act at the same time. Turning myself into Juvenile Hall was one of those mistakes.

The minute the matron locked me in my room I changed my mind. Trapped, I realized how my mother must have felt being institutionalized all those years. I began to cry and didn't stop until my mother and father came to see me on the weekend.

"You've embarrassed me," my father said when they entered the room, and he said it so quietly I was afraid. "Haven't I put up with enough?" he went on. "If I'd realized how you were going to turn out, I would have done things differently. I should have gotten the hell out the first time your mother broke down. You are a disappointment, Paula. You think you want a new home? I should leave you here."

I didn't realize, of course, that my father was speaking mostly about himself. It was his life that he was disappointed with. At this point I was just an outlet for his frustration and sorrow.

"Daddy," I said, "please take me home. I'll be better. I promise." I thought of all the ways I could improve. "I promise," I said again.

"Well, Paula Jean." My father folded his hands on the table between us and sighed. "I don't know if that's possible for you. I don't know if you can change."

"Bill," my mother said, "I think she should come home with us." Instantly I hated her for interfering. Caught between wanting to go home and not wanting to side with my mother, I was at a loss as to what to do.

My father looked at my mother. "Elaine," he said, "let me handle this."

My father left me in Juvenile Hall for another week. I met a pregnant twelve-year-old and an eight-year-old who was in for prostitution. Most of the other girls left me completely alone because I was such a baby, crying night and day. My roommate spent every night telling me to shut up and threatening me with bodily harm if I didn't stop bawling. By the end of the week the only inmate who would talk to me was the eight-year-old prostitute. But I did learn, finally, how to hide inside the corners of my eyes all the things I didn't want people to see, like hope.

CHAPTER 4

Growing Up Mad

In the movies after a siege of family pain and trouble everyone learns something profound, which is expressed by a main character in one or two unforgettable lines. Real life doesn't deal out profundity so easily. Often profundity lies undiscovered between the cracks, with no one to root it out and bring it to everyone's attention. If there was anything profound hiding in the cracks of our family life at this point, we were all too busy stepping over it to notice.

Whereas I rebelled in a loud enough fashion for everyone to see, my brother worked at becoming inscrutable. By the time he was nine years old, he was really getting quite good at it. He practiced keeping his face expressionless for long periods of time until finally no one could guess what was going on behind his eyes, nose, and mouth. He practiced inscrutability by staring at people. His favorite target was our father. As he grew older, my brother, whose temper was frightening when he lost it, learned self-control by driving our father's temper out into the open.

My father was caught between his own youthful dreams and the harsh reality he, like the rest of our family, endured. My father had certain expectations when he got married. First of all, he expected to be happy. He also wanted a family life with children. He would take the children to the zoo and the beach and go fishing, and every couple of weeks he and his wife would go out to the movies and dinner. My father would create a family life different from his own, where his family could be safe, happy, and secure. In short, he wanted the normal stuff we all imagine is our due.

Instead, his wife broke down mentally until she bore no resemblance to the woman he had married. His daughter loudly rebelled and rejected her own family in search of a new family and identity. And his son withdrew from family life so quietly that his escape was almost undetectable.

My father never showed us his sorrow. He did show us his anger. When I came home from Juvenile Hall my father's temper was cemented into the expression on his face, which never again looked relaxed. His brow had become permanently furrowed, and his mouth puckered as if he were always preparing to yell. He grew angrier by the month. His temper exploded in the middle of meals, on weekends, and during television programs. If he disagreed with the newscaster, he would scream at the television screen. Clerks in stores learned to dread his approach. Father became more and more demanding until my brother just stopped coming home, spending as much time as possible with his friends. I either stayed in my room or didn't come home myself. We all developed refuges to keep us away from our family life. My father's refuges were either work or his temper, and he kept to both of them as much as possible.

As for my mother, she never really gave up her dreams of teaching, even after she went crazy. As her daughter, I became her resident pupil. She continued to make me read the classics every summer until I was sixteen, when I refused to participate anymore. She insisted that I spend two hours each day in my room reading. I spent afternoons in my room lost in *Little Women, The Little Prince, The Wind in the Willows,* and *Alice in Wonderland.* As I grew older she gave me the works of Jane Austen to read. Each day, in the rare moments when she was lucid, my mother and I discussed what that day's reading meant in terms of feelings induced and literary style. She listened to my opinions about what I had read and slowly taught me to analyze literature. During the summers, my mother gave me a hunger for books and the gift of critical reading. Now, I can't read a book, poem, essay or article without wondering what my mother's opinion would have been of the writing and the message contained. One birthday the only presents I asked for were a book of poetry and a guitar. I read every poem in the book, *The Golden Treasury of Poetry,* silently to myself and then out loud. I still have the book, but the guitar got lost somewhere along the way.

My parents gifted me with an active intellectual life, but as I grew older examples of affection between them were harder to come by. I have fuzzy recollections of affection between my parents when I was very young. Before my mother's first major breakdown they laughed together, shared cigarettes, and held hands. Even now, romance to me is defined by the long-ago image of hands held between a car's bucket seats or intertwined feet sticking out from bedcovers. By the time I was a teenager, evidence of affection between my parents was either nonexistent or invisible. Based upon the fact that they stayed together, I suppose my parents still had a devotion of sorts, but they certainly never admitted to it, nor did it show by virtue of physical expression.

The physical side of my parents' marriage had ended after my mother came home from the hospital and we reunited as a family and moved to Hayward. They didn't touch each other in front of my brother and me after that, and my mother slept on the couch while my father used the bedroom. I did notice that my mother sometimes tried to hold his hand. In the car her hand would creep over to touch his as he held the steering wheel. My father always found a reason to change the channel on the radio or put his hand on the gear shift, anything to let go, shaking her off like something unpleasant had landed on his skin.

Not that my father was demonstrative in the best of circumstances. All through my life, whenever I've hugged him or kissed him on the cheek, he's ducked away: head bowed, chin tucked in towards his chest. My brother missed the intertwined feet part of our lives. All he got to see was the rejection. I don't know what he found to serve as a base for his ideas of what a healthy relationship should be. I grew up believing that affection was something you sought surreptitiously, and was often denied. Rejection panics me, spurring me on to prove my worth. More often now, I stayed away from my house and went looking for affection elsewhere. When I was home, my mother spent practically all her time on the living room couch, napping, waking up, smoking a cigarette, and napping.

My mother, however, had her own secrets. She was, as I've stated, by no means cut out for homemaking. I don't think it was the dust and dishes that drove her crazy. Schizophrenia is genetic, so it's probably just a coincidence that her being crazy went along with being a housewife. When I was a young girl I believed that the world had lost a good teacher and gained a crazy woman because of me. My guilt made me angrier as time passed. Like my father, I made anger my refuge. That kind of anger sets you apart.

My mother's secret life involved trying to get a job. One day every week she'd get dressed up in her one good suit and apply for the jobs available in town for which she was qualified. You'd think that being well educated and having experience as a teacher would have aided her job search, but the "crazy thing" must have gotten around. After all, employers must have reasoned, she'd been committed and in its own way that sort of incarceration carries more of a stigma than jail.

So, even with experience she couldn't find a teaching job. She couldn't type and so wasn't qualified for a secretarial job. Finally, she took the only job she was offered, on a graveyard shift, cutting film at a factory near the edge of town. Every night she put on her smock and went to work. All day long she slept on the couch. I was sixteen and not home very much myself anymore. Often I climbed out my window about the time she left for work and climbed back in a few minutes before she got home.

At sixteen, I was physically very different from my mother. I was taller for one thing, with waist-length hair and a very good figure. The only feature my mother and I had in common was our eyes. I inherited my mother's eyes, which were large, almond-shaped, and blue in color. Unfortunately, I also inherited the family myopia. I hated wearing glasses and generally walked around half blind. I did everything I could to accentuate my figure and wore lots of eyeliner around my huge, myopic blue eyes.

Mother had developed a fear of courts and hospitals. She didn't mind doctors' offices, but institutions and authority frightened her. She clung to her routines so tightly that after a while she even stopped looking up. As time went on, she hid her blue eyes from us more and more. When my mother did look up to meet my eyes, the lost expression in her's made me run away from her even faster than usual.

My brother had his appendix removed that year. My mother suffered through several days of anxiety visiting him in the hospital. I went with her one time. She walked behind me down the hospital hallways looking at her feet. I was afraid she would trip and kept telling her to look up. When doctors and nurses passed by us, she stopped and leaned into the wall. Sometimes she forced impatience right up and out of me.

"Come on," I said. "What's wrong with you?" Finally I took her by the arm and pulled her down the hallway. "You're embarrassing me," I whispered. I did not realize in her emotional state how much that visit cost her.

My mother almost never varied in her routine of sleep, work, grocery store. She hated and feared hospitals, but she braved them to bring my brother comic books and candy. I could not know then but I know now how much courage that must have taken.

While my mother held onto her own fears, my brother and I developed a fear of families. In all family photographs my brother and I are leaning a bit away from everyone else, halfway out of the picture.

Now that I was old enough, I cooked most of our family dinners. My mother was usually sleeping on the couch because she'd worked all night, or just sleeping on the couch because it was better to be asleep than awake. About this time I realized that I was as cut out for housework as my mother. Every now and then I looked up from whatever I was doing and caught my mother staring at me. "What do you want?" I would say, perplexed. "What is it?"

She wouldn't answer. She just closed her eyes, and lay back on the couch.

I wanted an explanation from her. I wanted to know why she was different from other people. I also wanted to know why she'd left me in the first place, and why she'd come back just when I was starting to become happy. But what I really wanted to know was if I was going to turn out like her. I wanted to be prepared for the eventuality of becoming lost inside my own mind, unable to find my way out.

I never understood how my mother kept her film-cutting job, because, in my opinion, she definitely didn't appear or act normal anymore. The medications she took to keep her hallucinations and paranoia at bay caused her to act spacey a good deal of the time. She suffered from medication-induced headaches and anxiety that made her jumpy while exhausting her. I suppose working the graveyard shift at the film-cutting factory kept her out of the way of management personnel who might have been put off by her strangeness.

Sometimes my mother had a normal week or two. When that happened, she cleaned the house, cooked dinner each night, and made my brother his school lunch. She sang as she went through those days, a sound so lovely that even the neighbors who usually avoided her stopped to listen as she hung the wash on the clothesline in our backyard. During my mother's normal times, she went shopping and bought clothes. I marveled, because even though she spent most days in a dazed condition, somehow she always picked fashionable things. Styles I was shocked that she knew existed. Once we spent a mother-daughter Saturday afternoon in our family's only bathroom as she helped curl my straight hair. Patiently she taught me to roll my hair in pin curls and secure each strand in place with bobby pins. I slept this way all night, and in the morning she brushed it out for me, standing next to me while she looked at me in the mirror and said, "See how pretty you look, Paula."

I tried to pretend that my home life didn't matter. I began to hang around with what I thought was a very cool crowd. After a while the people I looked up to were getting arrested, addicted, or worse. When heroin began to be the drug of choice I stopped hanging out with the fast crowd and spent most of my time at home in my room. School started, and I was sent home every other day because of the length of my skirts, which hovered somewhere around my crotch. After a while I discovered that I had developed a reputation for being "easy." None of the straightlaced girls would talk to me, and the girls I'd once been friendly with began bumping into me in the school hallway. Sometimes out of the blue I would feel a shove that would knock me down to the floor. Usually no one helped me up. One Friday I went to get my books out of my locker and found *slut* spray-painted across the front of it. I asked my friend Maryanne about it, and she said that no one wanted me around anymore and that she'd been told not to bring me to parties. No one would have anything to do with me but Maryanne and the boys. The only reason the boys wanted anything to do with me was that they believed the rumors.

One Saturday, I didn't get out of my bed until two o'clock in the afternoon. I woke up early, but lay in bed staring at the ceiling. I knew that nothing in my life was going to change, and I no longer cared whether it did. After I got up I went into the bathroom and took my father's straight razor from the cabinet. I felt a calm practicality about what I was going to do, underneath which lay my hope that one of my parents would break down the bathroom door to save me.

Father preferred old fashioned razors, the kind you unscrew, pop a blade into, and then clamp down. He claimed they brought him a closer shave. For me, they made the whole process risky. I'd cut my legs to ribbons my first try at shaving them. Today, I took my father's old-fashioned razor blade, unclamped it from the shaver, and cut my wrists. I hacked away until I made deep enough cuts to cause some serious bleeding, and I stood watching the blood drip into the sink. After a bit I left the bathroom, walked through the living room where my father was watching television and my mother was sleeping on the couch, left the house, and sat on the front steps. I sat for about thirty minutes, dripping blood onto the concrete. The mailman came to deliver the mail and looked at me. He knocked on the door. "Excuse me," he said, "your kid's sitting out here bleeding."

My father drove me to the hospital. On the way, he talked constantly, almost without taking a breath.

"Is this what you want?" he asked. "Do you want to be crazy like your mother? Do you want me to put you away like her? Well, I'm not going to do it. From now on I'm not letting you out of my sight. You come straight home from school, Paula Jean, every day. Do you hear me?"

"Yes, Dad."

"Between your mother and you I don't know what I'm going to do. I can't believe that this is my life." Once we got to the hospital, he continued screaming at the nurses and doctors until one of them told him to shut up.

My mother didn't talk to me after I got home from the hospital with my wrists bandaged. She didn't look at me either, but late that night as I lay in my bed I heard her crying. That Monday morning my father made me go to school, bandages and all. The school counselor suggested that my father take me to a psychologist. Father told her to mind her own business.

Our family pediatrician removed my stitches. I sat on the patient table while he pulled them out.

"Well, you did quite a job on yourself," the doctor said. I didn't answer. "Tell you what," he said. "The next time you want to try cutting your wrists, if you are really serious, cut down the vein, not across it." Then he turned to my father. "You can take her home now," he said before he left the room.

My mother's medications weren't keeping her sane, or even what passed for sane in our house. Through the years she'd had more setbacks, including extended trips away from home. A few times father packed her up and sent her home to her family in Tennessee, but they always sent her back to us. My mother spent part of my teenage years being shipped back and forth across the United States by bus like a package no one wants to claim. When she came back home, she always came to my room first. She woke me up and hugged me, telling me how glad she was to see me. By then my fears about her, about myself, were overwhelming. I always turned away from her, towards the wall. In the afternoons, she went to the neighbors because she was afraid to be alone. She walked to the store every day for cigarettes, one foot in and one foot out of the gutter. People either stared or turned away when she approached. With my father and brother staying away from home as much as possible, it was left to me when I got home from school to go out and discover where she'd taken refuge. Sometimes she didn't want to return home with me and then we would argue. I suppose they must have been desperate for people to work the graveyard shift at the film-cutting factory, because for a long time they overlooked everything and kept rehiring her.

Still, when I was sick, my mother was the one who held my hand and put a cool rag on my forehead. No matter what was going on inside her mind, she always pushed away her demons for me. Maybe this is what being a mother is about, being able to put away your demons to help your child. Often my father lost control of his temper with me and bore down ready to teach me a lesson. My mother always stood between us, her head down, her arms hugging her waist.

During my junior year in high school, I asked for a backpack for Christmas. I was going to hitchhike across the United States after graduation to escape my life in California. But I decided not to wait for graduation. Early one morning I left and headed to New Mexico to visit my cousin. From there I didn't know. I planned to go where I wanted and when I wanted. I didn't need the what-passed-for-a-normal-life family and friends crap. I would never need anyone again.

My cousin Beth was my Aunt Betty's eldest daughter. She was one of the trio of blond, beautiful cousins to whom I was constantly comparing myself. Beth was seven years older than I, and never paid much attention to me when I was young, skinny, and bratty. Still, I convinced myself that she would be happy to see me. Beth had shocked the family by veering off the course planned by our grandmother. She'd dropped out of San Jose State University when she decided acid and a good-looking guy named Frank held more promise. Beth and Frank hitchhiked around for a year, ate out of garbage cans, dropped acid, and took odd jobs. They showed up at our grandmother's house on Thanksgiving day, dirty and barefoot. Another time, Beth got frostbite from sleeping barefoot in the snow. Frank and Beth ended their relationship in New Mexico. There Beth met Carl, a jewelry maker, with whom she now lived in a teepee outside Taos.

I hitchhiked to Taos and hiked through the snow over land with no roads to my cousin's teepee. She was nine months pregnant. All day she begged in town for money, while her common-law husband made jewelry. This was not the free-spirited, unencumbered life I had envisioned. Three nights a week the local Indians came to Beth's teepee. Everyone drank peyote tea and danced.

There was only one sleeping pallet in the teepee so the three of us (three-and-a-half, if you include the unborn baby) slept on the same pallet.

One morning Carl rolled over and began poking me in the crotch area. He put his hand on my behind and began caressing me. I elbowed him out of the way. He turned to my cousin, and they had sex. "Oops," he laughed, "I thought your cousin was you."

I left the next day and after a few detours, arrived in Berkeley, California. Having nowhere to stay I sat on the curb on University Avenue with several other homeless free spirits and waited for life to happen.

There I made the acquaintance of Cole, a graduate student from England, who happened to be walking by. He said I could crash at his place for a couple of days. I followed him to his studio apartment. We talked for a while and began kissing. Before we could progress to a horizontal state, he gave me a tab which turned out to be acid. The world began to change shape. I pushed my companion away, backed into a corner, and sat down. Around me the walls undulated; all sound seemed to have stopped and at the same time began swirling in my head. My companion now had an elongated forehead and a rectangular mouth. "Cole, p-l-e-a-s-e call my father," I whimpered. My voice came slowly out of my mouth and hung in the air in a cartoon balloon. I could see the words.

My father came and took me home. For once he kept his temper to himself. In fact, he didn't talk to me at all for about a month. I stayed high for a couple of days, slept little, and talked less. My mother had finally lost her job for good and taken up permanent residence on the couch. After a month I went back to school. I stayed away from most of my old friends. I worked hard at school, graduated, and applied to college. The summer after I graduated high school, I fell in love.

Tyler was the most beautiful, talented, doomed person I'd ever met. He was certainly prettier than I ever hoped to be. Tyler was a musician, and his idols were Jimmy Hendrix and Jim Morrison. He told me that his plan was to become famous quickly, party hard, and die young. He was a wonderful, sensual kisser and an intense lover. He also suffered from melodramatically violent depressions. Tyler thought he was doomed to greatness and I had no doubt that he was correct. I loved his deep brown eyes and chiseled features, his talent, his obsessive self-destructiveness, and the fact that my parents hated him. Tyler trailed danger behind him the way most people drag their old coats across floors, unconsciously and with ease.

The first time Tyler hit me he was very sorry. He agonized over the sight of my bruised face, and I felt guilty and sad for his pain. His depressions were so severe that he would quit whatever job he held at the time and hibernate in the darkness of his room at his mother's house. He medicated himself with PCP and heroin.

We'd been seeing each other for six months when Tyler was arrested for being under the influence of drugs. He was in jail for three days because I didn't have enough money for bail. I couldn't sleep at night. My stomach stayed tied in a huge knot, and my back was so tight I thought it would snap in two. His own mother told me to leave him in jail. I went to Tyler's arraignment and watched from the cheap seats near the back of the courtroom as the bailiff led him in handcuffs, dressed in prison blue. Tyler pleaded no contest and received probation. After the judge passed sentence, Tyler turned around and gave me a little wink.

CHAPTER 5

Runaways

As soon as Tyler was released from jail we got married. My mother amazed me by disapproving in a quiet, stubborn fashion. She refused to help me make wedding plans or go with me to shop for a wedding dress. She wouldn't stay in the same room with Tyler, even leaving her place on the couch when he was present. Finally, I insisted that she tell my why she disapproved.

My mother, as usual, was laying on the couch. She sat up, lit a cigarette, and smoked quietly.

"What," I insisted into her silence and the cigarette smoke that surrounded her. "What is it?" After a childhood filled with adult silences I was still no good at dealing with them.

My mother rubbed her chin with a circular motion. Finally she turned to look at me. "You'll be unhappy," she said.

I stood up. "Why?" I asked. "Why wouldn't you want me to get married? Do you want me to be alone forever?"

Mother looked down. A long time passed before she answered me. "I don't want you to be unhappy. But being married doesn't mean that you won't end up alone." My mother crushed out her cigarette, lay down, and closed her eyes.

I stood up and began pacing the floor. "Hey," I said, "listen to me. I'm not you. Do you understand? I'm not you. I'm going to be happy. Hear me? Mother?"

My mother turned away from me and covered her head with her blanket.

The wedding was marred not only by my mother's silence but by my father's sarcasm, Tyler's hostility towards everyone, and the absence of well-wishers. As he was considered the family outlaw and was therefore something of an outcast, Tyler's family didn't attend the wedding. Only my father, mother, and brother came to stand up for me. Before the minister pronounced us man and wife, I heard my father mutter, "Just don't have kids."

The minister, thinking he'd misheard, leaned forward and said, "Excuse me?"

I turned around. My father was looking at the ground, shuffling his feet back and forth. After a minute he said, "Nothing. Go on." A lifetime of disappointment seemed to well up in him. A tear slid down his cheek.

When the minister pronounced us man and wife, Tyler turned to my father and smiled.

After I got married and moved from my family's house in Hayward to the tiny apartment Tyler and I shared in San Jose, I got into the habit of phoning home daily. I missed the disjointed patterns of my childhood. We were attached—my father, brother, mother and me—by my mother's insanity and the patterns we developed in defense of it. One year, on my father's birthday, I took him to the movies. We saw *One Flew Over the Cuckoo's Nest*. It was the shock therapy scenes that got to him. Sitting in the darkened theater next to my father, we watched a strapped-down Jack Nicholson act out the response of someone being shot through with electricity. As I watched Jack jerk against his restraints, I heard a sniffling sound next to me. I turned, and my father was looking at me. I reached over and felt his cheek, which was wet. It was the first time I'd ever touched my father in such an unrestrained fashion. In my family, we learned early not to touch each other, at least not without giving warning. We're a moving-away-from-each-other sort of family, and true to form, my father moved away from my hand, leaving my fingers suspended in the air between us. Later over dinner, we talked about other things until he suddenly changed the subject back to my mother and the shock therapy she endured.

"I didn't know," my father said, "I didn't know they were going to do that to her, but they did and she was never the same." He stopped talking as the waiter, sensing with waiter's intuition the most inappropriate moment to approach our table, refilled our water glasses.

After that, we dropped the subject of crazy mothers, shock therapy and what can happen to you while you are trying to survive your life. He asked me how things were going, how I liked living in San Jose with Tyler and being married. "Everything's going fine. Everything's great," I lied, my lips set in what I hoped was a reassuring smile. "How are you doing? How are things at home?" I asked. He told me things were hectic as always, but basically okay. He lied, too. But I knew the truth.

After I moved out, my brother told me that he could hear our mother laughing and crying late at night. When my father stayed out late, she laughed loudly and for a long time, and when my father didn't come home at all she cried. Since Tyler didn't believe in keeping me updated as to his whereabouts, I quickly understood about crying all night. Before we were married I thought Tyler was physically beautiful, talented, and intelligent. After we got married I learned that he was driven by a fundamental dislike of everyone he knew, especially himself. The more I loved him, the more he resented me, and the more he bragged about the girls with whom he spent his time.

Tyler's stepfather had a gay friend, a very nice middle-aged man named Fred. Often, Tyler dressed up, put on my makeup, and went to Fred's Friday night parties. Sometimes he brought me, stationed me in a corner, and ignored me all night. I watched as Tyler circled the room of men teasing and flirting, arousing all sorts of lust. But what neither the girls he spent nights with nor the men he teased understood and that I understood too well by then was that Tyler was not a sexual creature. He was just plain angry all the time.

I applied for a job and was hired to work the evening shift at a Silicon Valley semiconductor factory. For eight hours, from three o'clock in the afternoon until eleven at night, I spun silicon wafers in the developer, a huge machine that looked and sounded like a washing machine. I named it Ethel. During the daytime I attended San Jose City College. I had wanted to attend San Jose State University, but I didn't have the money for tuition, figured my father wouldn't lend it to me, and assumed that the university wouldn't accept me anyway. I had a million excuses ready each time I gave up on a dream. I didn't have an idea in the world where my life was heading. For two years I drifted along just letting things happen to me and not considering the consequences of just letting time pass me by.

Like me, my brother Michael began planning his escape from family life when he was thirteen years old. He saved enough money to buy an old Harley Davidson motorcycle, which was in pieces in a box. My father said it was unfixable.

Despite my father's predictions of failure, my brother had taken the pieces of the motorcycle from the box and built a running bike. He spent as much time as possible away from home. When Michael turned sixteen he took and passed the GED. The day after he learned the results of the test, Michael packed up and left home for Alaska, the farthest point he could think of away from our family.

With my brother and me out of the house, my father decided to get a divorce. He told my mother that his terms were no alimony and no encroachment into his retirement. In return, he would divide the savings accounts with her and give her the house. If she wanted a fight, they would go to court. Neither one of them wanted to go to court. My father feared a lifetime of alimony. To my mother, going to court was a step towards becoming institutionalized, which she would do anything to avoid.

My father never exactly told me that my mother was my responsibility now. I hadn't realized that he was planning on leaving. When he phoned to tell me about the divorce I asked him who would take care of her.

"She's not my responsibility," he said, "I've spent enough of my life making sure you and Mikey were okay. Now it's my turn."

"What does that mean, Daddy? What do you mean by 'it's my turn'? Who takes care of her?"

"That's not my problem anymore, Paula Jean."

I didn't realize my father had hung up the phone until I heard the dial tone. Father never did believe in long drawn-out goodbyes. He also apparently didn't believe in forwarding addresses, because he did not give me his new phone number for six months.

My father became a free man. My brother was in Alaska. At twenty years old I was now my mother's keeper.

Tyler and I had been married for two years. We still lived in San Jose, where I went to school and worked evenings. Spending more of my time in Hayward with my mother wasn't a problem with my husband, who after two years of marriage wasn't home much himself. It did prove to be a problem at school. I began to neglect my class work. The quarter after my father left my mother I flunked two classes and was put on academic probation. The following quarter I flunked two more and was suspended from school. When the counseling office advised me that I was no longer eligible for admission, I asked them to reconsider. Informed that their decision was final, I walked off the school grounds with my head down.

"Hey. Watch where you're going," an angry girl yelled at me. I had crashed into her, causing her to drop her books on the ground.

"Sorry," I mumbled and walked on. I came to a garbage can, opened the lid, and dropped my books and folders inside. As I walked away, I didn't look back at the school and I didn't cry. When I saw my mother and she asked me how I was doing in school, I lied and said that I was doing well. After all, my mother was an educated woman, and she would have been very disappointed in me.

For a while Mother and I managed to make things work. My mother was seeing a new psychiatrist, a woman whom she trusted and liked quite a bit. Since my mother didn't have a car and didn't want to take the bus, I drove up three times a week to take her to her sessions. I also went on Saturdays to help her clean the house and to take her grocery shopping.

My mother never asked about Tyler, which was fine because I wouldn't have known how to explain. I learned early in my marriage not to ask my husband any questions. Tyler didn't like to be questioned. His answers were always physical. He slapped and punched me. He liked the bruises to show.

"My mama always had bruises on her while I was growing up," he said. "My mama knew how to treat a man, knew what to do when the world came down on her man," Tyler said, running his words together. And then he'd want me. After a while the only time we had sex was after he got angry. I would lie still and quiet, and he would be loud above me.

About once every three months Tyler became depressed. He would lock me out of the bedroom and lie in bed, crying. If I offered to help, he came out of the bedroom, threw me repeatedly against the wall, and told me not to interfere.

Tyler's depressions usually lasted about a week. Afterwards he disappeared for a while. I heard from friends that he was never alone during these absences. Sometimes late at night the phone would ring. No one answered when I said hello, but I heard laughter in the background. When Tyler finally came home, it was because he, or his latest girlfriend, ran out of dope money. Naturally, he found it difficult to keep a job.

Tyler's dope preferences ran between heroin and PCP, two completely unrelated drug experiences. Heroin takes you down, and after a while only gets you normal, meaning that you slowly lose the high and then spend your time trying to get back to the level prior to the high.

I learned all about both drugs from observation, and the difference in Tyler while under the influence of one or the other drug was extreme. Heroin caused him to nod his head a lot, keeping his eyes at half mast, scratching his face, and slurring his words. The worst thing Tyler ever did to me while stoned on heroin was nod out and burn holes in the couch with his cigarette. So I learned not to mind heroin.

Tyler was completely different while on PCP: he was blank and zombie-like. His arms and legs moved stiffly, and his eyes became huge and round. The aftereffects were the scary part. Coming down from a PCP high made him irritable. He trusted no one and believed in hitting first and asking questions later. Tyler hated me to wear my hair behind my ears. He liked it long and flowing. If I put my hair behind my ears it was a good reason for a slap. If I wore a short skirt he accused me of trying to attract other men and punched me in the stomach. If I refused to get him a beer he opened every can in the six-pack and poured them over my head.

Sometimes I watched Tyler sleep and I could see an old man in his face, in the way the skin fell back when he lay snoring. Nothing was going by in Tyler's life but time. He and I were alike in that way. If he'd been home more, he might have refused to let me go to Hayward, but he wasn't and so I was free to take care of my mother.

My mother took her medication and liked speaking with the doctor, and things were fine for a while. We had regular mother-daughter conversations about clothes, makeup, and school. With surprise, I realized that I liked her. Mother had a good sense of humor and a beautiful laugh that she used often. She went shopping and updated her wardrobe. Now, instead of her usual sweatshirts and sweatpants, she wore slacks and blouses. We began going out to lunch every other week, and I found myself looking forward to these outings. We were feeling our way towards a relationship.

"I always missed teaching," my mother said during one of our lunches out. "I still do."

Not knowing what to say to this, I put my fork down on

the edge of my plate and wiped my mouth with the napkin. "Why didn't you go back then?" I asked.

My mother smiled. She looked up at me with her clear blue eyes. "People who have been committed to psychiatric institutions don't apply for jobs as teachers," she said. "That sort of experience just doesn't look good on a resume." My mother resumed eating as I sat staring, with my mouth slightly open. We ate silently for a while. Finally my mother put down her fork and looked at me.

"Please stay in college, Paula," she said. "You're very smart and I want you to have a happier, better life than I've had."

Filled with guilt that I'd been kicked out of school and without stopping to think, I said the first thing that popped into my mouth. "Going to college didn't help you any." I felt terrible after I'd said it, like some nasty, spoiled child for whom no gift is ever enough. I wanted to say *I love you, Mama*, or *I'm sorry, Mama*. Instead I just took a bite of my salad and said, "We're fine," to the waitress who had stopped at our table.

My mother sat smiling, looking down at her plate. "Remember when I had to take that factory job? Well, I applied for a job at our neighborhood library that year. You were about thirteen," she said.

I put down my fork. "I didn't know that," I said. She had my full attention.

"Yes," my mother said. "They turned me down because I was overqualified. They weren't afraid that I'd have a breakdown, they were just afraid that I'd quit." She looked up at me and continued talking. "I wore my favorite suit for the interview. Since it was a weekday your father had the car, so I walked to the library. After the interview, when I knew I didn't have the job, I walked home."

"I didn't know that," I said again.

"If you don't stay in college, Paula," she said, looking

me directly in the eyes, "you'll never have a chance to be rejected for a job that you want because you're overqualified. You will go through your life wishing for more and becoming angry and disillusioned with yourself. I want you to have a chance to try to either succeed or fail, but at least have the chance to try."

At that moment I wanted to be exactly like my mother, but I didn't tell her, and the moment passed unrecognized. I couldn't, after all, let her know that I was a failure at the one thing she valued: education.

Unfortunately, my mother began feeling so normal that she stopped taking her medication. All her life, my mother's diagnosis hung on her, made her separate. She always wanted to be just like everyone else. My mother never got over the hope that if she stopped taking her medication and tried really hard, miraculously she would be normal. A few weeks after she stopped taking her medication she stopped cleaning the house. She began spending her days sleeping on the couch and was back in the routine of waking up to smoke a cigarette and then going back to sleep. Sleep was where my mother went to be safe. Finally she stopped seeing her psychiatrist and our relationship deteriorated to its former state of anger and distrust.

Now when I went grocery shopping for my mother she insisted that I only visit one particular store, which was on the opposite side of town from where she lived. When I returned with the groceries, she checked the receipt to make certain I wasn't trying to trick her. She took everything out of the bag, checking the brands. If I accidentally bought the wrong brand she made me go back to the store and exchange it.

I always drove home to the apartment hoping that Tyler wouldn't be there. If I saw his car parked in front of our building I drove around waiting for him to leave. Sometimes he parked his car around the corner, and when I let myself into our apartment he was sitting on the couch. He liked to sit in the dark with the drapes pulled, no light except for the tip of his cigarette. And he laughed when I came through the door, a sound real low and soft.

"Where you been, baby?" he said. "Where you been, sweetheart?"

My body took on a chill then, like before the flu, when you know you're going to be sick but don't want to quite believe it yet. "I've been with my mother. It's Saturday. You know I always see her on Saturdays. Do you want a beer?" I walked towards the kitchen.

"Where you really been, baby?" He sat smoking his cigarette. I flipped the light switch. "Don't turn on the light, sugar."

I knew I was in trouble then. For Tyler, dark moods required dark rooms. So I turned off the light and knew that it was just a matter of time before he came after me. "I had to buy groceries for her. Look, I got some stuff for us too. Are you sure you don't want a beer?"

Tyler put his cigarette down in the ashtray. "I think you're lying to me. Is that so, Paula Jean? Just my little liar." He stood up then and walked towards me.

I always left the light out for a long time after that.

Money seemed to run out all the time. Tyler grew up poor and didn't mind, but I couldn't get used to being broke. I began borrowing from my mother.

One day while driving I overshot a turn coming onto the freeway and drove over the embankment. I kept going even though my car began to rattle and sway. A mile up the road a highway patrolman pulled me over and insisted upon giving me a sobriety test. I passed the test, and he let me drive on. Unfortunately, the accident had done something to the underside of my car. The cost for fixing it was $500.

After the mechanic gave me the bad news, I drove to my mother's house, woke her up, and asked her to loan me the money to fix my car. "Of course, Paula," she said. But when we got to the bank, she wouldn't get out of the car. I pulled at her arm, and she turned to look at me. I thought of Tyler and school. I thought about getting out of my car and running away. Everything seemed hopeless. Suddenly I began to laugh. We sat in my car for a while, and I laughed. My mother wrapped an arm around her head and watched me.

Finally I stopped laughing and told her, "I won't be able to help you anymore unless you get me the money. I have to have it or I can't get to work." My mother cowered in the corner of the seat. I got angrier. Didn't she see that I was doing everything I could to support her? "I won't have anything to do with you. You'll be completely alone." My mother got out of the car and went into the bank. I looked through the windshield for a long time. After a bit I thought it had started to rain, but it turned out I was crying. My mother got back into the car and handed me the money. We didn't speak all the way back to her house.

My mother began insisting that I take her to appointments with new doctors: general practitioners and internists. She called me at the last minute to tell me about her appointments. I was fired from my job for missing work and making too many mistakes when I was there. It was humiliating to fail at a job that only required me to load a machine with silicon wafers and wait until it completed a cycle so that I could reload. Now Tyler and I had only the money he brought home occasionally. I didn't know how he made his money and was afraid to ask. When I thought about the future I was terrified.

At my mother's house one Saturday I found a bottle of sleeping pills in her medicine cabinet, and I realized what these doctors' visits were about. *She must want to stay asleep all the time now*, I thought. I could understand the urge to stay unconscious, but that didn't mean it wasn't my responsibility to try to keep her awake.

I continued to take her to new doctors, but I got sneaky. At the beginning of each doctor's visit, I asked the receptionist to let me see the doctor first. After telling my mother I was going to the bathroom, I slipped down the hall to see the doctor. My mother always chose female doctors. They sat across from me in neat white medical coats smiling professionally while I told them about my mother's schizophrenia and my belief that she was medicating herself into unconsciousness. The doctors were always skeptical. "Let's see," they said. "Let's have a talk with her."

"What seems to be the problem, Mrs. Rothwell?" each doctor asked my mother.

"Well." My mother leaned forward and spoke softly. She never lost her southern accent, and madness did not erase her beautiful voice. Everything my mother said came out of her mouth with a lilting cadence. "I can't seem to get to sleep at night, Doctor. I have to get some rest."

"Why is it that you can't rest, Mrs. Rothwell?" each doctor said, looking my mother over.

Sometimes my mother laughed at this point. "I don't know. I just can't. I need to rest. I need to get some sleep."

Now there was a standoff: the doctor tapping the desk with a pen, my mother wrapping an arm around her head, and me staring up at the ceiling.

"I'll tell you what, Mrs. Rothwell. I'm going to give you a couple of sleeping pills, enough for a few nights. And you make an appointment to see me in about a week." The doctor stood up then and looked down at my mother.

"But I can't rest. Can't you give me a prescription?" my mother said to the doctor's feet.

"You come and see me in about a week, and we'll see then." The doctor usually left the room at this point. And my mother would turn to look at me, her big blue eyes staring at my face. I always had to fight the urge to cover up my guilt with my hands.

We never went back to the same doctor twice.

After a couple of months my mother figured out what was going on. As we drove home from a doctor's appointment one afternoon, she began staring at me. I glanced in her direction. She didn't look away. Her eyes were dark blue and unblinking. She began hitting herself on the top of the head. Then she began slapping her face.

"Mother, please stop," I said, but she wouldn't. She began moaning. "Mother, stop," I yelled at her.

We came to an intersection, and when I stopped the car she opened the door. I grabbed her arm, put the car in park, and reached across her body to lock the door. She covered her head with her arms.

"Why are you doing this to me, Paula Jean?" she began to yell. "That hurts. Don't touch me." She moved away from me, leaning against the door.

"I'm not hurting you. I'm trying to get you home."

She turned to stare at me. "Why are you doing this to me, Paula Jean? Get away from me. Let me out." Her eyes stayed that dark blue, and I knew mine were identical as I looked back at her. We hated each other then. I knew it for sure.

The light changed, and I turned onto the freeway in the middle of rush hour traffic.

"I should let you," I said. "I should let you get those stupid pills and kill yourself, but I just can't."

My mother began hitting herself on the top of the head again. "Let me out. I want to get out. Get away from me."

We drove down the freeway screaming at each other.

The traffic didn't help being stop, go, stop, go. My mother kept banging at her head with her fists, and I alternated between trying to restrain her and trying to drive. Traffic came to a complete stop, and I slammed on the brakes, swerving, and barely missed the car in front of me. We sat in the car staring straight ahead into traffic.

My mother sat beside me moaning, and I thought of how easy it would be to open the door, get out, and leave her there in the car. She'd paid to fix it, after all. But where would I go? I was shocked by the thought that I had nowhere to go.

The driver in the car behind me honked his horn, and I glanced in the rearview mirror. My mother opened the car door, got out, and began running down the freeway. I watched her go.

"I should let her," I said out loud. "Let her go." She ran in between cars. Horns honked and people yelled.

I pulled my car out of traffic, parked on the side of the freeway, and ran after her. Drivers stared and pointed and talked to their companions. Some laughed. I felt shame and a strong anger take over until I felt like another person. I caught up with my mother, grabbed her arm, and dragged her over to the side of the road. When I got her back to the car a highway patrolman was waiting. He asked what was wrong. My mother, whose history included police officers driving her to psychiatric facilities, shut up immediately. I explained to the officer that my mother was reacting to medication. He warned us to get off the freeway as soon as possible and let us go.

My mother and I didn't speak to each other on the way home.

At my mother's house I parked the car in the driveway. I still felt a strange, strong anger. It sat in my stomach, making me feel sick. Finally, I got out of the car and opened the door on my mother's side. She sat in her seat, looking down at her knees.

"Okay," I said. "Here we are. You can get out of the car now." She sat in her seat, looking at her knees. "Okay, you can get out now. You're home."

She turned to look at me. Her eyes were clear, light blue and sad. They were the eyes I'd grown up with again. Her face wore the same look it always had when she came home from the hospital or her parents' house: glad and confused at the same time.

Slowly she got out of the car. I couldn't take anymore. Without looking back, I drove away.

My mother ran away the next day. I discovered her absence when I went to do the grocery shopping. The front door was unlocked, and all the lights in the house were on. I noticed that some of the back windows of the house were broken, but this didn't worry me. My mother had a reputation as the neighborhood crazy lady, and kids always dared each other to sneak up onto the porch or throw things at the house. I was always chasing them away. My stomach clenched at the thought.

I sat on the couch and waited for her to come home. The house was dirty. There were piles of mail and magazines strewn throughout. My mother had stopped letting me clean her house. She was afraid that I was planting listening devices in the rug when I vacuumed and under the coffee table when I dusted.

I waited until nighttime; then I called the police. They told me they had no way of knowing how long she'd been missing. "You have to wait seventy-two hours to file a report," they said. "Go home," they said. "Try to relax," they advised.

"You don't understand," I said. "My mother is mentally ill. She's schizophrenic. She can't take care of herself." I began to cry.

"How do you know?" the police officer on the other end of the telephone asked. "Do you have proof?"

I hung up the phone and wondered who to call next. I thought about who in my mother's family would help me. The only one of my mother's ten siblings to keep in touch with my mother was her older sister, Gayle. I remembered my Aunt Gayle from the summer we visited my mother's parents. She was tall, smart, and beautiful. Aunt Gayle looked enough like my mother so that you knew they were related, but my aunt was a more robust version.

My mother's other brothers and sisters kept their distance. In the South where my mother grew up, blood ties are telling things. It was too easy for my aunts and uncles to identify with my mother's insanity when it was right in front of them. Grandmother Mildred was so comfortable with the thousands of miles between California and Tennessee that when my grandfather Lucian died she waited until a week after the funeral before she told my mother.

"There was no need for you to bother yourself with the trip, Lucia Elaine," my grandmother wrote in a letter. "We know you were with us in spirit."

Unlike the others, Aunt Gayle always loved and protected her younger sister. She thought my mother brilliant, gentle, and free-spirited. Gayle phoned our house once a week no matter what my mother's mental state and whether or not her calls were welcome. So now that my mother was gone, I phoned the only other person I assumed would care.

"Aunt Gayle, Mother has run away," I said. "What should I do? Can you come?"

My aunt became upset. "What did you do to her, Paula Jean? Why, your mother is the most gentle, loving woman in the world. She would do anything for you. What did you do to her?"

I hung up the phone and went home.

Tyler's car was parked in front of the building. As soon as I opened the door to our apartment, I noticed he was coming down from something, and I hoped it wasn't PCP.

"Hey, baby," he said, smiling. "Hey, my little Paula Jean." Tyler laughed. "I'm leaving you, sugar. I've got me a new woman. Twice the woman. Younger too, she's fifteen. She says I am the best thing she's ever seen."

"Fine," I said. "Go." I felt exhausted and didn't care what happened. He could do his worst.

"I'll go when I want to go, bitch," he said, and smiled.

Tyler walked through our apartment throwing lamps, cups, plates, glasses, and anything breakable onto the floor. When he'd created a big enough mess, he held me by the neck and made me crawl around picking up the broken pieces. For two hours we went through the apartment, Tyler breaking things and me crawling around cleaning them up. Finally, he pushed my face into the carpet, held me by the throat, and raped me. I lay underneath him while he raped me and did not have one clear thought. He left the next morning to move in with his girlfriend and her parents.

A week later, I received a letter from Tyler's girlfriend. She wrote that I should let Tyler go because they truly loved each other and belonged together. She understood him. When he came home frustrated and angry, she would say, "Beat me, Tyler, hit me. It will make you feel better." Somewhere inside me a little Paula Jean kicked up, and I wrote back telling her to keep him.

I still hadn't heard from my mother. I did not fill out a missing person's report. Neither my aunt nor my father asked about her, and my brother was far away. *She's okay*, I kept telling myself. And then, almost as an afterthought, added, *People can disappear so easily, with no one to care or wonder where they went.* I began to feel detached. I got a job at a local pizza parlor and kept to myself over the next months.

Lacking the desire for anything, especially romance, I of course met someone new. Tom was tall, blond, gainfully employed by the electric and gas company, and so stable that I couldn't believe he was for real. He was like a real big quiet in contrast to all my noise. I'd grown up to be the type of woman that men looked at twice, with long brown hair, large blue eyes, and a good figure. In an off-kilter sort of way, I resembled a Barbie Doll. I knew I was sexy and didn't work at hiding it, but when I attracted attention, I was often made uncomfortable by it. We met in a country western bar. I'd gone there with a girlfriend who was worried about me being alone too much. He'd stopped in after a bachelor party. I looked up and saw a tall, muscular blond man smiling down at me. After he asked me to dance, we didn't sit down again. A few weeks later Tom introduced me to his family. I couldn't relate to his parents, who told stories about family vacations and what their son was like growing up. Yet I felt that I'd found a place to escape into, where I'd never be scared or feel hunted or be alone again. I think that, initially, Tom and I were both attracted to the fact that we were complete opposites. Tom loved being in a crowd and liked to socialize in groups. He liked nothing better than a good party. He also was completely open with everyone. I learned his entire life story on our first date. Tom and I met at a time in our lives when we needed to be in love more than we needed to consider whether we were basically compatible.

In contrast to Tom's openness, I was careful with my confidences. Actually, I was secretive. For example, I didn't tell Tom anything true about my childhood and nothing about my mother. How do you tell someone, after all, that you are the daughter of a crazy runaway?

After two months, we moved in together. Tom was kind to me. He hugged me often and didn't have mood swings. I wanted a quiet life where I would never again think of the past or worry about anything. For a while we had what I'd wished for. I worked a series of part-time jobs without settling on anything for more than a month or two. I tried to forget that once I'd wanted to go to college and become something meaningful. Usually I succeeded, only remembering at night when I couldn't sleep.

Tom and I had been living together for a year. The mortgage on my mother's house was paid in full so the only bills she had paid were for the gas and electric and the telephone. After she disappeared, I turned the utilities off and paid the insurance and house taxes from my salary. I had her mail routed to my father's house and picked it up from him. Tom was kind and never questioned what I did with my salary. He seemed happy to have me to come home to, and I was glad he was there.

One morning, I received a phone call from the Oakland Police. They had tracked down and phoned my father first, and he gave them my phone number. My mother had been picked up at a downtown hotel. Her choices: a seventy-two-hour hold in jail, or she could go home with me. I'd learned from my childhood what secrets to keep and truths to tell, so Tom still didn't know about my mother. I'd managed to create a whole new past for myself, including a mother who was a lovely woman who taught school and died when I was six years old. My father helped with my fantasy childhood by answering no family-based questions.

Now all my carefully hidden truths would have to come out.

I didn't know what to do, but I also didn't have the

luxury of a lot of time to think over the alternatives. I tried to think of a way to both take care of my mother and keep her hidden at the same time. Finally, I settled on a solution. I decided to take my mother to her own home in Hayward.

The police told me that, after leaving her house, my mother had checked into the same hotel in Oakland from which she'd now been evicted. According to the hotel clerk, she rarely left her room except to go to the bank to get money and to convenience stores to get cigarettes and food. Her room bill was one hundred dollars a night. My mother had run through her entire savings. After she ran out of money, she barricaded herself in her room. The hotel manager couldn't get her to leave and finally called the police. When they kicked in the door, they found her huddled in the corner of the room muttering to herself. She put up a fight and had to be carried through the lobby screaming.

Someone else's mother, I thought. *She can't be mine.*

I phoned my mother's old psychiatrist, who agreed to see her immediately. I picked up my mother from the police station and took her directly to the psychiatrist's office. After her session I filled Mother's prescription and took her back to her house. During all of this my mother was silent. She clung to my arm. Every now and then she looked into my face. Her eyes were clear blue and innocent as a child who hasn't been hurt yet.

The house desperately needed cleaning and there was no food, so groceries needed to be bought; the lights didn't work and the utilities needed to be turned back on, and Tom needed an explanation.

"My God," he said, when I told him about my mother in a careful explanation, which was descriptive but lacked certain facts. After all, what did he know about insanity, about what can happen during one short lifetime. Better to keep the truth to myself and serve him up just the edges of my reality. "That's quite a secret. I feel so sorry for you," Tom said and got himself a beer from the refrigerator. But I noticed that he avoided looking at me for a while after that. He looked at the refrigerator or whatever he was holding in his hand, but not directly at me.

Arrangements needed to be made to sell the house to provide my mother with some money. I went back to Hayward, made certain my mother took her medication, and left her sleeping on the couch while I went out to phone my father.

At first, my father didn't want to become involved and kept finding reasons to get off the phone. Eventually, he gave me the name of a good and trustworthy real estate agent. My plan was to put my mother in a small apartment near where I lived in San Jose. I would manage her money and sign her up for Social Security disability benefits. Until I could arrange to sell her house, I would have to pay for her groceries. I was making pretty good money at my current job and had recently become efficient, so this did not present a problem.

My mother responded to her medication and began to be aware of her surroundings. She started cleaning the house. She showed an interest in reading, taking walks, and going shopping for groceries and clothes. I knew, however, that this was just an intermission and that before long my real mother, the crazy one, would be back.

We had three quiet months before she cut down her dosage. "I feel fine," she said. "I'll be all right this time," she promised, her eyes filled with hope.

"It's just like all the other times," my father warned. "That's what she always says." He sighed. "Now you know a little of the life I've had to lead."

Somehow, Tom adjusted to the change in our domestic circumstances. He understood that I needed to go to

Hayward almost every day to check on my mother, but he showed no interest in meeting her. In fact, he didn't want to talk about her at all. In his eyes I sometimes saw the same look of disappointment I'd grown up seeing in my father's.

Three months later, just as in the past, my mother stopped taking her medication altogether. The psychiatrist appointments were forgotten, and the doctor told me that she could not force my mother to get treatment.

I became the enemy now. My mother ducked her head and watched me from the corners of her eyes, stared at me when I spoke to her, and did not answer when I asked her questions. She reminded me of some half-wild animal, impossible to completely tame, who sticks with you because you feed it.

One day the real estate agent and I arrived at her house and found the door locked and the locks changed. My mother screamed through the door, "You were trying to steal my house from me!" She stood at the window yelling, "I know what you're up to!"

I walked the real estate agent to her car. She told me there was nothing further she could do, patted me on the shoulder, and wished me luck. I stood on the porch all afternoon, but my mother would not let me into the house.

The next day I went back. My mother didn't answer my knock, so I looked through the front window. She sat on the couch talking to a large, red-haired woman. Every now and then my mother said something that caused the red-haired woman to throw back her head and laugh.

I later learned that the woman was a real estate agent who had come to my mother's door the previous day. Houses in the neighborhood were suddenly hot items, selling fast and with little effort.

In answer to my knock, my mother opened the door but left the chain in the hook. She spoke through the opening.

"Go away, Paula Jean," she said. "I don't need you. I have a friend now, and she'll help me." Then she shut and locked the door.

I stood on the porch and listened to them laughing. After a while, I left feeling hurt and angry. Why couldn't she trust me? As I drove, my feelings of responsibility for her care began to overwhelm me, and soon to scare me. How could I hope to take care of her when everyone else had failed? I stayed away from my mother's house for two weeks. When I went back to see her again, she was gone. The house was sold. I did not know the name of the new real estate agent, so I could not get in touch with her. None of the neighbors knew where my mother had gone, and the new owners of the house were not moving in for three months.

I didn't know what to do.

I drove back to San Jose.

Tom put his arms around me when I told him. "Oh, honey," he said, "you did everything you could. I know you did. You did your best."

We were sitting on the couch. I scooted a bit away, just enough so that it would be an effort for him to touch me, and so I could see his face when I spoke to him. Because something else was on my mind.

"Tom," I said, "my period is a month late. I think I'm pregnant."

CHAPTER 6

Paula Jean

"I thought you were on birth control," Tom said in a puzzled voice and moved away from me until we had a barrier of empty space between us. "I'm confused here. How can you be pregnant?" He rubbed his face with one hand, as if he were trying to wake up from some deep sleep, and I noticed again how good looking he was, tall, blond, and athletic.

"Things happen," I said. The truth was that I wasn't consistent in taking my birth control pills, and two months prior I'd forgotten to take my pills for a week straight. This was my version of birth control Russian roulette, since I was secure in my belief that I couldn't get pregnant because I didn't deserve to.

"Did you forget to take your pill or something?" Tom leaned forward, looking distressed.

My choice was clear. Tell the truth or lie. "Of course not," I said. "Sometimes it doesn't work, I guess." I shrugged. "I mean, I don't really know for sure yet." I sighed. "I guess I should buy one of those home pregnancy tests."

"As soon as you're sure, you'll let me know, won't you?" Tom asked.

"Of course. Sure I will." I looked down, and he left the room.

For about a week after that we moved around each other carefully, saying "excuse me" a lot and leaving wide spaces in the hallway, so we could walk past each other without touching. Every day Tom asked me if I'd had a pregnancy test yet, and every day I told him that I'd forgotten or hadn't had the time or some other excuse for not wanting to find out the truth. On the one hand, if I was pregnant I would have someone to care for, who would some day care for me. On the other hand, I knew what could happen to little children that people forgot to care for.

One night a couple of weeks after I made my announcement, I woke up and found myself alone in our bed. I got out of bed, pulled on the old T-shirt that I used for a robe (a cheerful thing, too bright to wear in public, with pink and blue kittens imprinted all over the front and back), and walked barefoot into the living room. I turned on the light. Tom was lying on the couch with his arm over his eyes.

"What are you doing out here?" I yawned. "It's after midnight, you know." I pointed at the clock.

"When are you going to get tested?" he asked, keeping his arm over his eyes. "And, Paula, is there anything more you have to tell me about yourself? Any other secrets you're keeping?"

"What do you mean?" I perched on the edge of the couch near his feet. He moved his feet away from me, but slowly, so that the movement was hard to identify as escape.

"I'm beginning to feel you've never been completely honest about yourself. That's what hurts me," Tom said from underneath his arm. "I just found out about your mother, and now I find out that you might be pregnant. I was just wondering what else I'm going to find out as time goes on."

"Babe." I reached out and touched his knee. He jerked away from my touch. I folded my hands in my lap. "I think you know it all now," I said, wondering how I could keep the details of my first marriage a secret. After all, I'd learned how to keep the realities of my life away from prying eyes when I was just a little kid. Protecting the truth from intruders was a hard habit to break. And I'd grown up to believe that everyone was an intruder.

Tom took his arm away from his eyes and looked intently at me. "Really? So, I know everything there is to know about Paula Jean Rothwell now, hmm?"

I felt my stomach tighten. "Well, I was married once before. I didn't think that was important, you know, to tell." My hands were sweating, and I rubbed them on my nightshirt.

Tom sat up and put his head in his hands. After a couple of minutes he looked up at the clock. He kept his eyes on the clock as he talked. "When were you married?" he asked. His face was haggard, as if he were putting on extra years with each passing minute.

I crossed my arms underneath my breasts and began rocking back and forth. The movement reminded me too much of my mother so I made myself stop and sat up straight with my hands at my sides. "I was young. It only lasted a couple of years," I said.

"Are you divorced?" Tom asked.

My chest felt as if invisible hands were pushing into it, pushing me back where I didn't want to go. "No."

"Why?" Tom asked. "Do you still see him?" He looked

straight at me, and I could see his intake of breath. Then he said quietly, "Do you still love him?"

I thought about Tyler and how beautiful he was physically and how angry he was underneath. I thought about the bruises and other women he bragged about. I thought about the money he spent on drugs and the food we went without because of not having that money. And I remembered how it felt to be scared all the time and also to be shamed by that fear. I thought about having to see him again to ask for a divorce.

"I didn't have the money for a divorce," I said. "And besides, I don't even know where he is now." I shrugged. "I don't think I ever loved him. I know everyone says that about their old relationship when they break up, but we were hardly what I'd call devoted."

Tom stood up and walked over to the fireplace. "Okay," he said and looked down at the rug, rubbing his toe back and forth until he made a little pattern in the carpeting. "I have an attorney friend you can see. We'll work it out so you can get a divorce. If that's what you want, that is." He looked over at me, letting the question hang in the air between us.

I stood up too. "Of course it is," I said. "I love you," I said, hoping it was true.

"I love you too, even though you sure make it hard sometimes. There is so much hidden inside you that I don't know if I'll ever really learn who you are." Tom leaned against the fireplace and crossed his arms over his chest. We were both quiet for a moment while the clock ticked and the refrigerator hummed and sounds of normal domesticity surrounded us. It was, after all, the middle of the night when domestic tranquillity and its accompanying noises can be both calming and oppressive.

Tom came and stood close to me, leaned down, and

took my chin in his hands. "I love you, and I don't want to lose you." He let go of my chin and straightened up. "Paula, you've got to have the pregnancy test. This week. I don't even want to talk to you about anything more until after we find out whether or not you're pregnant."

"What'll we do if I am?" I asked, not sure at that point what I wanted to happen.

Tom rubbed his face. "It's lousy timing, but we'll work it out." He looked up at the ceiling. "But I have to be able to trust you, and I need you to trust me. Nothing will work without that." He paused. "I can tell you are keeping a lot about yourself back from me. I don't know if you are capable of completely trusting me or anyone else."

We both went back to bed. I was wide awake and was hypersensitive to every sound and movement. From the twisting and turning on Tom's side of the bed, I don't think he slept either.

I stayed in bed for three days after our conversation. I pulled the sheets around me until I looked mummified and only got out of bed to get a drink of water, eat something or go to the bathroom. When I got out of bed, I dragged the sheet with me. Tom and I didn't talk about the possible baby, my mother, or anything else. I understood that he felt that he'd gotten more than he bargained for: a girlfriend with a crazy mother and now possibly an unplanned pregnancy. I piled up the burdens in my mind, and then I added myself to the top of the heap. I imagined aiming a finger at the whole pile, giving it a little poke, and standing back while my sins scattered everywhere. When I finally got out of bed, Tom didn't press me. For the next few days we continued to walk around the house, edging away from each other and being way too polite in an oppressive excuse-me-please, thank-you and oh-I'm-sorry sort of way.

When I went to bed at night I didn't want to go to

sleep for fear of dreaming. My mother came to me in my dreams warning me about children and all the disappointment that accompanies being a crazy adult in a supposedly sane world.

"You don't know what having children does to you, Paula Jean," my dream mother said. "If I hadn't had children, I'd be fine now. Just ripped my mind and heart out having you, Paula Jean."

"Is that why you left me?" I demanded of my dream mother. "Was I such a bad child? Is that why you always leave me, Mother? Will everyone always leave me?"

"I couldn't help it," her image would answer. "It was all too hard."

I always woke up from this dream screaming. Each time, Tom rolled over and patted me on the back. "Just a dream, babe," he said in a husky, sleepy voice and put his arms around me. "Go back to sleep."

I began lying in bed at night forcing my eyes to stay open in order to ward off my dreams. It always caught up with me though. I would drop off to sleep, and back my mother would come, turning my dreams into nightmares and taking away my peace.

Finally, I bought a home-pregnancy test from the local drug store. It was negative. According to the result, I wasn't pregnant. Not completely trusting so easy a result, I bought three more tests. Each one proved negative. Instead of relief, I felt disappointment, as if I'd lost something precious, as if there were one more unachievable thing in my life to regret.

Tom seemed relieved when I told him that I wasn't pregnant. He brought me roses the next day. He offered again to pay for my divorce and took me to see his attorney friend, who immediately went to work so that he would be able to find Tyler and secure the divorce quickly.

After my divorce was final, I asked Tom if we could get

married. He agreed, and one weekend we drove to Reno and had a simple ceremony. Afterward, we decided to keep our marriage a secret. We wanted to prove to each other that we were happy together and that our commitment was a private matter.

After we got home from Reno, we spent our evenings planning our future. We spoke of buying a second house, getting a dog, and going on vacation, but neither of us mentioned whether having children fit into our plan.

Our life together was a calm oasis. Tom never again asked about the painful details of my first marriage. I didn't want to explain or talk about what it was like to be married to a someone who didn't come home most nights and when he was home hit you just so that he could make you cry. Tom seemed to have picked up my habit of not talking about painful things, so he didn't ask. I also needed to keep myself safe from thinking about my mother and from a vague dissatisfaction with my lack of accomplishments, so I surrounded myself with rituals. The only way I could continue pretending to be happy was to organize my life in such a way that nothing was ever out of place or unplanned. I focused on the little rituals of life so that the larger disappointments would fade into the background. I knew what to do, when to do it, and why it needed doing. Each weekday morning when I left the house for work, I tried the door three times after I turned the key, to make certain it was locked. After I started my car, I flipped on the radio. If the news came on instead of music, I turned off the engine and went back into the house to make certain I'd turned off the coffee pot.

Of course, after that, I had to try the door lock another three times.

Sometimes it took me an hour to leave my driveway,

and I was late for work. But I felt it couldn't be helped—
it was just the price I paid for keeping my life orderly.

On the first Saturday morning in January, my tra-
ditional day to take down the Christmas decorations, I
was arranging boxes in the correct positions when the
phone rang. I took an ornament from the top branch of
the tree and answered the phone. The person on the
other end of the line identified himself as the manager
of a motel in Hayward. He told me that a woman claiming to be my mother was in one of the rooms. She'd
been there a month and had now barricaded herself in
the room so that the maids couldn't go in. When he'd
threatened to call the police she'd given him my phone
number. Would I come? he asked.

"Yes," I said. No sense in wondering if the woman in
question was really my mother. Who else could she be?
"I'll come. Could you give me the address, please?" Little
slivers of glass fell onto the carpet. I'd crushed the ornament I was holding, and my palm was bleeding. I shook
my hand free of glass, picked up a pen, and wrote down
the address of the motel on a napkin. After I hung up
the phone, I had to rewrite the address on a clean piece
of paper because the napkin was covered with blood.

Tom wasn't home, so I didn't need to come up with
an explanation about my mother's reappearance. I
picked the remaining glass out of my palm, wrapped another napkin around my hand, and left the house to
pick up my mother. By the time I drove from San Jose to
Hayward, blood had seeped through the napkin and my
jeans were stained.

The motel manager met me in the parking lot. He
looked from my napkin-wrapped hand to my stained
jeans. "Are you okay, ma'am?" he asked.

I hid my bleeding hand behind my back. "I'm fine.
Which room is my mother in?"

He pointed up at the second level. I followed his pointing finger. My mother stood in a window, smiling and waving. I shut my eyes for a moment and took a deep breath. When I opened my eyes, the motel manager was leaning forward and staring at my face.

"Are you sure you're okay?" He clasped his hands in front of his chest. "Can I get you a glass of water?"

"No, I've already had my daily allotment of water," I said wearily.

He leaned closer. He had very thick eyebrows, and they were pulled together forming one hairy line over his eyes. "Excuse me?" he asked.

Well, I thought, now he knows for certain that she's my mother. We're both crazy as all hell. "Never mind," I said. I looked upstairs again. My mother still stood at the window, waving and smiling. For a minute I felt dizzy, and the ground underneath me seemed to be moving.

The motel manager grabbed my arms. "Ma'am," he said and leaned closer to my face. He had terrible breath, and it revived me. "Would you like to go inside the office for a minute?" he asked.

I shook my head. "No," I answered, "I'll be fine." I went up the stairs and knocked at my mother's door. "Mother," I called, "open the door."

I listened to her scrambling around inside the room. The door opened.

"My girl," she said. "My little girl."

"Please get your things, Mother," I said and watched shaking as she picked up her purse and a can of Coke. "I'm going to take you home."

The manager said he wouldn't charge us for the room. He was just happy to help. I thanked him while my mother held onto my waist. I had to unpry her hands in order to get her into the car. We began our journey to San Jose with my mother in high spirits. She smiled and smoked but didn't talk to me. However, as we got farther from Hayward she began to fidget, becoming more and more agitated. She lit one cigarette after another, throwing them half smoked out the car window. When she ran out of cigarettes, she turned to look at me.

"Where are you taking me, Paula Jean?" she asked, wrapping one arm around her head and covering her mouth with her other hand. "I want to go home."

"I am taking you home, Mother," I said, wishing that I'd remembered to lock the car door on her side. My heart began to pound. *I'm having a heart attack*, I thought.

"I want to go to my house," she said. "Take me to my house." She began to yell. "What have you done with my house, Paula Jean?" She began to moan and rock in her seat.

"You don't have a house," I said through gritted teeth. "You sold your house, don't you remember?" I gripped the steering wheel. The cuts on my palm opened and began to bleed.

When we arrived at my house, my mother wouldn't get out of the car. It was a warm California winter's day and all my neighbors were outside their houses. I got out of the car, opened the door on her side, and knelt down in the driveway.

"Mother," I said softly. "This is the only place you have to go. Please get out of the car." She turned to look at me.

"But, Paula Jean, I don't live here. I want to go home to your father. Please take me home."

"Mommy," I said, "this is the only place I have to bring you. Please get out of the car." I lowered my head. I noticed my hand was bleeding harder.

My mother reached out and began to stroke my hair. "Your hair is always in your eyes, Paula," she said softly.

Finally, we worked our way into the house. I got down

a bowl for her to use as an ashtray and put her in the spare bedroom.

Tom came home. When he heard moaning from the spare room, he looked in and found my mother curled up in a corner. The reality of my mother was about to detonate our marriage, exposing our vulnerabilities and fears to each other.

"How long is she going to stay?" he asked me.

"I don't know. I guess until I can get her medicated and into her own apartment."

Tom looked nervous. I felt sorry for him, annoyed with him, and also terrified that he might leave me. If the dose of reality my mother represented was too much for my own family, how could an outsider be expected to cope?

My mother got up after midnight and paced through the house for the rest of the night, smoking and talking to herself. She turned on all the lights, and Tom and I sat in our bedroom, watching her shadow pass underneath our door. In the morning she hid in her room and refused to come out. Tom tried to understand and help me, but he walked through our house in a trance, bumping into furniture and dropping breakable things like glassware and knickknacks. I tried to see the situation through his eyes, to look at my mother from an outsider's point of view. I explained to him that she was behaving so strangely because she'd been off her medication for a long time. During my explanation his face changed until he looked like someone who had been in a terrible automobile accident, almost as vague and disoriented as my mother. Truthfully, what seemed perfectly normal to me was completely out of his experience. He had no coping mechanisms for this sort of family crisis.

Things became tenser every day. One morning we were sitting at our kitchen table drinking coffee when

Tom blurted out, "She acts like the bums that sleep in the park downtown. I don't mean that your mother is a bum, but that's what she acts like." He took a gulp of coffee. "I know how that sounds. I'm so sorry, but I don't know what else to say."

"Maybe you should visit family or some friends for a while," I suggested. "Go on. It's okay."

Tom looked miserable, but the next day he went to his parents' house. "Just for a few days," he said. "I have to have some time to pull myself together."

I nodded but said nothing.

A few days after Tom had gone, I phoned my father. "Daddy," I said, "I have Mother here." There was silence. "Daddy," I asked, "did you hear me? I have Mother here."

"How is she?" my father finally asked.

"Not so good," I said. My heart began to pound again. *I'm dying*, I thought. *My heart is giving out.* "Can you come help?" I held the receiver in both hands.

"I'll think about it," he said and hung up.

I redialed his number and counted the rings. The answering machine finally picked up. "Daddy," I said, "I know you're there. Please pick up." I hung up the phone and redialed. "Daddy," I said when the answering machine picked up, "you have to come help me. I don't know what to do. Please call me back." I phoned again in a few minutes and got a busy signal. After a while, I phoned the operator who told me that the phone was off the hook.

In the middle of the afternoon I went into the spare bedroom. My mother was asleep clutching her purse. I pried it away from her. Inside I found a little spiral notebook. Most of the writing was just scribbling, but on one page there was an address and a phone number.

I dialed the number. A cheerful female voice answered.

"Starside Apartments," the voice said. I asked if the woman knew my mother.

"Why, yes," the woman, who identified herself as Mrs. Ramirez, said. Apparently, my mother had been a tenant there until a month ago.

"What happened then?" I asked.

Mrs. Ramirez paused before answering. "Well, honey," she said, "your mama couldn't pay the rent and we had to put her out."

I told Mrs. Ramirez that I would be up in about an hour to see her. Then I called my grandmother Lillian and asked her to come watch my mother while I went to Hayward to collect her things.

Grandmother Lillian was now a widow. One morning a year before, as was his daily habit, my step-grandfather got up at five-thirty and went out to his junk yard. When my grandmother brought him his lunch he was happily hammering license plates onto a fence. He was late coming home for dinner, but that was not unusual. Grandmother went to tell him that his dinner was getting cold and found him leaning against the fence, dead and smiling. The doctor told her that he'd died of a heart attack. Grandmother was a rich and independent woman now. She was fond of saying that even though some might call it an eyesore, there was big money in junk.

Grandmother arrived twenty minutes after I phoned her. She must have driven quite fast, probably intimidating all the traffic in her way. Despite her new financial status, Grandmother still drove the same Rambler station wagon she'd owned when I was a child. I always hated riding with Grandmother. She aimed her car at the traffic ahead and maneuvered forcefully around anyone in her path.

Grandmother had aged into a small artillery-unit of a woman. Her hair was slate gray, her clothes all crisp angles. She marched into my front room and looked around. In all the years I'd lived here Grandmother had never visited.

"This is a nice house," she said, and frowned. Grandmother looked me over. "You're too thin. I'll have to take a look in your refrigerator."

"Grandmother." I looked down at the floor. No matter my age, around Grandmother Lillian I became an eight-year-old girl who could never get the linen napkins folded correctly or her slip to stop showing below the edge of her skirt. "Thank you. I don't know what I would have done if you hadn't been able to come." Tears ran down my face.

My grandmother stepped forward and put her hand on my face, touching me gently. She turned my face so that I was looking at her. "Don't worry now." She patted my cheek and then walked into the kitchen to look over the contents of my refrigerator.

I carefully followed the directions my mother's landlady had given me and had no trouble finding the Starside Apartments. Mrs. Ramirez was a friendly, chubby lady. She invited me into her apartment, which was filled with knickknacks, throw pillows, and stuffed animals. Mrs. Ramirez cleared a place on the couch for me to sit, settled herself on a rocking chair, and scooted it close enough to the couch for our knees to touch.

"Your mother's real estate agent made the arrangements for your mother's apartment and paid the first and last month's rent." Mrs. Ramirez couldn't remember the real estate lady's name, but that didn't matter because once she deposited my mother in her new apartment, the real estate lady left and never returned.

"Imagine that," Mrs. Ramirez said and patted me on the knee.

My mother's apartment was unfurnished. In the five

years my mother lived there she never arranged for a phone or for the electricity to be hooked up.

"Didn't you think that was strange?" I asked, moving my knees aside so that Mrs. Ramirez and I were no longer connected. "A woman living alone with no furniture and electricity?"

"Well, dear," Mrs. Ramirez said, "I believe in minding my own business. I let well enough alone. Live and let live, I always say."

"Ah," I replied. Mrs. Ramirez gazed expectantly at me. "Hmm," I said.

Mrs. Ramirez told me that my mother walked to the store every day to buy food that wouldn't spoil and that every month she took the bus to the bank to get her rent money.

"How do you know all this," I asked, "if you were so busy minding your own business?"

Mrs. Ramirez sat up straight, her spine stiffened, and she scooted her chair back a bit. "What do you mean?" Her mouth puckered and stuck out from her face. She resembled an angry hen ready to do battle.

"I don't mean to offend you," I said. "I was just wondering how you knew what my mother did with her time."

Mrs. Raimrez folded her arms across her chest. Finally she spoke. "I asked her when she paid the rent. I was sorry to make her leave, but my husband insisted. 'We're not in the charity business,' he said. 'No rent, no apartment,' he said. And frankly, it was getting to be a little difficult to rent the apartments next to your mother's." Mrs. Ramirez leaned forward. "She was a little strange, God rest her soul."

"She's not dead," I said.

"Excuse me?" Mrs. Ramirez asked.

"Well, you said 'God rest her soul,' which kind of implies that she's dead." I looked at Mrs. Ramirez's face.

Her head was tilted to the side, and she wore a confused expression. "Never mind," I said and stood up. Mrs. Ramirez stood also.

"I have some of your mother's things. Just a minute." She scurried into the kitchen. Mrs. Ramirez moved with small, quick steps that made her bottom wiggle.

She gave me a grocery bag filled with my mother's belongings: mostly little spiral-bound notebooks, but also a gray sweatshirt, a bank passbook, and a picture of my brother and me. I looked closely at the picture. My brother and I stood at opposite edges, and in the middle of the picture was a couch. It must have been taken, I thought, at my grandmother's house. My brother and I appeared out of focus. It was probably the best photograph of us I'd ever seen.

Before I left, I asked Mrs. Ramirez one more question. "What did my mother say when you evicted her?" I asked.

"Oh," Mrs. Ramirez said. "Eviction is such a harsh word." She wiped her hands on her dress. "Well, when the police . . ."

"The police," I interrupted. "You called the police to ask a ninety-pound woman to leave her apartment?"

Mrs. Ramirez looked at her hands. "You just never know," she said, "what someone like that will do. I mean, I realize she's your mother. But you never know." She sighed and looked up at me. "She went with the police quietly. They released her out on the sidewalk, and the last I saw of her she was walking down the road."

"Thank you for your time," I said.

I sat in my car going through the grocery bag filled with my mother's things. The bank book showed that her last withdrawal was a month before in the amount of two thousand dollars. The beginning balance had been sixty-five thousand dollars, which I supposed to be the proceeds from the sale of the house. The final balance was marked zero. My mother had spent the entire proceeds from selling her house in the five years since I last saw her. I decided to go to the bank and make sure.

Before going, I looked through her notebooks. In them my mother had made notations of her days.

"Found a rotten egg today, no more eggs."

"Almost hit a small boy with grocery cart. Be very careful from now on. Cute boy."

"Cold today. No heat."

I closed the last notebook, started my car, and drove to the bank. After speaking with several tellers and working my way up through the manager to a vice president, I was told that my mother's bank balance was indeed zero. No mistake. She'd withdrawn the last of her money a month ago.

When I got home, Tom had replaced my grandmother as my mother's baby-sitter. He sat in an armchair clutching a half-drunk bottle of beer. "I thought I'd come back home and try again," he said. "I know you are used to this, but I'm not."

I nodded and went into the kitchen to get something to drink. I opened the refrigerator. My grandmother had arranged all the food in straight orderly lines. Even the vegetables were arranged in alphabetical order. It looked like a little food and drink army. I picked a Coke out of the soft drink battalion and began again trying to phone my father. I could understand how Tom felt—explaining what living with my mother was like was one thing, really living with her was another.

Father remained unreachable. I left messages that progressed in degrees of hysteria until after three days I began screaming into the telephone.

"Call me," I shrieked. "I'm your daughter, call me."

Meanwhile, Tom and I adjusted to a vampire-like lifestyle. I took time off work. My mother slept all day and prowled the house all night. Since it was hard to sleep, I did the same. Midnight found me vacuuming and dusting, while by nine in the morning I lay on my bed trying to sleep. Tom marched through the house with his eyes half closed, almost dazed. Two weeks after my mother came to stay, I found him sitting on the porch after midnight, his head in his hands, crying.

"What is it?" I said and sat down beside him.

"Oh man." He rubbed his eyes and looked sadly at me. His face was swollen. "I can't take it. I'm sorry." He put a hand on my knee. "Paula, I want to do this for you, but I can't. You can see that, can't you? I can't take it."

I tried to reassure him that everything would be okay. "It's nowhere near as bad as when I was a kid. Wait until we get her medicated." I placed a hand over his. "You'll see. She's very quiet then."

"Paula, I'm trying but I don't have the experience to do this. It's not the life we planned, I planned." He stood up. "I can't eat. I can't sleep. I'm screwing up at work. I can't let everything I've worked for go down the drain because your mother is crazy. I want to support you, but I don't think I can do this. Keep trying to get your father on the phone. I'm going back to my parents' house for a couple more days."

"Whatever," I said, frustrated. My life had prepared me for a different sort of normal than his had. I felt sorry for him. I felt sorry for myself.

I got up and went into the house. I'd imagined that my marriage to Tom would erase the sad parts of my childhood and be the saving of me. Instead I was stuck having to save myself.

After Tom left, I was all alone in the house with my mother. We didn't talk to each other. At night she turned on all the lights throughout the house. During the day she shut all the drapes and slept curled up in a corner of her room. I wasn't sleeping at all. All my reactions teetered on going over the edge. I'd been working part-time at a glassware shop, but now I was afraid to be around breakable things, especially things with sharp edges. I called my boss and quit my job. "Take some time to think it over," my boss said.

"Just mail my check. I have to take care of my mother," I answered and hung up the phone.

One night I sat on the couch watching my mother pace through the house. She carried on a conversation with herself and smoked an entire pack of cigarettes in an hour. After a while she came and sat beside me on the couch. She put her arms around me.

"My girl," she said. "We'll always be together."

I shivered and then began to laugh. I put my head in my hands and laughed until my laughter turned into tears and finally became a groan.

"My girl," my mother kept repeating.

I got up and went into my bedroom. I dialed my father's number. This time, he answered.

"Hello?" he said. His voice was sleepy in a who-dares-to-call-at-three-in-the-morning way.

"Daddy," I yelled. "This is your daughter. Remember me?" There was silence on the other end of the phone. "Daddy, you have to come and help me. If you don't come tomorrow—tomorrow, Daddy—I won't ever see you again." I hung up and lay on my bed, my head aching. Next, I called Tom. "Please take the day off work and come home tomorrow. My father is coming to help," I said and hung up.

"Paula?" my mother said. I looked up. She was standing in my doorway. "Is your father coming?" She stood with her arms wrapped around her body, hugging herself. "Is my man coming to take me home?"

I looked down at my hands. "Yes, Mother. He's coming tomorrow. Please get some sleep."

Tom and my father arrived at the same time. My mother heard my father's voice and came out of her room. "My man," she said. "I have my man back." She put her arms around him and lay her head on his shoulder.

My father looked terrified.

"I'll be right back," I said and went to phone Dr. Karen Feldman, my mother's psychiatrist from my teenage years. Even after my mother stopped being her patient, Dr. Feldman had been kind enough to give me advice regarding her care. She was still at the old number and answered on the first ring. Dr. Feldman was pleased to hear from me and listened to me describe the last few weeks with my mother.

"What is it you want to do?" Dr. Feldman asked.

"What do you think I should do?" I asked back.

"What would you like to do?" Dr. Feldman countered.

I sighed heavily. "I don't know."

"Do you want to keep your mother with you?"

I thought about that for a moment "No. I've tried. I can't take care of her." I started to cry and spilled out some of the things that had been occurring. "I tried, but I can't. Can you help?"

"Paula, if you are asking me for permission to have your mother committed, it is not my place to give it to you. From what you are saying though, I doubt you can provide the care she needs," Dr. Feldman said. She went on to explain the difficulty of having a person committed against their will. "It's just not as easy as it used to be. But please feel free to call me anytime."

I thanked her, and we hung up. I sat on my bed looking down at the phone. *I'm no better than Mrs. Ramirez*, I thought, and dialed the police. After explaining the situation to them, I went into the living room and motioned to my father and husband. My father unpeeled himself from my mother's arms. The three of us met in the kitchen. I spoke in a whisper.

"I've phoned the police. They're on their way."

None of us looked directly at the others. We looked at the refrigerator instead. I counted my magnets.

My mother called to us from the living room. "Is something wrong?" she asked.

She sounded calm and sane. *Maybe it's us,* I thought. *Maybe we're the crazy ones.*

We sat on the living room couch with my mother. She held onto my father. "Isn't it wonderful to be a family again?" she kept saying. When the police arrived, Tom jumped up to let them into the house. When they came into the living room, my mother let go of my father and looked up at them. She sat quietly with her hands folded in her lap, looking up and blinking.

They'd sent two police officers to take my mother to Valley Medical Center. They were huge, muscular men who looked to be in their mid-thirties. "Ma'am," the bigger officer said to my mother, "you need to come with us."

My mother clasped her hands together. "Why?" she asked. "I want to stay here with my family," she said.

The police officers stood on either side of her and lifted her up. They each took an arm and began walking her towards the door. My mother looked over her shoulder at my father. "Bill," she said, "Bill." My father started to cry.

My mother did not look at me.

Outside the house my neighbors stood on the sidewalk watching. I felt dizzy. Tom put his arm around me as I started to fall and held me up. The police officers put my mother into the back seat of their car. The bigger officer came to where the three of us stood.

"We'll meet you at the hospital," he said.

I drove us to the hospital, keeping pace with the police car. My mother watched through the back window. She didn't look away until we got to the hospital. All the way there I concentrated on feeling my heart beat. Thud, thud, thud it went against my chest, just that dull sound marking my progress behind the police car.

At the Valley Medical Center psychiatric wing, my mother, father, husband, and I sat on an uncomfortable vinyl couch while the policemen spoke to the doctors. Finally, a doctor came over and knelt in front of my mother. He asked her what her name was, what the date was, what city she was in, what country, what county, and the names of the last three presidents. My mother answered all their questions clearly, correctly, and quickly.

The police officers and the doctor talked. Then the doctor consulted with other doctors. They huddled together, occasionally turning to point in our direction. My mother wrapped her arms around her knees and began rocking back and forth. I looked up and saw our designated psychiatrist gesturing at me.

I walked over to him. "Yes?" I said.

"We have a problem," the doctor said.

"You have a problem," I said. "My mother is crazy. My father has become the world's most efficient escape artist, my husband has been living with his parents for the duration, and I haven't slept for a week. You say that you have a problem?"

The doctor leaned forward and looked into my eyes. "Calm down," he said in a low voice. "I understand your pain and frustration."

"The only way you could possibly understand my frustration," I said, "would be to go back twenty-eight years and relive my entire life."

"Now, now," he said. "Look, obviously your mother is

not well." He glanced over at her. "But, unfortunately,
she answered all our questions." He looked down at the
ground. "You can still make the choice to commit her,
but I have to warn you that she'll be locked up with some
dangerously psychotic patients. I can't assure her safety."
He shrugged.

"I can't take her home," I said. "I can't take care of
her. I can't get her to take her medication." I waved my
arms in the air. The doctor watched them levitate.

"Is there another relative? Somewhere else she could
go?" I looked at my mother sitting on a couch with her
hands folded around her knees. She was rocking and
humming. Aunt Gayle, I thought. "There is someone,"
I said to the doctor. "My mother's older sister. She lives
in Florida. She should be able to handle Mother. She's a
social worker, and my uncle is a doctor."

"Good." The psychiatrist smiled and patted me on the
shoulder. "Great. Well, you can use our phone. Listen,
one other thing." He leaned forward and looked into
my eyes. "Consider getting some counseling. You are
under more stress than you realize." He smiled. "Does
your insurance cover psychiatric care?" he asked.

Any moment, I thought, they'll break out the strait-
jackets, take both my mother and myself away, attach elec-
trodes to our skin, and blow our brain cells out our ears.

I phoned my aunt. She answered the phone cheerfully. I interrupted her greeting. "I have Mother with
me," I said.

"Oh, how wonderful, Paula. I'm so glad she's with you."

"We're at Valley Medical Center. I'm having her committed."

"What?"

"I'm having her committed."

"What? Paula Jean, have you taken leave of your
senses? There is nothing wrong with your mother. She's

the kindest, most gentle person in the world. This must be your father's idea." Since my mother's first commitment when I was a child, a family war had existed between my father and my aunt. The sort of war that no one ever wins and no one ever backs down from: a war of bitter disagreement and festering disappointment.

"No, Aunt Gayle. It's mine. I can't take care of her. She's out of her mind."

"Paula Jean. Don't you talk about your mama like that. I'm ashamed of you. You take her home now."

I took a deep breath. "Aunt Gayle, you're wrong. Mother is sick, and I've tried, but I can't take care of her. I want to send her to you." There was silence on the other end of the phone. "If you won't take her, I'm going to have to commit her."

I waited. It seemed like a long time until my aunt spoke.

"Fine," she said quietly. "Put her on a plane and let me know when to expect her." She hung up.

I drove home from the hospital recklessly, at least twenty miles over the speed limit and running all lights and stop signs. Once home, I sat Tom down by the phone and instructed him to make flight arrangements, pushed a sandwich in front of my mother, and packed an old suitcase of mine with clothes I no longer wore. For some reason, the thought of sending my mother across country with no luggage shamed me more than sending her away did.

My father came into my bedroom and sat on the bed while I packed. "Well," he said, "I guess I'll be on my way."

I threw the packed suitcase on the floor and grabbed his arm. It felt thin underneath his clothes. I could feel his bones. *My God*, I thought, *they're both dissolving. There will be nothing left of either of them soon.* I let go of his arm.

"Daddy." I sat on the bed and hugged him. "You have

to see this through with me." I pulled back and looked at him. He nodded his head. He was crying.

Traffic was heavy for late in the day. Finally we arrived at the airport, checked my mother in, and sat in the airport lounge. They announced pre-boarding. My father and I walked my mother to the attendant while Tom stayed back. My mother started down the ramp to the plane. The hood of her sweatshirt was around her face. She stopped, turned, and stood for a moment smiling as people walked around her. Finally, she put her hands in the front pocket of her sweatshirt and walked down the ramp, around a corner, and was gone.

"Mommy," I murmured.

"What?" Tom asked. "What did you say?"

"Nothing. Let's wait for the plane to take off," I said. "Make sure everything is all right." My heart was pounding, and I spoke loudly to make certain I could be heard over it. My father nodded, and we walked to the window. The three of us stood in a row gripping the railing, waiting for the plane to depart.

They called final boarding. The doors closed. After a few minutes the plane pulled away from the gate. I felt relieved, then suddenly the plane stopped its forward movement and returned to the gate. I began to walk backwards. Tom turned towards me and reached out, but I shook him off. My father turned, began running, and Tom caught him. I dropped my purse and ran past the place where they check your belongings for firearms, past where they sell the tickets, past all the restaurants, and down the escalator. People stared and called out after me, but I kept running. I ran down the road towards the freeway. When I got to the freeway, I stopped and sat down on the curb crying.

After a while Tom drove up and stopped the car next to me. My father was in the back seat. Tom opened the door. "Please get in," he said. "Some guy loaded his dog in baggage and forgot to get on the plane." Tom reached across the car to me. "It's all right, Paula. The plane took off. We'll be all right now. Please get in." I picked myself up and got in.

I turned my head to the side and leaned my forehead against the window as Tom pulled the car onto the freeway. I didn't want to know the person who lived inside my body anymore. She was capable of any sort of betrayal.

Two weeks after my mother left, I received a letter and a box from her. The box held towels and a yellow T-shirt that read "Fort Lauderdale" on the front in black lettering. I didn't read the letter. I tore it up and threw it away. I put the towels and the T-shirt in the attic.

One day my husband came home from work and found me sitting in the bathtub wearing the T-shirt my mother had sent me. The bathroom was dark, and there was no water in the tub.

Tom turned on the lights and knelt by the bathtub. "Honey," he said, "what's wrong?"

"You'd think she'd know," I answered, "that I look terrible in yellow. It's not my color. You'd think she'd know that."

Tom stood up. "Who? Who are you talking about?"

My eyes narrowed. I turned my face so that I was looking up at him through my eyelashes. "My mother," I snarled. He took a step backwards. "Who do you think we're talking about? Don't you listen? Don't you understand anything?" I began to cry. "Please leave me alone."

Tom backed up into the hallway. "All right, Paula," he said quietly. "I'll leave you alone now. I'll be in our room if you need me." He turned off the light and shut the door.

I laid back in the bathtub. I thought, *This is how it feels not to care about staying sane anymore. This is how it feels to be my mother.*

Each night I laid in bed next to Tom, concentrating on falling asleep. "Sleep, sleep," I commanded my body. Each inch of me felt tense. I couldn't stop thinking, not even for a minute and certainly not long enough to fall asleep. "Stop thinking," I ordered my mind, but it showed no mercy.

I began staying up later and later, hoping for exhaustion. Once I hit the bed I was wide awake again. "I'm not my mother," I whispered to the bedroom walls, careful not to wake up Tom.

I bought a bottle of Jack Daniels at the liquor store, hid it underneath the sink, and began spiking my tea. At first I used a teaspoon of whiskey mixed in with the chamomile, but after a month this became a teaspoon of tea mixed with my whiskey. Eventually I progressed to several cups of tea before bedtime. Tom began leaning towards me and sniffing my breath.

"What's wrong with you?" I demanded, backing away. "Leave me alone," I said and made myself another cup of tea.

One morning I woke up crouched in a corner of my bedroom. I didn't remember how I got there. I had a headache and was sore all over from crouching. Tom had gone to work. If Tom saw me now he would probably think that he had to call the police to come get me. I imagined myself riding in the back of a police car and arriving at a hospital trying to convince strange doctors of my sanity. I would need to memorize the names of the presidents in order to defend myself.

My heart began pounding. I got up and paced the house with my hands over my ears. "No," I said. "No." I went into the bathroom for a tissue and stopped at the sight of myself in the mirror. My hair was uncombed and I wore no makeup. My eyes were bloodshot. "You used to be such a pretty girl," I told my reflection. I went into the kitchen, got the telephone book down from the cupboard, and turned to the psychologist section. I pointed a finger at the first psychologist's name in the book and began dialing. It was very early, and some doctors were not in their offices yet. The first psychologist I reached could not see me until the following week. The fourth psychologist could not see me for ten days.

Ten psychologists down the list, I laid down on the floor and made calls between panic attacks. After each phone call I had to shut my eyes and clench my fists against the panic in my chest. "You're not dying," I said to myself. "But you're probably crazy." Four hours and twenty phone calls later one of the psychologists, Dr. Farron, returned my call. He'd had a cancellation and could see me in an hour. "Thank you," I said to the phone after the doctor had hung up.

I arrived at Dr. Farron's office thirty minutes early. His office consisted of a waiting room into which patients let themselves, and then the door to his office. I stared at the door to his office for thirty minutes, crossing and uncrossing my legs, changing position on the couch, and shaking my foot. Sometimes I imagined that the doorknob turned and I stood up, leaned forward, and then sat down again. *Open*, I thought at the door, *open*. Finally the knob really turned, and the door opened. The angle of the door obscured the departure of the patient. I leaned forward on the couch and listened to the hum of his voice saying goodbye. Dr. Farron shut the door and turned to face me, catching me leaning forward obviously trying to eavesdrop.

He smiled. "Mrs. Mints?" he asked.

Dr. Farron was a tall, heavyset man with a soft voice and an expressionless face containing tiny features. His eyes, nose, and mouth were all squished into the middle of his face. I imagined him as Santa Claus at Christmastime, brimming with good cheer and presents. We entered his office, which was furnished with an overstuffed sofa and two leather chairs, all smelling new. He cheerfully informed me that he'd recently been robbed of all office furniture including his rug.

"Your patient files too?" I asked from deep inside the comfortable cushions of his sofa.

"No, I keep those with me." He looked at me and smiled. Then he took out a yellow pad, sat back, and waited.

I looked down at the coffee table. It was made of simulated redwood. The top was covered with magazines and one huge box of tissues. I took a tissue and blew my nose.

"What brings you here today?" he asked.

"I can't get any rest," I said and began to laugh. "I'm laughing because that's something my mother used to say." I cleared my throat. "So, anyway." I sighed. Dr. Farron sat patiently in his chair holding a pen poised over the yellow pad. "I can't sleep," I said.

"For how long?" he asked.

"I don't know. Forever, I guess."

"So you suffer from chronic insomnia?"

"No. My mind won't shut up. I can't stop thinking." I took a deep breath. "I think I'm crazy. I'm going crazy." My leg began to shake, kicking the coffee table and knocking a magazine to the floor.

"Why do you think you're crazy?" Dr. Farron asked.

"My mother is schizophrenic. I'm afraid I'm like her. I'm going to end up like her. Even the not-resting thing. That's just my mother coming out in me. I don't know what to do. I feel as if my chest is going to explode."

Dr. Farron canceled his next two appointments. He shot questions at me without looking up from his yellow pad about my exact age and symptoms. Finally he looked up and smiled. "Good news, Paula. You're too old to be schizophrenic. If you were going to be, you would have been years ago. The worst you can be is neurotic at this point. I'm joking of course."

"What do you mean?" I asked.

Dr. Farron leaned forward in his chair. "I mean that the chance of an onset of schizophrenia at this late date, in someone with no history of mental illness, is very slim." He sat back. "My job is to help you learn to channel your thoughts in a different direction, to teach you to think about your life differently. This will require hard work from both of us. We need to get you to the point where you can look at your childhood and think about your mother without fear. Right now, I think you would benefit from some relaxation exercises. They'll get you through the weekend until we can start on a regular schedule." He paused. "Do you keep a journal?"

I shut my eyes and took a deep breath. I was relieved to be merely neurotic. In fact, my possibly neurotic nature made me feel downright euphoric. "No. I mean, not really."

"Hmm?" Dr. Farron said, looking down at his yellow pad.

"Well." I giggled, a nervous sound that came out of my mouth in a squeak and embarrassed me. "I write. Sort of." I sat up straight. "I write short stories."

"Really?" Dr. Farron looked up and smiled at me. "Have you ever tried to have any of them published?"

"No." I giggled again. *Stop that*, I told myself. "It's just a hobby. They're not very good." I looked down at my hands.

"Hmm," Dr. Farron said and looked down at his yellow pad.

When I got home I told Tom I had visited Dr. Farron, a psychologist.

"What does that mean?" he asked. "Paula, does this

mean years of therapy?" He paced the living room. His body shook as he sat down on the couch.

He's as scared as I am, I thought. My heart began to skip along underneath my skin. I crawled into Tom's lap, and we sat like that until evening fell and I had to get up and turn on the lights. "I'll be okay," I said. "I promise."

"Okay" takes time, in this case three months of time. Hard work kind of time. I unpeeled years of lies. I was unused to talking about myself honestly, and my confidences came out rusty. I dropped them in the middle of Dr. Farron's office, weary of the strain of holding them back.

"My heavens," Dr. Farron said. "You've survived a great deal. You should be proud of yourself."

"Proud?" I pulled a handful of tissues from the box.

Dr. Farron leaned forward in his chair. "Yes, proud. Close your eyes," he said. "I want you to see that little girl trapped in the bathroom with her mother, thinking her mother is dead." I heard him sit back in his chair and opened my eyes. Dr. Farron was smiling. "That little girl was not responsible for what happened between her parents. She was not responsible for her mother's mental illness. She was just a little girl living in what must have seemed like a war zone. You can forgive her now." He leaned forward again. "You can love her now."

"Who?" I asked.

"Why, Paula Jean," he said. "That's who."

I began to sleep through the night. I saw Dr. Farron at least two days a week for two months, graduated to one day a week and then told him I didn't need him anymore.

"That's wonderful," he said and smiled. "Well, you have forty-five minutes left. Is there anything you'd like to talk about?"

I thought for a minute, searching around my mind for any hidden obsessions. I smiled. "Nope," I said.

I paid him, and we stood up and walked to the door. Before I left, he put his hand on my shoulder. "What do you intend to do now?"

"Get a job, for one thing." I looked down. "Write more stories. I submitted one to a magazine. Work on my marriage. We'll see what happens." I sighed. "Doctor, if you hadn't been available to see me that day, I don't know what I would have done. I was on the edge." I laughed. "I was over the edge."

"Paula, whatever you choose to do now, you're in charge," Dr. Farron said. "And, Paula Jean, I couldn't have done it without you." He smiled. "Keep in touch."

I drove home. While I drove I went over my plans. I would finish college and go on for my master's degree. "Like mother like daughter, at least scholastically," I said to the windshield. I would take a risk and make a career as a writer. "I am a writer," I said to the steering wheel of my car. And I would take care of my mother, or at least offer to. Once I got home, I went into my house and immediately called my Aunt Gayle.

She answered on the third ring. "Aunt Gayle," I said. "May I talk to my mother?" I wrapped the phone cord around my hand.

"Why, Paula Jean," my aunt said, "it's about time you phoned your mama."

"You're right." I sighed. Responsibility, I thought. Now that I was willing to accept it, I also had to accept everything that went with it. "May I talk to her, please?"

"Your mama isn't here."

"I beg your pardon? Where is she?"

"You know your mama," Gayle said. "Never can keep her tied down to one place. She just has to go her own way."

"So, where did she go?"

"Well, a month after she got here she wanted to leave, and she went."

"Okay." I swallowed. "So, are you telling me she took the bus? Where did she go?"

"No, Paula Jean. Your mama doesn't like the bus. She just left. You know what a free spirit your mama is. She likes to hitchhike."

"Wait a minute." I sat down. "Are you telling me that my mother, a mentally ill woman, is hitchhiking around the country? And that you let her?"

"Don't you speak to me like that, Paula Jean," my aunt said. "You certainly haven't made any attempt to keep in touch with your mama. She wanted to go, and she left. Your mama isn't like the rest of us."

"That's right, she's schizophrenic. I can't believe this. You let a mentally ill woman hitchhike off into the sunset. What were you thinking?"

"Paula Jean, I certainly don't need to put up with this abuse from you." My aunt hung up the phone.

I sat at my kitchen table and listened to the dial tone. My heart froze. *Mother*, I thought, *where in the world are you?*

I learned later that my mother was closer than I thought. When, a month after she arrived at my aunt's house, my mother told her sister that she wanted to leave, my aunt gave my mother some money. Unfortunately, my mother had been off her medication for a long time, and she was no longer in control of her hallucinations. She landed in Arizona where she first began living as a homeless person, so there are no records of what happened to her there. Eventually, she made her way back to San Jose, California, to be near me. Her regular home for the rest of her life was underneath a tree, next to an office building near the intersection of North First Street and Highway 880. She was known by the people in the office building as Little Elaine. Since she didn't panhandle, the people in the office building helped her with money, food, coffee, and clothes. When the weather was bad, she slept at one of the city's homeless shelters. The other homeless citizens living in the area knew her by sight only, as she kept to herself, spending most of her time sitting under a lamppost, smoking and staring. Though many people knew who she was, she had no friends. Nor did anyone in the family know where she was.

So, when I spoke to my aunt, my mother was living in a cardboard box, underneath a tree, fifteen minutes from my house.

CHAPTER 7

Discoveries

After coroner's investigator Minor told me that my mother, Lucia Elaine Rothwell, was dead and I began to scream, I forgot to care what my co-workers thought of me. But hysteria has rules, one of them being that you must stop screaming sometime, if only to take a breath. Finally I shut my mouth, then opened it again to breathe in deeply, with my hands on my diaphragm. When I had calmed down, I picked the telephone receiver up off of the floor.

"Mr. Minor?" I said. "Mr. Minor, are you still there?"

"Are you calm now, Mrs. Mints?" Mr. Minor asked.

"Yes. I am. Quite calm now."

"When can we expect you?" he asked.

"Soon. I'll be there soon."

"Mrs. Mints, I need to be here when you come. Can you give me a more specific time than soon?"

"Mr. Minor, I realize this is your job, but it is a bit of a shock to me."

"Well, you knew your mother was missing, didn't you? You knew she was homeless, didn't you?"

"I haven't seen my mother in quite a while. I didn't know where she was. I didn't know she was homeless." I paused. "I'll be there in an hour or so."

"Fine. I'll expect you in about an hour." Mr. Minor hung up the phone.

When I looked up, my four officemates were watching me. There was a standoff of time in which no one made an attempt at conversation. I realized that it was left to me, the screamer, to make the first verbal move.

Since I'd left therapy with Dr. Farron, I'd worked hard at redirecting my life. I'd gone back to school and earned an associate of arts degree in general education. I'd begun attending writing workshops and classes. I was planning to go back to college at San Jose State University and work towards a bachelor of science in business administration. After I completed that degree, I wanted to work towards my MBA. Finally, I was becoming the educated woman with choices about her future that my mother had always hoped I'd be.

Also, Tom and I were working at getting our lives back onto an even keel, but my mother's stay at our house had left us too far apart. We were becoming caring strangers living separate lives inside the same house.

Another problem I had to face now was that I'd allowed my officemates to believe that my mother was already dead. The year I began this job someone asked me what my plans were for Mother's Day. "Oh," I replied, sighing and hanging my head, "I don't like to talk about that." I continued to hang my head for a moment, allowing time for the pronouncing of muttered sentiments and the phone to ring.

During my three years of employment I'd developed a fable of a gentle and loving mama who read books at bedtime, cooked huge southern meals, and taught school in her spare time. At this point, to my office-mates, my mother was not only a saint but an icon, rep-resentative of perfect childhoods and other cherished images. Now I had to admit to the homeless schizo-phrenic my mother had been when she died.

"Could I see you for a moment, Jim?" I said to my boss. "Privately." We walked back into the room where the travel brochures were kept. Up and down all the walls were colorful magazines showing smiling families throw-ing beach balls and pointing cameras in pursuit of fun. For a moment I imagined my family among them, the ball whizzing by me. Always in times of crisis my mind in-vents places to humorously hide in until reality catches up and takes over.

Jim turned and looked at me. I noticed he had a small crescent-shaped scar on his chin which I had not seen before. I focused on the scar. "That call was about my mother."

Jim stood with his hands folded in front of him. I real-ized that in the three years I'd been employed at the travel agency we had never held a personal conversation. Office talk was of the how-was-your-weekend, did-you-have-a-nice-vacation variety. I looked up and noticed a concerned expression on his face.

"My mother has been missing for a few years, and now I have to go identify her body."

"I'm sorry." Jim reached out and patted my shoulder. He pulled a handkerchief out of his back pocket and handed it to me.

I touched my face and found that my cheeks were wet. I realized that I'd probably been crying since I got off the phone. I wiped my face with Jim's handkerchief. As I handed it back, I noticed his initials embroidered in the corner. The letters were stitched in blue. How old-fashioned, I thought, and smiled.

I decided to wait until I could get home to phone my husband. I supposed the normal reaction would be to lean on someone else for support, but I found it difficult. After I drove home, I paced the house for a while wondering how to ask Tom for help. Finally I gave up wondering and dialed the phone. It was then I realized how much I wanted him with me.

"Dispatch." I recognized the voice of Steve, who worked at Pacific Gas and Electric with my husband.

"Hi, Steve. This is Paula. I need Tom to call me as soon as possible."

"Sure. I'll get the message to him right away." Tom did not have a phone with him, and Steve would have to reach him by radio. "Is it urgent?" Steve asked.

"No, no. I just need him soon." I rang off and sat on the couch. For a few minutes I sat crossing and uncrossing my legs. The newspaper lay on the dining room table. I got up and straightened it until all the corners lined up perfectly.

Thirty minutes passed.

"Dispatch."

"Steve, sorry to bother you, but did you get that message to Tom?"

"Yeah, he hasn't called you yet?"

"No. Could you call him back and tell him it's important? I hate to be a bother."

"Don't worry. I'll get him on the radio right now."

I paced through the living room. My cat ran up to me, and I pushed him away. I went into the bathroom, washed my face, and reapplied my makeup. Looking at myself in the mirror, I noticed my blue eyes staring back at me: they were identical to my mother's in shape and size, huge and inquisitive. Now, they were also haunted and anguished.

I went into the kitchen, took all of the dishes out of the dishwasher, and rewashed them.

Another forty minutes passed.

"Dispatch."

"Steve." My voice broke. I took a rumbling breath. "Please call him again. Please call him again. Please."

"Paula, calm down. When I talked to him he said he'd call you as soon as possible."

"As soon as possible?" I pulled the receiver away from my ear and slapped it against the palm of my hand. It made a red mark in the center. I took a deep breath and spoke into the receiver. "You don't understand. I have to go to the morgue. My mother's body is there. Tell him to come home." I realized I was screaming into the phone.

"Whoa. Slow down. Your mother?"

"Yes, my mother." I paused for a moment and wrapped the phone cord around my hand. *I've come unglued*, I thought. *I've lost it completely.* I sighed. "I haven't seen her for three years. She was homeless. I didn't know where she was, it wasn't my fault. Look, I can't do this alone. I shouldn't do this alone." I held the receiver underneath my chin, grabbed a section of the newspaper and began shredding it.

"Okay, calm down. I'll get Tom right away. Stay where you are."

I left the house.

In extreme circumstances I use driving as a substitute for thinking and feeling. Because I once in a while turn the wrong way and miss street signs, I now concentrated on not getting lost. By the time I arrived at the coroner's office, my hands gripped the steering wheel in little fists. I had to unpeel them and flex for a minute to bring the feeling back into my fingers.

Sven Holton, my friend from the coroner's office, came rushing down the pathway towards my car. Sven was tall with long legs that seemed to gather up the concrete as he moved. He arrived at my car, gripped the door handle, and looked through the window at me. I got out of the car, and he hugged me. Keeping one arm around my shoulder, he walked me towards the building.

"Paula," he said, looking pained. "I'm sorry. I'm so sorry."

I felt badly for his discomfort but wished he'd take his arm away. There seemed no good way to ask him to, and I let him keep it on my shoulder.

The lobby had a dirty linoleum floor and a tired looking rubber tree plant in one corner. The linoleum floor had brown and green flecks in it and was in a pattern I would not have chosen.

"I would have brought you in the back way," Sven whispered in my ear, "but there is a smell back there today. I was afraid it would make you feel sick."

"No." I smiled. "I have a strong stomach." And I remembered when I was a teenager throwing an orange through our kitchen window, smashing it and hitting my mother in the head as she stood in our backyard. I'd been so afraid of my father's reaction that I threw up. My mother told my father she'd broken the window. You can safely blame anything on the insane; no one doubts their ability to behave irrationally.

"Are you okay?" Sven asked. "Would you like some water?" We were in a reception room now. There was a formica table next to one wall, and Sven and I sat by it on plastic chairs and waited. "Doctor Cochran performed the autopsy," Sven said.

"Who?"

"Dr. Cochran, the coroner. He's my boss." Sven smiled.

I realized that Sven expected me to show appreciation

for what I supposed was some sort of gruesome honor, so I smiled back. "Ah," I said.

After a short while, a man came into the room carrying a paper grocery bag and a clipboard. The man put the bag on the table.

"This is Investigator Minor, and these are your mother's things," Sven said. The bag seemed to get bigger as I looked at it, until it seemed to take up the entire top of the table. I thought about the groceries it once held, someone's jam and eggs, and now my mother's last effects.

"Paula Jean Rothwell. Oh, excuse me. Mints? Paula Jean Mints." Mr. Minor said my name as a statement and continued looking down at the clipboard. He was a tall, thin man, and he wore a little gray hat with the brim turned up. I imagined fishhooks stuck in the brim on the weekends while he sat in a boat, with his fishing line out.

"Paula, just Paula. Yes, that's me." I wanted to be certain he got my name right. "Paula Mints," I said again. "Not Rothwell, Mints."

"When did you last see your mother?" Mr. Minor asked a list of identifying questions: where, when, how kinds of things. I answered each of them trying to match my voice to his: clipped, short sentences, showing no expressions, and giving nothing away. Mr. Minor didn't look up from his clipboard. After a while he stopped talking and began writing something on the stack of papers attached to his clipboard.

Sven leaned over to me. "Your mother had identification from the shelter, but nothing to point to you. We were all quite sure she was going to end up cremated at the county's expense."

"Really," I said, taking a nervous gulp of air and eyeing the grocery bag.

"It's extraordinary. This wasn't even my case. I had nothing to do today, so I was helping Investigator Minor go through her things, and there was a picture of you. Well, I recognized you right away. Your eyes—you know they're quite distinctive. She'd written 'my children' on the back of the picture." Sven patted my shoulder. "Really, quite amazing."

"You can have a look in the bag now," Mr. Minor said.

Inside the grocery bag was a red vinyl purse with a broken strap. The purse was stuffed with little spiral notebooks. Underneath the purse was a pair of broken glasses with one of the earpieces missing, the photograph of my brother and me, and underneath that a half-empty pack of cigarettes. I smiled. The cigarettes were Marlboros. My mother smoked Winstons. If the cigarettes were wrong, maybe it was someone else's body. Maybe she'd given a picture of my brother and me to a friend.

"Is this it?" I asked Mr. Minor. "Didn't she have any clothes? Was she found naked?" I felt myself shivering.

"Evidence," Mr. Minor said without looking at me. He stood up. Sven stood up, gripping my shoulder and dragging me up with him.

"Evidence? What for? What do you mean?" I said. Mr. Minor did not turn around. "Excuse me, what do you mean?" I asked his back. "Doesn't the existence of evidence imply a crime? How did my mother die? What happened to her?"

Mr. Minor opened a door and waited for Sven and me to walk through. Sven propelled me through the doorway. He rubbed my shoulders, moving his hand in a circular motion. I wondered if there was a polite way to ask him to stop. I concentrated on the thought: *stop, Sven, stop*, but he increased the pressure and made faster circles. The door clicked shut, and Mr. Minor walked around us.

"Well," Sven said and cleared his throat. "Well."

This room had no furniture. In the corner stood another sad little rubber tree plant. It was bent over and needed watering. At the end of the room there was a door, and next to the door a window covered by blinds, which were closed. Mr. Minor stood by the window, ready to open the blinds.

I stopped and backed up a bit into Sven's arm. "Wait a minute. Where is she?"

"Behind the window," Sven said and pushed me forward. At last, he took his arm away.

Mr. Minor began opening the blinds. "Stop," I said, struggling to breathe. There seemed to be no air whatsoever in the room. It was just a tiny, closed-in little space with no air. "What does she look like?" I finally asked. "Does she look okay?"

Mr. Minor looked at me. He had pale green eyes, and I could find no reflection of myself there. "She looks like an old lady that no one cared for," he said, and then he pulled open the blinds.

I closed my eyes. When I opened them, Mother lay on the other side of the window with a white sheet pulled up to her neck. Her hair fell back from her face, and I noticed it was beginning to turn gray. She was pale, and her skin sagged. I ran my hand across the glass, which felt cool and soft. My mother didn't look dead to me. I half expected her to open her eyes and turn her head towards me. "Paula," she would say, "are you all right?"

Sometimes when my mother called me Paula, she could fill my name up with love. She took me with her when she ran errands in those early days when I couldn't have been more than two years old, so these memories have gauze over them to keep them young and pretty. My mother drove from errand to errand with me sitting next to her in the car, bouncing up and down on the seat. My mother laughed and turned towards me. Her hair, freshly curled, fine and soft, swung with her head as she turned in my direction. "Paula," she would say and then with a laugh, "you settle down now."

The image faded away, and I was back in the airless little room. "That's her," I said quietly, trying to keep my voice steady. "That's my mother." I put my hand over my mouth.

Mr. Minor nodded and drew the blinds. Sven gripped my shoulders, turned me around, and walked me back through the door. Mr. Minor followed and stood for a few minutes looking at the papers on his clipboard.

"Sign here," he said and held the clipboard towards me. I signed my name, and he pulled back the clipboard and walked through the door.

"That's it," Sven said and handed me the grocery bag. I noticed it was a brown Safeway bag.

Outside, the day was very bright, and I put my hand up to shield my eyes. The sky should be gloomy, cloudy and threatening on the day you identify your mother's body. *I am handling this okay*, I thought. *I haven't collapsed.* No one would suspect what I'd just done.

"Wow." Sven wiped his forehead with the back of his sleeve. "I'm shaking. I was so afraid you would faint in there. I thought you would faint."

He stood looking down at his hands, so I looked too. They were shaking. I looked at his face and noticed that little veins stood out in his temples. Sven had carrot-red hair, and his face looked very pale underneath it.

"What should I do now?" I asked. "With her body, I mean. Is there a bill I should pay?"

"You just ask the funeral home to arrange to pick up the body. There's no bill." He patted me on my shoulder and shifted his weight from foot to foot. "Are you certain you're going to be okay?" He leaned forward and studied my face. After a moment he moved back. "Go home and talk to your husband." He backed towards the building. "I'll call you in a few days."

When I got home, Tom was there. "Why didn't you wait?" he said. "You're so secretive. You never ask for help. I want to, you know." His forehead crinkled at me.

"I'm sorry," I said. As much as he wanted to, I wanted him to, but I couldn't. I had to hold myself together, not reach out, not now. "I should have waited for you," I said. We stood in silence for a moment. Then I went in to call my brother who had come back from Alaska a few years ago.

"Our mother is dead," I said when he answered the phone. "You need to come home."

To my brother and me, home was a place we were in together. Since that was a rare occurrence, the concept of home held no satisfying place in our lives. In my immediate family none of us live close. We cling to distance and find comfort in the fact that we are not home. It's one of our secret family tragedies that no matter how far we get away from each other, in the end we're still a family.

My brother took the news about our mother's death calmly, saying he would be up in six hours. "Have you called Dad?" he said.

"No." A few years had passed since we all put my mother on the plane to Aunt Gayle's, and I just had not thought about phoning my father.

"I'll call him. See you soon, Sister."

At midnight my brother was at my door with a bottle of Jack Daniels and a twelve-pack of beer. He embraced me and said, "There's nothing to say, is there?" Tom and he spent the rest of the night drinking.

My brother had moved to Los Angeles. He bought a house in the roughest neighborhood he could find, where every day was a near riot, and kept to himself. My brother prized being tough above all things and disliked most people on principle. Still, he could be kind to the elderly and children, and both seemed to like him immediately.

I was surprised to learn that my mother had been in touch with my brother. Michael told me that he'd seen her about a year before. "I opened the door one morning, and I found her sitting on my porch. After a couple of hours, I coaxed her into the house. My plan was to have her live with me. I went to the local Social Security office to arrange for conservatorship. I told the woman there that I wanted to become the conservator for our mother's disability benefits. The woman looked me over." I knew what she'd seen: a young man, mid-twenties or so, with a long beard, long hair, and a torn shirt. Around his forehead he wore a blue bandana. He must have looked to her like someone not to mess with. She excused herself and went to consult her supervisor. When the woman returned, she told my brother that there was nothing they could do right then. He would have to go home and wait for a caseworker to phone him. The paperwork was delayed, and before it could be completed my mother disappeared.

My father arrived the next morning. I was the one who opened the door. He stood on the porch crying. My father is now a frail, small man who has grown more sensitive with age. He cries often.

"I don't want you to blame me," he said as he passed me in the doorway on his way inside. "I waited until you and your brother left the house to get a divorce. I'm not responsible for what happened to her after that." He walked towards the living room. "I tried to help. You know I did. You don't know what kind of a life I had with her."

I didn't answer him. There was no answer. I was silent.

We picked out a funeral home from the Telephone

Directory Yellow Pages and went as a family to make arrangements. At the funeral home we were assisted by the funeral director, a tall, emaciated man with a long black beard. We decided on cremation. As my brother discussed price, I watched a small spider make its way down the director's black beard and drop off onto his suit. I stared at his beard wondering if the spider was alone, or if more would crawl out. I looked up and noticed my brother, father, and the funeral director watching me.

"I was just discussing the type of urn with your brother and father." The funeral director smiled, as I tried to keep my eyes off his beard. "I was suggesting that your mother certainly deserves something a bit nicer than a plastic container." Everyone looked at me.

"Whatever my brother and father want," I said. "I think I'll wait in the car."

When we got home we discussed what to do with the ashes. My brother wanted to scatter them somewhere, but no one could think of a place. My father thought we should invest in a nice grave site, but no one wanted to pay for it. Finally, I settled it by deciding that her ashes, in their plastic container, would stay with me. I put them in my attic next to the Christmas things.

As the week went on, my family grew concerned about my lack of tears, so I manufactured some, and everyone relaxed. All week I welcomed guests and fielded phone calls.

My Uncle Sam, who was my mother's youngest brother, phoned. "Paula Jean, honey," he said, "what can I do? When is the funeral?" As he spoke I remembered all in a flash the last time he telephoned. I was sixteen years old and he was coming to California on business. My mother asked him to dinner, and when he said yes she was excited. She bought cookbooks and rechecked recipes. The day of the dinner she recooked anything that did not turn out perfectly. The house was spotless. We all dressed up for dinner. Six o'clock came, then seven, then eight o'clock. I went to bed around eleven o'clock that night. My mother was still sitting at the dining room table, which was set with her best china and silver for her brother's arrival—just sitting in the dark, smoking cigarette after cigarette.

"Where were you?" I screamed into the phone, and my body felt hot with anger. "I remember her waiting that evening you were supposed to come for dinner. Where were you?" I slammed down the receiver and looked up to see my father, brother, and husband watching me.

They all phoned then, all her family, asking about the funeral, shocked at the decision to cremate her without asking their preferences. My Uncle Lee, her oldest brother, phoned. "Where were you?" I said again.

My Aunt Gayle called early on the day my brother and father were to leave. She was the last family member to see my mother alive. "Where were you?" I said wearily. I was used to and comforted by these words now.

"Well," my aunt said, "I might ask you the same thing, Paula Jean. Where were you?"

I slammed down the receiver hoping for a damaged eardrum on the other end. When I looked up, my brother was standing next to me. We looked at each other in silence. "Do you want breakfast before you go?" I asked. He shook his head.

I returned to work a week after my brother left.

Three weeks went by during which I tried to look like I was recovering from the shock of my mother's death. I wasn't done, however, dealing with shocks. One morning a month after my mother's death I opened my front door on my way out to work and found a man preparing to ring my bell. I startled him mid-ring, with his index finger aimed forward accusingly.

"May I help you?" I stood clutching my purse, trying to appear brisk, rushed, and at the same time friendly.

"Paula Jean Mints?" the man asked, as he looked into a little leather-bound notebook.

People calling me by my whole name never meant good news. I gripped the doorknob. "Yes."

"Sergeant Morgan with the San Jose Police Department." He held out identification, which I did not look at. "I wonder if I could ask you some questions about your mother." He made it a statement, not a request.

"Come in." I stood to the side and let Sergeant Morgan into my house. Once he was inside, I asked, "I don't understand. Is there a problem? Did my mother commit a crime?"

Sergeant Morgan turned to look at me. "I'm with Homicide, Mrs. Mints. I'm investigating your mother's death."

I closed the door, and we walked into the dining room. "Can I get you a cup of coffee or tea?" I asked. I wondered how I was supposed to behave. Maybe I should cry. Everyone seemed to expect it. I was certain that Sergeant Morgan was no different from anyone else. The Sergeant wanted tea, so as I made it, I took the opportunity that boiling the water provided to look him over.

He was about five-foot-ten with blond hair and a thin brown mustache hovering above his upper lip like a well-trimmed caterpillar. I watched him looking around my living room. He gave careful attention to all my furniture. My cat came into the room, and he smiled at it. Finally he turned to me. "You have a nice house," he said.

The teakettle whistled, and I busied myself with dropping a tea bag into a cup and pouring the boiling water. "Sugar?" I asked. "No? Well, here's your tea." I smiled and handed him a cup. "Be careful, it's hot." I sat down across the table from him. I crossed and uncrossed my legs, folded my hands on the table, and cleared my throat. "Are you saying my mother was murdered?"

Sergeant Morgan looked at his tea, put the cup on the table, and opened his notebook. "Your mother was apparently the victim of a homicide."

"I'm confused," I said slowly. "What do you mean *apparently* the victim of a homicide? Why wasn't I told this before?"

"Could you tell me a little about her past, how she became homeless?" Sergeant Morgan took a pen from his jacket pocket. He wore an itchy-looking tweed coat, which I imagined must be uncomfortable, since it was a warm day.

I thought about what to say next. What kind of picture to paint. Instead of manufacturing a tale, I told a bit of the truth, about my mother's breakdowns and some things about the last time I'd seen her when I'd tried to have her committed. "She never trusted me again," I said softly. What I told the sergeant was true, but just the edges of true, like a black and white photograph that leaves you wondering what color things were.

Sergeant Morgan took a handkerchief from his shirt pocket and handed it to me. There were no initials stitched on the corners, I noticed, and then another thought came into my mind: *People are always handing me handkerchiefs; I should really buy one of my own.*

I wiped my face. When I pulled the handkerchief away, it was wet. "I'm sorry," I said. "I'll have it cleaned." But he just took it back. I looked at his hands for a minute. They looked like well-used hands, very clean but knobby. The nails were neatly trimmed. "It's my fault," I said. "I'm responsible. I should have kept her with me. If I could go back, I would find a way to make it different." I looked down at the table.

Sergeant Morgan closed his notebook. "What happened to your mother was not your fault. You shouldn't blame yourself."

I looked up. Sergeant Morgan had soft brown eyes. I smiled. After all, he just knew the part of the truth I brought out for strangers: which, when no one knows your heart, your fears, and your dreams, is basically everyone. "At the coroner's office they didn't tell me very much about what happened to my mother. Can you tell me how she died?" I asked.

Sergeant Morgan's face turned a little grayish. I worried for him. He seemed so uncomfortable. "Mrs. Mints, I'm not certain I should tell you." We were quiet then. The only sound was my cat cleaning himself: his licking and stretching seemed the most activity in the whole world. "Your mother was the victim of a sexual assault." He looked down at his shirtfront and straightened his tie, which he somehow managed to turn upside down.

"Are you saying my mother was raped?" The room seemed very still. "Are you saying my mother was raped and murdered?" I said again.

"Your mother was the victim of a sexual assault, and the assault caused her death." Sergeant Morgan stood up. "We believe," he added.

"Can you tell me more than that? What happened to her? What do you mean?" I stood also.

"That's all I can tell you at this time." He began walking towards the door. I followed. He paused in the doorway for a minute and said without looking at me, "You can't blame yourself. Sometimes it isn't possible to take care of yourself and the people you love without destroying something. I know. My sister is mentally ill. I haven't seen her for two years." He looked me directly in the eyes, and his had tears in them. "I have no idea where she is or what she's doing."

Alone, I washed the teacup the investigator had used and put it away. I remembered I hadn't told anyone at my office that I would be late. *My mother was murdered*, I thought, and the thought was so clear and large that it seemed to hang in the air.

I gave up the idea of going to work and called in sick. My boss was solicitous in a when-will-you-get-on-with-life kind of fashion. After a short while, tragedy wears on those watching from the periphery. You get to hear a lot of "time heals" kind of advice. When time doesn't heal, employers and intimates become uncomfortable with your pain. Tucking it in is the safest thing.

I climbed to my attic, pushing aside cobwebs, spiders, and boxes of old dishes. I located the Christmas things. I'd placed my mother's ashes in their neat plastic container next to the marked boxes. I thought, half amused, if I wasn't careful my husband would recycle her in a fit of environmental concern. I ran my hands along the container, which felt cool. Finally, I pulled it onto my lap. "Mommy," I said. "Mommy." And now I was crying. Tears fell down my face, dripping from my chin onto my mother's resting place.

I sat there in the attic with my mother's ashes in my arms, rocking back and forth.

CHAPTER 8

Some Questions

As the daughter of a murder victim, I considered how to behave. All around me, intimates wished I'd get on with my life while strangers responded to the news with horror, and something else: a greed for information. For them my mother's murder had made me a gossip tidbit.

One afternoon I received a phone call from a woman who said that she worked as a district attorney for the County of Santa Clara. "I'm so sorry," she said. "Every weekday morning I bought your mother a donut and gave her a hug. I could see in her eyes that she didn't belong on the streets."

"How could you tell she didn't belong on the streets?"

"Hmm? Something in her eyes. Your mother had wise eyes."

"Really? What do you mean by wise?" I asked.

"I saw your mother every day. If you'd like to get together and talk about her, let me know."

"I'd like that. When can we get together?" I asked.

"Pardon me?"

"I would like to get together with you to talk about my mother. I want to know what she was like towards the end of her life. When would be good for you?"

"Uh. Well. Right now is busy. I'm going on vacation in a month. Maybe when I get back. I'll call you."

"Maybe I could call you? What's your number?"

"You know, I just realized that I'm late for a meeting. I'll call you."

"Excuse me, what was your name again?" I asked.

She hung up.

When my mother was alive I was able to hide from her and still I never felt safe. Now that she was dead I wanted to know her, and still she'd slipped out of my grasp.

It seemed the closest I would be able to get to my mother at this point would be through her photograph, but I had none. In fact, I had no photos of my family. The few that exist are both scarce and too precious to be entrusted to me. Some people get to be family archivists of memories, keeping pictures in albums and saving mementos of the past. My grandmother Lillian has always been the great compiler of our family mementos. She keeps us all piled neatly in boxes and in albums stuck in place by glue. She has piles of drawings and handmade cards from my cousins in her boxes. From my brother and me there is only one plaster pie tin in which one of our tiny hands is captured. My grandmother Lillian claims the hand belongs to either my brother or me but can't remember which one of us. From my mother there is an ashtray she made while committed to Agnews State Mental Hospital, and photographs in which my mother exists as background. You see my cousins in the foreground mugging for the camera, and behind them my mother is sitting in the corner, staring away from the camera so that all you have is the back or side of her head. My brother, mother, and I leave slight evidence with which to connect us to anything.

I knew that my grandmother did not have any decent photos of my mother, or for that matter, of my father, my brother or myself. However, I was pretty sure my father had the only good photographs of my mother. I asked him for them and he sent what he had to me. They arrived alone in an envelope with no note. I attached them to my refrigerator door with little magnets. *Welcome home, Mother*, I thought. Her trapped image stared back at me. Mother hated having her picture taken. She always turned away just as the camera clicked, so her resulting image was fuzzy. My refrigerator door was now covered with out-of-focus bits and pieces of my mother.

I looked up the word *murder* in the dictionary. Taking my favorite pen, I slowly and carefully copied every word of the definition onto a piece of paper: "to commit a murder; also to kill brutally; to put an end to; to spoil by performing poorly: murderer." I read the words over and over again, read them aloud, and repeated them in the shower. My husband became concerned.

"Don't you think you're becoming a bit fixated?" Tom asked.

"Someone has to find out what happened to her," I answered and slammed a door in his face. All the doors in our house were shut now, with one of us on the other side either waiting to get in or trying to get out.

My father was horrified by the latest twist to my mother's death. "Oh my God," he said. "If I ever get my hands on the son of the bitch that did this. . . ." He stopped talking.

"You'd what, Dad?"

"Well, it wouldn't be pretty."

"So what would you do?"

"It just wouldn't be pretty."

My father is good at threats. He is prone to bursts of

temper with store clerks and other hapless persons who through some innocent act manage to offend him. His mouth becomes pursed and his face red. Pointing his finger in the air, he promises to bring about job loss, legal action, or a punch in the nose. My father has ruined many a store clerk's day with his temper.

My brother inherited our father's temper but is inclined to keep it to himself. The only evidence of temper you ever see in my brother is the appearance of a blue vein that bulges out from his forehead and throbs slowly, pulsating in time to his mood. As a kid I knew by the vein when to stop egging him on and run away. My brother has a great poker face for others, but his forehead can't hide a thing from me.

My brother and I talked about our mother's murder over the phone, so I had no clue as to the true state of his emotions. He took the news calmly.

"Oh yeah?" he said. "Hmm."

It was my brother who suggested I solve the crime. "Someone in the family has to take responsibility," he said. Unfortunately, I had no idea where to begin my sleuthing. When I was a little girl, I could never figure out the answer when we played who-done-it, and I'm always shocked when the murderer is revealed at the end of a television show, movie, or mystery novel.

Two weeks later I was still planless. I had heard nothing further from the police and wondered if I was a suspect.

"Too much television, Sister," my brother said when I broached this theory of guilt to him.

"Would that be matricide?" I asked him. Little twinges of guilt pricked at me. *I should confess,* I thought, *to the crime of wishing my mother dead so often that it actually happened.*

"Look, they talked to all of us. They even talked to Aunt Gayle." He paused for a moment. "Sis, call me when they know something."

But as time passed and no one from the police called, it became clear to me that the murder of my mother, a homeless person, had little importance to the authorities. Even though I wasn't sure how to go about finding information myself, the realization that it would be left to me to become the pursuer of justice and my mother's advocate strengthened my resolve to take action. I dialed the number on Sergeant Morgan's business card. I was told that he'd retired two weeks prior. I left a message for Officer Henry Cabot, who was now in charge of my mother's case.

A week after I left my message, when he hadn't called, I went to see him on my lunch hour.

"What can you tell me about my mother's murder? Do you have any leads?" I asked.

"Nothing, Mrs. Mints. We have no leads at this time."

"Nothing?"

"Nothing further at this time," Officer Cabot said. He cleared his throat. "We've been receiving phone calls from people who knew your mother."

"Really?" I said and shut up. During my pause Officer Cabot cleared his throat again. I cleared mine in response.

"Yes. Apparently she was well known in the area." Officer Cabot cleared his throat again, and I wondered if it indicated a medical condition of some sort. "Anyway, people are wondering where to send flowers."

I considered what to say. Should I suggest my attic? I imagined telling Officer Cabot, Yes, have them sent to my house. We have her enshrined in my attic, homeless no more. Weary of our throat clearing communication, I sighed. "Well," I sighed again. "Have them donate money to a homeless charity. That's probably what my mother would have wanted."

There was a long pause.

"Well," Officer Cabot said, "okay."

I got up. "Will you keep me updated, you know, regarding developments, I guess they're called?"

"Certainly, but I wouldn't expect to hear anything anytime soon."

When I got back to my office, for a long while I sat facing the wall. When I swiveled my chair around, my boss was standing in front of my desk.

"We've got to stop meeting like this," I said.

"Can I see you in the back room?" Jim frowned, turned, and walked towards the back of the office. I followed.

We stood in the room surrounded by colorful brochures.

"Paula, I know you are going through a difficult time, and I don't want to make things worse, but," Jim stopped talking and looked at the floor.

Fired, I thought. *I'm going to be fired.* I felt a flush start up from my chest. *Back*, I silently ordered my blushing skin, *back*.

"I guess what I am trying to say," Jim continued, "is that you need to keep your personal life out of the office."

"It's amazing," I said. Jim looked at me. I continued, "I mean, the lack of depth to most people's sympathy. Amazing." The inability to keep my mouth shut inherited from my father rose up and refused to let me remain quiet. Jim and I stared at each other for a minute.

"Paula, this is a place of business," Jim said. "I'm sorry for your loss, but you need to act professionally while you are in the office." His mouth formed a prim little line above his chin.

I smiled and didn't look away from his face. "Sorry for the inconvenience," I said, clipping my words. I was through being ashamed of my mother, and myself. There is always a moment, sometimes more than one if you're lucky, when a person can choose to change their life's direction. This was one of mine.

Sven Holton, my friend at the medical examiner's office, was the only person I knew personally who was also legally attached to the case. I phoned him during my lunch hour.

"Paula, how are you?" Sven's cheerful voice filtered through the phone line at me.

"I'm fine, Sven. How are you?" In response, he began to seriously tell me about his life, including a detailed description of his marriage, which seemed to be disintegrating. I must remember, I thought, to reserve the how-are-you questions for when I have time to listen. "Sven," I interrupted, "I wondered if I could ask you some questions about my mother's death."

"Hmm," Sven said. "Okay, Paula, what would you like to know?"

"Um," I said. "Everything. I want to know everything."

"Well, Paula, you need to be more specific than that." Sven paused, "And I probably shouldn't talk about this while I'm at work."

"Okay, I understand."

"I'll call you later, okay?"

At work that afternoon I made lists of the questions I wanted to ask about my mother's death. By the end of the day I decided to ask to see the autopsy report, the official document where I assumed all the information could be found.

Sven phoned me that evening. "Paula, I didn't mean to cut you off before, but Minor doesn't like me discussing his cases. I'm sure you figured out that he can be a little unpleasant." Sven sighed. "Luckily, he's thinking of retiring." Sven stopped talking. "Well," his voice returned in a rush of air. "I've been thinking about you since your call, and I've decided I want to help you."

"Could it get you in trouble, helping me, I mean?"

"It could get me fired," Sven said. "But I'm sick of this place. Sick of watching people get screwed over. You don't know, Paula, how close your mother came to being cremated before you had a chance to identify her body. You don't know how things are handled here."

"How are things handled?"

"Let me give you an example. About a month ago one of our investigators notified a woman of her son's death by leaving a note in her mailbox. Okay, Paula? Do you understand? I'm on the verge, we're all on the verge, so if I can help you I will."

"Sven, I don't want to get you in trouble, but I have to know." I got up and paced a small path back and forth in front of my television set.

"I don't care, Paula. I can't watch this anymore. My wife and I, remember I told you we were having problems? Right? She told the counselor we're seeing that I don't know anything about life anymore. All I know is death. Can you imagine that? Only knowing about death? So I'll help you, Paula. What is it you want me to do?"

"I want to see the autopsy report. Can you get me a copy?" There was no answer, and no breathing noises from the other side of the phone. I listened carefully to the quiet. My cat meowed, and I threw a section of the newspaper at him. "Sven?" I said into the phone.

"Okay. Let me think of how I can get it to you. I'll call you in a few days."

"Sven, I don't want you to lose your job."

Sven sighed. "Let me think of how to go about this. I'll call you in a few days."

Sven worked out a complicated plan involving car changes, phone booths, and parking lots. He chose a time when he wasn't on body-viewing call, and I took a day off work to accommodate his arrangements.

At eight-thirty on the appointed morning I waited at a phone booth for Sven's call. He had searched the neighborhood near the medical examiner's office and had chosen this phone booth as a safe place. It was a chilly morning filled with horn-honking traffic. I stood outside the phone booth trying to look inconspicuous. When passersby made a move towards the phone, I darted into the booth and pretended to make a call. As nine o'clock approached, my mood swung from feeling like a clever investigative reporter to merely feeling stupid.

Exactly at nine o'clock the phone rang. "Paula," Sven said, "go to the parking lot in front of San Jose City College. I'll meet you there in thirty minutes." He hung up.

I drove to the San Jose City College parking lot and sat in my car. A minute later, Sven drove up and parked several spaces away. He walked towards my car looking over his shoulder.

Sven stood by the front window of my car looking towards the school. "Follow me," he said.

I opened the door of my car. "No, no." Sven pushed my door closed. "In your car, follow me in your car." He turned away, stumbled over a raised portion of cement, steadied himself before falling, and got into his car.

I followed Sven for about thirty minutes. Following was no easy task as Sven changed lanes often, drove fast, didn't signal for turns, sped up through yellow lights, and came to abrupt halts when the light turned red, often in the middle of an intersection. By the time we arrived at a grocery store parking lot I was sweating.

We parked our cars in the back of the lot. Sven motioned for me to stay in my car. He walked towards me holding a manila folder and glancing over his shoulder.

He got in beside me. "I think we should go somewhere else, Paula. I don't feel quite safe here."

"Okay. Where?"

"Just drive for a while."

I drove. Sven gestured for lane changes and turns. We ended up in a shopping mall parking lot where finally Sven relaxed.

"All right, I don't think anyone I know will see me here." He turned to me and smiled. "How are you?"

"I'm fine. I feel like I'm putting you at risk, but no one else will answer my questions."

"Don't worry about it. I want to help you. I brought the report." He patted the folder. "Why don't you read it, and if you have any questions you can ask me."

"I should probably take notes." I fumbled in my purse for a pen.

"No, this is yours to keep. I took it from the file. That's why we have to be very careful."

"How did you get it out of the building?" I asked.

"Never mind." He handed me the folder. For a moment I thought of not opening it. A tab on the top of the folder read "Lucia Elaine Rothwell." Sven watched me. I opened the folder. The investigation report was on top. Case number: 90-092-005. Decedent: Lucia Elaine Rothwell. Address: Homeless person, San Jose, California.

I closed my eyes.

"Are you okay?" Sven asked.

"I'm fine," I said. "I was just thinking of all the safe places I've never been."

"What? Excuse me?" Sven leaned forward and looked into my eyes. His eyebrows drew together, and his mouth pursed. I patted him on the knee.

"Never mind," I said and continued reading. "So she was found underneath some trees?"

"Yes. Your mother was found in a field near an office building. A man who usually said hello to her noticed the body when he parked his car."

I read the rest of the investigation report. Basic information, telling me no more than the names of those involved with identifying her body. "Lots of misspellings." I smiled, trying to lighten both our moods.

Sven smiled. "Investigator Minor was in a hurry."

"Must have been," I said and turned the page. Page two of the report included a description of the scene and the details of what had happened after my mother's body had been discovered. I glanced up at Sven. He was watching me.

I continued reading the report: my mother was found partially nude with her hose and panties wrapped around her left thigh and her jeans lying on the grass beside her body.

"What does this mean?" I asked Sven. "There was blood on the ground." I paused and then said, "Does this mean she was raped? Is this where they got the idea she was assaulted?"

"Well," Sven drummed his fingers against his jeans, "yes, it could indicate a rape." Sven leaned against the door of my car.

I turned to the autopsy report. The first page was a more precise retelling of the investigative report details. I turned to page two, where across the top my mother's name was typed in capital letters beneath the case number. They called her Lucia rather than Elaine as she preferred. *Poor Mother*, I thought, a *Lucia forevermore*.

"What's this?" I asked Sven. I read aloud from the report. "'There is a diagonal laceration which starts from the vaginal opening and extending posteriorly to just right of the anus for a distance of approximately one-and-one-half inches. The laceration involves the entire thickness of the skin and subcutaneous tissue.'" I stopped reading. "Below the skin, right?" I looked at Sven.

"That's right, it was quite a deep cut," Sven said.

I continued reading from the report. "'As well as a

portion of the underlying muscle.'" I paused. "Wait a minute, is this what killed her? Was she stabbed in the, uh," I looked at the report, "privates?"

"Possibly. I'm not sure."

"Why?"

"I don't know if she lost enough blood for the cut to be the cause of her death. I'm sorry, I just can't give you a good answer to your question."

"Oh." I looked at the report. "I don't understand. Could a penis do this, or was she raped with something else? Did someone stick something inside her?"

"Possibly," Sven said.

I slapped the report against the steering wheel. "Sven," I said, "you are possibly-ing me to death. Can I get a yes or no out of you?"

"I'd like to be more positive with you, but it just isn't that easy. Your mother was postmenopausal, so the lining of her vagina was very thin. It's possible a penis could have caused the rupture, but maybe not."

"Oh," I said. I shut up and read on.

"'Scattered along the inner vaginal wall are a few patches of genital warts,'" I read aloud. Down in the autopsy report, in black and white, evidence of my mother's sex life.

"Sven," I said, "does the presence of genital warts mean my mother was having sex?"

"Yes," he said.

"Could she have gotten them from a dirty toilet seat?" I looked out the windshield.

"No," Sven said quietly.

"So, this probably wasn't the first time she was raped, because she absolutely would not have consented." I looked at an invisible spot on the windshield and bit my lip.

Sven sat back against the car door and watched me.

His face was all straight lines, the calmest face I'd ever seen. I imagined this was the expression he wore when he untangled bodies.

"Because my mother would never have consented to having sex. My mother hated to be touched, it was part of her sickness. She wouldn't have voluntarily had a sex life," I said to the windshield.

"I understand," Sven said.

"No, you don't," I said. "My mother would never let a man touch her." Sven patted my shoulder, and I shrugged his hand away.

"Paula, are you okay?" Sven leaned towards me. His face was so close to mine that it seemed blurry.

"Fine. I'm fine." I continued reading. "Wait a minute, there's nothing down here for cause of death except something about muscle wasting. How did she die? I'm confused," I said.

"I feel badly for you," Sven said. "I don't think you're finding out what you want to know."

"Do you have any ideas? I'm confused. This is so sketchy. Is that because she was homeless? Did they just not care?"

Sven raised his hands: they floated, palms up in the air. "Look, this wasn't handled very well. It's sloppy work. Obviously, there is evidence of sexual assault. I don't know what to say." His hands dropped back into his lap.

"You mean that no one cared enough to do a good job."

Sven sighed. "She was a homeless person." He shook his head. "I hate it, but that's the way it is here. They did take a vaginal swab. At least that."

"Huh? Excuse me, but you need to spell it out for me. I don't speak medical examiner." I shook my head. "I mean, I'm certain they didn't take a vaginal swab in order to give her a PAP smear."

Sven frowned. "Hardly. Since it was a probable rape,

they took a sample of her vaginal secretions. For DNA testing."

I bit my bottom lip again. "Okay, what would you say caused her death? All this other stuff aside, what is your opinion?"

"Off the record?"

"Sven, how much further off the record can we get?"

He leaned close to my face. "I believe your mother suffered a trauma to her lower extremities, possibly caused by the insertion of a foreign object." Sven sighed. "Look, this isn't very pleasant. Your mother was postmenopausal."

"So?" I asked. I could feel a hot redness creeping up from my neck to my face. "What does being postmenopausal have to do with anything?"

"It means that her vaginal wall would not have been very, um, elastic. And also," Sven paused, "that entering her wouldn't have been easy."

"And this means what?" I began hitting the steering wheel with my hands.

"Okay," Sven said, "this is what I believe. I think her attacker became frustrated when he couldn't get his penis inside of her and used something, a beer bottle maybe, to open her up before he raped her. Shoving something inside her vaginal opening would have brought about the bleeding you read about." Sven looked out the front window of my car. "If I had to guess, I'd say she bled to death."

"Who would do that to her?" I said. "She couldn't possibly have been considered sexually attractive." I shook my head. "I don't understand."

Sven patted me on the knee again. I looked at his hand. He pulled his hand back and put it on his own knee.

I could hear her in the back of my mind talking through an exhale of cigarette smoke. "Paula, what did you expect to find here? Put all that stuff away and go find something useful to do."

"Okay," I said. I put the report back into its manila folder. All these facts described a person whose mind and heart I barely knew the patterns of when she was alive. I couldn't find her on the pages of this report. This was no one I knew.

I put the folder in the back seat of my car. *I am the solver of nothing*, I thought. *I am the savior of no one.*

"There's no way to know, is there? No way to ever really know what happened," I said.

"What is it you really want to find out?" Sven asked.

"I guess what I really want is to know what the last minute of her life was like. Even if it was ugly." I leaned my head back against the seat and shut my eyes.

I opened my eyes.

"What are you thinking?" Sven asked.

"I don't know. Trying to imagine what happened to her, I guess. My mother once told me that, no matter what was happening to her, I was always on her mind." I looked down at the autopsy report. "I was wondering if I was on her mind when she died."

"Did reading the report help?" Sven asked.

"I don't think so," I said as I turned the key in the ignition. "I think that maybe some questions shouldn't be answered." *Then again*, I thought as I drove away, *maybe the answers would save me.*

That night as I lay in bed unable to sleep, I could think of nothing else but the last weeks of my mother's life.

CHAPTER 9

Patterns

Every Sunday before April, Lucia Elaine Rothwell sat on the curb near the street where a man named Alex Cavello lived. He passed her corner during the week on the way to work and on Sundays on the way to and from church. Alex lived in a poor neighborhood in San Jose, California, a place where after dark was not a time to be out. After Alex and his daughter came home from church, Alex sent his daughter to ask Elaine to Sunday dinner. Elaine never answered the girl's invitation or looked up to acknowledge her presence. Each time, the girl told her father that the woman would not be coming to dinner. Alex always sent his daughter back with money, which Elaine took.

Elaine's days followed a pattern. She knew where the truck stopped twice a week to take orders from the homeless for clothes and personal supplies. She knew where to go for a free meal and where to be at night if she wanted an indoor place to sleep. She was a regular in the neighborhood around the San Jose Civic Center and people made special trips to give her money and food. Once, a man noticed that her shoes had holes in them and bought her some socks and a new pair of tennis shoes.

For the past month, Elaine had been sleeping most week nights at the armory in North San Jose, which had been turned into a homeless shelter. In the mornings she always went back to her campsite near the office building at North First and Highway 880. Elaine woke up April Fools' Day 1990 in her cot with the blanket pulled over her head. Instead of the provided pillow, she used her purse, a red vinyl tote bag. She sat up on the edge of her cot. There were too many people around her. They kept talking to her, asking questions, and saying good morning. Elaine put her head down and her hands over her ears. There was noise inside her head, an insistent buzzing. The sound never went away. She even heard little buzzing whispers in her sleep. Elaine fumbled through her pants pocket, found some quarters, and bought a Coke from the machine in the hallway. After drinking her Coke, she gathered her things and went outside to smoke a cigarette. She stood in front of the shelter holding her cigarette in two fingers and rubbing her nose with her thumb while wrapping her other arm around her waist. No matter the weather, Elaine always wore something over her head so that the only parts of her which were visible were her black horn-rimmed glasses and her nose. Today, despite the warm weather, she wore a gray shirt covered by two jackets: one blue and the other red. A black shirt was tied around her head. Elaine preferred hooded gray sweatshirts. One night she had taken her clothes off in order to take a shower, and someone had stolen her sweatshirt.

Elaine finished smoking her cigarette and walked downtown. There was a donut shop she sat in front of each day where people knew her, and someone would usually buy her a cup of coffee and a donut. She sat on

the curb. Sure enough, a donut shop customer brought
her a cup of coffee. After Elaine finished her coffee, she
set the cup on the curb next to her. Sometimes people
walking by dropped change into the cup. After a while
the owner of the donut shop brought Elaine a sandwich
and another cup of coffee. "You should eat better," the
shop owner said. "You are so thin. Don't you have family,
honey?" Elaine didn't answer, and the shop owner left
her alone on the curb to eat and went back inside.

Alex and his daughter noticed that Elaine was not in her
usual spot this Sunday. They watched for her all afternoon.
In the evening Alex grew concerned and called the police.
The police officer who answered the phone told Alex that
there was probably nothing to worry about. "Sometimes
those people just wander off," the officer said.

Elaine sat on the curb. Every now and then her chin
dropped, and she slept for a while. There was a lot of
noise inside her head today. Around six o'clock in the
evening she collected her identification and a carton of
cigarettes from the armory, and told them she was leaving. The shelter's chaplain took her into his office and
tried to persuade her to stay, but she would not change
her mind or say why she was leaving. While the chaplain talked, Elaine wrapped one arm around her head.
She put her free hand over her mouth and stared at the
chaplain with large, blank blue eyes. Finally he gave up
and walked her to the door. He stood in the doorway
and watched her walk down the street, a tiny woman
under five feet tall and very thin. The chaplain sighed
and went back to his office.

Late that night Elaine walked past Alex's house. She
kept going down the block and finally turned into a
field. The field was next to a freeway underpass, bordered by a chain-link fence. It was a warm night. There
wasn't much traffic, so it was very peaceful. Sometimes

the people in the office building on the other side of the fence gave her money or food. Everyone who parked by the fence said hello when they saw her. This was a good place to wake up on a Monday morning.

Elaine stood by the chain-link fence smoking a cigarette. The night was warm and pleasant. She noticed someone crossing the field towards her. As the person drew closer, Elaine saw that it was a teenage boy. He was smiling. "Hey, lady," he said. "Hey, got a cigarette?" He began to circle around her.

Elaine put her head down and didn't answer.

"Hey, bitch." The teenager shoved her. Elaine stepped backwards and her cigarette dropped to the ground.

The teenager became agitated and said to her, "Now look what you've done. You could've given that to me."

The teenager began pushing Elaine with both hands. He wasn't tall, but he was strong. Still Elaine didn't lose her balance. She wrapped her arms around her head and began to moan. The teenager grabbed her and began to shake her. "Shut up or I'll have to shut you up," he said. "Come on now. You want it, don't you, bitch? You want me to give it to you?"

The teenager pushed Elaine down onto the grass and lay on top of her. He unzipped her jeans and yanked them down. "Damn, how many pairs of pants you got on?" he said and pulled off both pairs of her jeans. "You want it, don't you, bitch? You want some of what I got." Elaine's shoes and one sock came off, and she lay on the ground looking up. "Close your eyes, bitch," the man yelled. He pulled at her pantyhose and panties until they were wrapped around one leg. Finally he began trying to push himself inside her. Elaine stayed quiet while he stabbed at her with his penis. "Damn it," he said, frustrated with his inability to penetrate her. The teenager knelt over Elaine's body. He noticed an empty beer bottle a couple of feet from where they lay. "Okay, I got it now," he said. The teenager retrieved the beer bottle and knelt over Elaine again. "Okay, bitch," he said, "now I'm gonna give you what you want, 'cause I know you want it bad. So just shut up and lay there or I'll kill you." And he shoved the beer bottle inside Elaine's vagina, once, twice, three times until finally the bottle was wet with blood. Then he raped her. Elaine began to moan and cry. "Shut up, bitch," he said. He grabbed a pair of Elaine's jeans and pressed them down over her face. Her glasses made a tiny crunching sound, and an earpiece fell off onto the grass. After he was finished, the boy rolled off her, stood up, and ran away.

The morning of April 2, workers arriving at the office building looked for Elaine but didn't see her. One man arriving for work around nine usually brought her a cup of coffee. Since he didn't see her when he got out of his car this morning, he walked over to the chain-link fence that separated the office complex from the freeway underpass, and took a closer look.

He was almost ready to forget about her and go to work when he noticed Elaine's pink blanket and what looked like a body lying on the ground next to it. The man didn't investigate further. He called the police.

Since she was found naked on the ground with her legs spread and a sweatshirt covering her face, Elaine Rothwell's death was ruled "suspicious." As of then there were not enough dues to conclude she had been murdered, so her body was sent to the coroner's office to be autopsied and identified. During his autopsy, the coroner discovered a six-inch-long laceration through the muscles and skin from Elaine's vagina to her anus. From this he deduced that she did not die of natural causes and ruled her death a homicide.

CHAPTER 10

The Persistence of Memory

Reading my mother's autopsy report was stultifying. I told myself I didn't want to spend my life rethinking my mother's murder, and I didn't want any more ghosts in my life either. What I really wished for was my mother to be alive again, this time safe. Unfortunately, I found that if I didn't keep my thoughts focused on the present, not only did her death haunt me but my mind conjured up every thoughtless cruelty I'd ever inflicted on my mother during my misspent adolescence. I remembered every Mother's Day when I had not given her a card. The times when I hadn't remembered her birthday startled me out of sound sleeps and jogged along behind me during my morning run. I was haunted by all the things about my relationship with my mother that I couldn't change now that she was dead. Sad memories were taking over my life. Memories have their own substance and their own lives. Our memories don't really belong to us at all, but to themselves. I decided that if I couldn't choose what to remember, I didn't want to remember anything, and I set my mind on looking forward.

Despite my resolve, I began seeing ghosts. One morning I was driving to work taking my usual route, when, stopped at a light waiting to make a left turn, I glanced to my left. Sometimes a homeless man spent his mornings on this particular island. Usually he held a sign reading: **Will work for food.** When I noticed him sitting underneath the light, I always smiled and said good morning to him. This morning when I turned my head, it was my mother I saw sitting on the cement. There was no mistaking her profile, the way her chin tucked into her chest and sweatshirt hood pulled up around her face. She didn't look in my direction.

"Not dead," I said out loud, "she's not dead." Despite my repeated wish to have the chance to change my mother's fate, erasing her death and altering my present, my first instinct was to drive like hell through the intersection and keep on going. Instead, I sucked in my breath until I felt it tighten in my throat and looked straight ahead through the windshield of my car. The light changed and cars behind me began to honk. I turned my head to the left again. Smiling up at me from the concrete was the homeless man I was used to seeing in that spot and not my mother after all. For a moment I just stared at the man until his smile faded away. Finally I smiled at him and drove on to work as usual.

After that morning, I saw my mother everywhere. Out of the corner of my eye I would glimpse her standing next to me, but when I turned to look she was gone. While in line waiting to buy a movie ticket, I would see her crossing the parking lot, but when I chased after her she disappeared. Leaving the grocery store I would see her standing by the soft drink machines with her head bent and her arms around her waist, but when I approached it always turned out to be some other poor lost person. Sometimes I thought I heard her voice, that slow, soft southern drawl that couldn't belong to anyone else. I was constantly chasing around corners, expecting to catch her in the act of being crazy. Bits and pieces of her were scattered all over my life.

By this time, everyday stuff like grocery shopping or watching television seemed pointless to me, and I gave up the effort of keeping my thoughts fixed on the present and future. My life reorganized itself around my mother's murder, until the world around me took on a different color and body shape. In my perspective, almost any other problem seemed petty and everyday life trivial. It became difficult to see my way out of my pain, which I did not recognize as guilt. My mother, enemy, protector, stranger, lifeline when I was an infant, was dead. Every time I looked in the mirror and saw her almond-shaped blue eyes looking back I knew that I was responsible. I'd killed her with apathy and my fear that I had more in common with her than just beautiful eyes. I couldn't stop her murder. I couldn't make her sane. And now, with the legal system seemingly bent on forgetting her, I couldn't solve the case and bring peace to my family or myself.

Friends phoned to cheer me up and as they told me about their daily tragedies such as flat tires, dead batteries or sick cats, my thoughts snapped. *So what,* I mouthed as they talked, *you think you know pain? My mother was murdered. Now that's pain.* Finally I began saying it out loud: "So what," I'd say. "My mother was raped. Not only was she raped, she was murdered. And not only was she raped, murdered and homeless, she was schizophrenic. Try living with that."

Eventually, my friends ran out of comforting words. Trapped inside their own fears of making things worse for me, they stopped phoning.

Left by myself to remember and mourn, I began fanta-
sizing about being a child again. In these daydreams my
parents realized they couldn't care for me and gave me up
for adoption. I was adopted by normal, calm people, and
from that point on my childhood was filled with things
like family picnics, birthday parties, and summer vacations
camping in the mountains. I grew up happy and was
spared all the pain that comes along with homeless, schizophrenic, raped and murdered mothers.

Tom tried to help, but I could not, would not, share
this agony, and I closed him out. My pain was mine alone.
At this point we had separate interests, separate friends,
and different goals for the future. So, Tom stopped
asking if I wanted to talk about what was wrong, and I
didn't ask for his help.

I was finding my work as a travel agent difficult to concentrate on. I couldn't drum up the enthusiasm necessary
to explain to a prospective client why a cruise offered more
vacation dollar value than a trip to Hawaii. I wanted more
from my career and life. I began to realize I wanted to
be someone my mother would have been proud of, an educated, accomplished woman. I needed to start setting
goals.

I found that setting goals is the easy part. I could sit
around all day setting goals. I began to see this was only
the first step. Once you set goals, you have to work towards making them happen or they become something
you only talk about at parties to impress other people. I
didn't want to spend any more time being the kind of
person who talked about what they wanted to do and
then made no effort to do it.

Part of making your goals into a reality involves a thing
called paying your dues. Basically, you have to prove that
you can do it. Paying your dues involves hard work and
risk and often isn't much fun. I wanted to move my life

in a different direction, but I didn't know how to go about it. Luck, as it often will when you recognize it as an opportunity, intervened. A client of mine who ran a software company offered me a marketing position. I accepted. I didn't know anything about computers or software, and I didn't think about whether or not I could succeed at the new job: I just wanted a different job to do. When I gave notice my boss at the travel agency, Jim, didn't look at me.

For a while he looked down at his desktop while I stood waiting. He arranged papers in little piles and then rearranged the piles. Finally he rubbed his eyebrows and scratched the bridge of his nose. "Ah," Jim said, "well, good luck then." He began typing on his computer keyboard, and I started walking back to my desk. "May as well leave now," he called after me. "No sense in giving two weeks notice and pretending you'll actually get any work done," he said, concentrating his gaze on the computer screen.

I gathered my things. After putting the boxes in my car, I went back inside and looked around my cubicle to make sure I hadn't left anything behind. I felt nostalgic for some reason. I realized that for a long while, being a travel agent had kept me focused and helped me feel good about myself, even if it had not brought me closer to fulfillment.

As I walked through the office, saying goodbye to my co-workers, I felt the relief that comes with a welcome change. I was finally moving on, hopefully moving forward. My future lay elsewhere.

My new job proved to be both exactly what I had hoped for and something less than I'd imagined. It involved learning an entirely new industry, software, plus the industry jargon and a working knowledge of the technology. It involved becoming familiar with the UNIX computer language. My job also involved wresting professional respect from a group of people who, though very nice as individuals, didn't exactly view me as a technical peer. For the first time in my life I recognized that my mother's hopes for me to become an educated woman had to have some real world basis. I was going to have to return to school.

I also had to learn the technical basics of my new job. I set about the task and found the process exhausting. Every day I was confronted with concepts and technical knowledge about which I hadn't a clue. I learned more about becoming a business woman from the first three months on my new job than I'd ever learned anywhere else. One thing I learned was that I was good at it. Another thing I learned was that I wanted more from my life. I began filling up my life with goals and plans and thought I left no room for ghosts of regrets past. I didn't realize that the ghosts were still inside me.

One evening I came home from my new job, took my laptop computer out of its case and placed it in the middle of the kitchen table. It looked ill at ease in the center of the table and would be difficult to reach. I moved it closer to the edge. I sat in front of it for a while with my fingers dangling over the keys and my mind a blank. I typed the letter "m" for a page. Then I went to bed.

After that, whenever I was at home, I was writing. I woke up early and wrote for an hour, went to my job, came home and wrote until bedtime. I wrote constantly, and everything, every poem, story, essay and article I produced, was about my mother. Sometimes she was hidden inside another character, but she was always there. The story of my life hung before me on the computer screen. I didn't know what to do with it.

During the day I worked hard. Exhaustion kept my memories and my pain at bay. If I found that there was an hour in the day during which I couldn't stop thinking

Paula Mints at six months.
(Photo by William Rothwell)

Baby Paula and her mother in
Eureka, California.
(Photo by William Rothwell)

Baby Paula at the Morgan Hill
home, taken by her mother.
(Photo by Elaine Rothwell)

Paula and her father at their
home in Morgan Hill, California.
(Photo by Elaine Rothwell)

Paula as toddler riding her stuffed dog at home in Morgan Hill, California.
(Photo by William Rothwell)

Young Paula in front of a makeshift Christmas tree constructed from pine branches by her father, at the family's home in Morgan Hill.
(Photo by William Rothwell)

Paula's fifth birthday at the Morgan Hill house.
(Photo by William Rothwell)

Paula's father at thirty-five.
(Photo by Elaine Rothwell)

Paula's parents at a party
in the early 1970s.
(Photo by Paula Mints)

Paula's father at a Santa
Cruz beach. This photo
was taken by her mother
when they were dating.
(Photo by Elaine Rothwell)

Paula's father fishing at a Santa Cruz pier.
(Photo by Elaine Rothwell)

Paula's mother with a fishing pole at a Santa Cruz pier.
(Photo by William Rothwell)

Paula's mother in the kitchen of the family's Hayward, California home.
(Photo by William Rothwell)

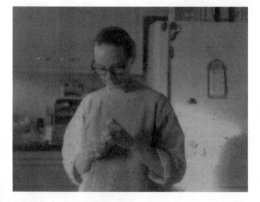

Young Paula in a Brownie
uniform, at the family's
Morgan Hill home.
(Photo by William Rothwell)

Paula and her
mother at San
Francisco Zoo.
*(Photo by
William Rothwell)*

Paula at ten, at
the family's
Hayward home.
*(Photo by
William Rothwell)*

Paula by the fireplace at the San Jose house with the family cat, shortly before her mother's breakdown.
(Photo by William Rothwell)

Paula's house in Hayward.
(Photo by William Rothwell)

Paula at 14 in the backyard of the Hayward home.
(Photo by William Rothwell)

Paula at 18 at the Hayward home.
(Photo by William Rothwell)

Paula at 23, in the home she shared with Tom in San Jose, California. *(Photo by Tom Mints)*

Paula at 30 in San Jose, trying to get her dog Chuck into the pool. *(Photo by Tom Mints)*

about my mother, I found something to do during that hour, anything. I didn't realize she was still inside me. I didn't confide in anyone else about her murder. I'd had enough of curious, though sympathetic, expressions. I didn't realize that by hiding my feelings about my mother's murder I was repeating my childhood patterns. Those sad patterns that kept everyone, no matter how intimate they believed they were, strangers in my life. I still had not faced my mother's murder. Though I thought that I'd placed her death in the background, it still lurked in my dreams.

As time went on, even though I tried to push my memories of my mother into the background to escape them, I would be damned if the legal profession would do the same thing. It was easier to be angry with professional strangers than it was to be angry with myself for my past childish cruelties, or with my mother for being crazy, leaving me alone, and then dying on top of it all. I began pestering the police in earnest, asking about their progress on my mother's case. Each time I called I marked the date on the calendar in red ink. With my new goal-oriented, focused personality, I was relentless in my pursuit of unanswered questions and unreturned telephone calls.

In order to avoid job burnout, officers with the San Jose Police Department rotate through different tours of duty, from homicide to sexual assault to patrol, so the various detectives assigned to my mother's case kept changing. It was hard to keep track. At first each new detective was polite and concerned, but after a while preoccupied sounds would creep into their voices, and finally after many unreturned phone calls I began getting the feeling that I was being avoided.

"Keep at them, Sister," my brother said. "Don't let them forget."

Michael didn't have to worry about the possibility of my forgetting. I may have filled my life up with busy work, goals, and plans, but on April 2, I allowed myself the realization of my inner suffering. I enshrined the day my mother was murdered and kept it with the reverence most people attach to religious holidays. For two years following my mother's murder, I saved all my pain up for the anniversary of the day she died. I filled that day with rituals. In the morning I cried. Since my mother had loved walking the beach at Santa Cruz, I drove there in the afternoon and walked the beach. I let my emotions build to a crescendo so that I was exhausted by bedtime. The next morning I was calm again. Tom usually came with me on my day of atonement and pain. It was one time we were able to share our deeper feelings with each other. The rest of the year we kept to a respectful, caring distance from each other.

My brother and I didn't talk about our feelings; I didn't know what he did with his pain over our mother's death. Michael asked for a copy of the autopsy report, but his only comment after reading it was a grunt. Maybe he saved his comments for other people. True to our past, we weren't in the habit of sharing our burden, or our joy for that matter. A childhood of planning our separate escapes from our family had not prepared us to be close now that we needed to be. I read about other families for whom pain and struggle form a bond, but that just wasn't true for Michael and me.

Michael had gotten married. He told me about his marriage after the fact, which didn't bother me at the time. From our father we'd learned the family secretiveness and we kept the legacy alive. At this point we were experts at keeping feelings and events to ourselves. So, Michael didn't ask me to attend his wedding and I only met his wife twice. They came to visit when she was six months pregnant and then again when my niece was two years old. He didn't tell me when his marriage broke up, and I didn't ask what had caused the breach. Apart from a few anecdotes about my niece and the occasional bit of news about our mother's case, conversations between Michael and me were awkward and quick to end.

It was becoming plainer all the time that the investigation into my mother's death was going nowhere. I began to realize that if I did nothing, the murderer would probably never be found. Not knowing where to turn, I visited the crime scene myself.

I was a little apprehensive at the thought of seeing the site of my mother's last, painful moments, but I was surprised by what I found. The area where my mother once lived and died was a very ordinary looking patch of land. A plastic bag and some food wrappers had been dropped there by a careless passerby and the traffic rumblings of the nearby freeway could be faintly heard; but to my relief, there was no sign of my mother there. I was ready to begin looking for answers.

I scoured the area for clues, finding little beyond the stray garbage recently left there. The police had probably already retrieved anything of value from the scene. Undaunted, I returned the next day and began canvassing the neighborhood for any scraps of information I could obtain. I spoke to homeless people and storekeepers. Many of them remembered seeing my mother around, but few seemed to know who she was. Only a handful even knew her name. I heard a lot of responses like, "She kept to herself," "She didn't say much," and "She didn't bother anybody." I quickly came to realize that the likelihood of finding anyone who really knew my mother was slim, so I widened my search.

I began walking around neighborhoods close to the crime scene asking residents and anyone who would listen what, if anything, they knew about the crime. Did anyone see or hear anything unusual the night of my mother's murder? Have there been similar attacks on other women in the area? Most people were kind and tried to be helpful, but they could not give me answers that brought me closer to the truth.

At the same time, I began reading the crime news in the newspaper. Every time I noticed a scenario similar to my mother's murder, I clipped the item. Then I put together all the information I knew and tried to find any connections to my growing collection of news clippings. Finally, I came across an article that was about a man who had been arrested for attacking a woman. The attack occurred in the same neighborhood where my mother's murder took place. I did a computer search and found several articles in which the accused attacker, Richard Carrasco, was named in connection with similar crimes.

The following day I returned to the scene of the crime. I thought about all that I had discovered and came to one conclusion: My gut told me that Carrasco was our man. I wrote up all the facts that I had gathered and along with the newspaper clippings, took them to the police.

It was one week after the anniversary of my mother's death. Officer Maler had recently taken over the investigation and had not yet begun to avoid me. He was a calm sort of homicide cop. His voice never rose above a careful monotone. "I think we finally have a lead in my mother's case," I told him.

"Let's see what you have, Paula." I showed him the information I'd accumulated on Richard Carrasco. "You don't give up easily, do you?"

For the first time in many years I thought of my mother without feeling shame. "I'm my mother's daughter," I said quietly, firmly.

After some checking, Maler deflated my sense of accomplishment. "Unfortunately, Carrasco is now free," he said. "First, we have to find him."

I thought that solving the case would give me the right to remember my mother and talk about her without guilt and pain. Yet her murder haunted me more now than ever. In my dreams I saw my mother's face, lucid and smiling. When I was awake, I imagined calling my brother and saying, *Michael, this is the person who killed our mother. Now you can forget the past and get on with your life.* I needed answers, I needed the truth.

I began checking with Officer Maler all the time.

"Hello, Officer Maler," I said at the beginning of my calls. "Any progress in finding him?"

"These things take time," he answered, his voice growing quieter with each call. Three months of weekly phone calls later, Officer Maler's voice passed from monotone to annoyance, and he said, "Look, I'll call you. Really, trust me. When we have him, I'll call you."

"It's no problem for me to keep checking," I replied.

"Really. I'll call you."

"I don't mind calling you."

"Look, really, Mrs. Mints. If there is anything new, I'll call." He sighed. "These things take time, you know."

"When do you think you will be able to arrest him?" I began to hop up and down. Safely behind the distance of the telephone line, I was free to behave like an idiot.

"I can't say," he said. "These things take time. I'll call you."

During this period, I worked fourteen-hour days, wrote stories when I was home, began taking college classes, and forced myself to imagine a future where I was successful. Despite my attempts to pretend my life was normal and though Tom and I still had deep feelings for each other, we said little and made love silently. I began to feel pressured, as if there was somewhere I had to get to in a hurry, but I wasn't exactly sure where that was. I was determined now to become the person my mother had always wanted me to be, and my determination left no room for anyone else. I thought that I'd moved on with my life and feelings.

Then, in late April 1994, my father got married again.

They'd been dating for five years. Jenny was very different from my mother. For one thing, she was sane, but there were other differences that served to illustrate just how much my father must have wanted to forget his first marriage. Where my mother had earned an advanced degree, Jenny was only a high school graduate. Where my mother had been thin all her life, Jenny was plump; her face very pretty but very round. My mother, even at her craziest, had been quiet, more given to staring than shouting and making scenes. Jenny was extroverted and boisterous, telling jokes and asking endless personal questions. My mother had always been respectful of other people's privacy.

As I've said, we'd never been a family that shared our private thoughts and feelings. Until I grew up I thought we were just reserved. We required our privacy like other families and needed hugs and three square meals a day. To us, secrecy was a basic need.

Jenny asked questions about my childhood to which she believed she already knew the answers. My father, it seemed, had turned into quite a teller of family fairy tales. Of course, in my father's version of our family life, my mother was the villain. With my father, memory did not persist—it was forcefully altered into something more palatable. I'd never realized how much my father needed to blame my mother for his own disappointments. Even dead my mother was the focus of all our family guilt and pain. I managed to avoid answering Jenny's questions by seeming to agree. "Oh really," "I don't recall," and "Maybe so," can be lifesavers when you are in the middle of an uncomfortable conversation.

My father's behavior after he announced his engagement was harder for me to cope with. He was very affectionate towards Jenny, holding her hand, kissing her, buying her little gifts, and telling her that he loved her publicly. I'd never seen him behave that way with my mother. Sometimes I wondered if behind closed doors he'd been as romantic and smitten with my mother, but mostly I just would have preferred that he kept his romantic feelings a bit more to himself.

The father I grew up with had loved us but had not been an affectionate person. Even when we were kids he didn't give hugs, say "I love you," or even hold hands. My father did family outing types of things with us. Once a year we all went to visit the San Francisco Zoo. We also went to drive-in movies, and twice we went to Disneyland. My mother's favorite outing was the beach. On the beach, her hair blowing in the wind, I could visualize her young again as she walked up and down the sand while my brother and I played in the water and my father lay on his towel. The place I remember my mother liking best during my childhood was the beach. Of course, I'd never really let myself know who she was, so my mother may have had many favorite places that remain unknown to me.

With Jenny, my father was like an infatuated kid. He never strayed far from her side and rarely took his eyes from her face. For me, it was a difficult thing to see. Though my father might not have lavished affection on us, he also didn't abandon us. If he wasn't emotionally there for us much of the time, well, he had his own demons to fight off. The truth was that in our family there was enough rejection, pain, and fear to warp a person's perception of the facts. Now that I'm older, I think that in the wrong hands the truth can be used to batter a person. Perhaps, armed with his illusions, my father would be a different sort of husband the second time around.

Towards the end of my parents' marriage my father had not been a faithful husband. In this way he brought some of my mother's worst hallucinations to reality and crossed over the line somewhat to participate in her craziness. When I was fifteen years old, one of his girlfriends began calling the house. She hung up when my mother answered and asked to speak with my father when my brother or I picked up the phone. This went on for about six months until I finally confronted my father. He told me that the woman was pregnant and that he thought he was the father. I was shocked and not happy to be the recipient of his secret. At fifteen I found both the thought of my father having sex and the possible reality of a new sibling repulsive and frightening. My brother was more than enough family for me. I didn't want to have a new family at this late date. Still, for a while this new secret brought my father and me closer, and in this way he made me his ally in the war waged between him and my mother.

The woman eventually admitted that her baby was fathered by someone else. She broke up with my father, leaving him with a pile of bills and a grudge against my mother for forcing him into having an affair. At that point, I began to wonder if the tendency to blame others, like schizophrenia, was a hereditary trait.

This was not my father's last affair, just the last one of which I was aware. My brother, however, listened to every phone call, monitored my father's every move, and became angrier by the year. He kept track of my father's affairs in the same way he tallied yearly baseball statistics, keeping a careful, mental tally of my father's wrongs.

Now, my father was going to marry again.

I tried to act like an adult. I had more success at this than my brother, who refused to attend the wedding or even talk about it. To my brother, my father's new wife became the one who had broken up our parents' marriage. He crammed all the other women in my father's life into the person of our new stepmother-to-be.

"Michael," I said during our one and only conversation about our father's upcoming wedding, "Jenny didn't break up our parents' marriage. It broke up because mother was sick. We all wanted to get away. It wasn't just Dad."

"Don't stand up for him, Sister. He was keeping her. I know he was. Just drop the subject."

"Michael," I began, "he didn't even know Jenny when he was married to our mother." A garbled grunting sound came through the phone at me. "Okay then," I said, "what do you think, his screwing around drove our mother crazy?"

"Maybe."

"That's not reasonable, Michael," I said, speaking from my years of practice at behaving semi-rationally. My brother didn't answer. I imagined him on the other end of the phone line tightening his jaw and grinding his back teeth. I am the family member least able to take silence as an answer. The old fear of abandonment always comes back to haunt me. "Okay, but will you go to the wedding with me?"

"Nope."

"Come on. Look, Tom is working and can't come. Don't make me go alone." I waited for him to answer. I could hear his breathing coming through the telephone line like the panting of some wild cornered beast. Finally he spoke.

"No," he said and hung up.

My father was getting married in Reno. His bride's

brother owned a condominium there, and this was to be their honeymoon suite. Jenny was fifty years old and had five children ranging in age from sixteen to twenty-five. Suddenly, I was going to belong to a family. They might expect to spend holidays together, go on picnics in the summer and call me up just to talk. The thought of all that made me a little nauseous.

I couldn't be expected to learn at this late date how to belong to a normal family. I tried to get out of going to the wedding. Suddenly my father, difficult to reach and un-communicative when he chose, wouldn't leave me alone. He nagged. He begged. He called constantly. When he cried, I agreed to go to the wedding.

I spent the night before the wedding at a friend's cabin in South Lake Tahoe, not sleeping and fretting the night away feeling disloyal to my mother. I arrived at the chapel in Reno just in time for the wedding, not getting there early enough to get involved with any pre-wedding con-versations. I parked my car down the block and walked to the chapel, which was small and badly in need of paint. It was only two o'clock in the afternoon, so the neon sign proclaiming "The Little Love Chapel" was not lit up. My father stood in front of the building smoking a cigar.

He didn't turn in my direction right away, so I had a moment to observe him. He wore a black velveteen tuxedo coat at least three sizes too big for him. Only the tips of his fingers protruded from the sleeves. The cuffs of his pants were rolled up to his ankles.

"Dad," I said.

He turned and smiled. Each time I saw my father I was shocked anew by how old and fragile he looked. It is tough to hold a grudge for the crimes of your childhood with one of the perpetrators dead and the other physi-cally deteriorating.

"Oh hi, honey," he said looking startled, as if my

coming to his wedding was a shock after all. He hugged me and kissed me on the cheek. "How are you?"

He didn't seem to need a reply as to my state and turned his attention immediately back to his cigar. I noticed that his hands shook. My cheek felt wet from the unaccustomed kiss.

"Are you nervous?" I asked.

My father held his cigar between his teeth. "Oh no," he said around it.

Suddenly, I was curious about my parents wedding. I'd never seen any pictures. I wondered if they had taken any.

"Were you nervous when you married Mother?" I asked, not caring whether or not my question was inappropriate to the occasion.

He slowly turned his head to look at me. His eyes were bloodshot. "Who?" he asked.

"My mother," I said impatiently. "Were you nervous when you married my mother?"

My father looked back at his feet. "Oh no," he said.

I felt annoyed. "Did you have a big wedding when you married my mother?"

"Oh no," he said.

One of my new stepbrothers stuck his head out of the chapel door. "It's time," he said and disappeared.

"That's Kurt," my father said. "He's my best man."

To get into the chapel we had to walk through a small store selling religious and wedding related artifacts. The walls were covered by shelves. Stacked on the shelves were dusty items with dustier price tags. Next to the cash register a small sign boasted 1,000,000 weddings performed since 1965. My father was getting married in the McDonald's of wedding chapels.

The wedding chapel itself was a small, white room with a podium in front and four rows of benches with an aisle in the center. Almost every seat was taken. My father introduced me to one of Jenny's aunts. He suggested I sit next to her and took his place before the podium.

"How are you, honey?" the aunt said. She was very old, anywhere between seventy-five and one hundred and eight. "They make a lovely couple, don't they?" Not wanting to speak, I smiled in answer.

Jenny started up from the back of the chapel. She wore a long purple dress and had purple feathers in her hair. I turned back to the front of the room. My father was glowing. His hands were clasped. Since I was sitting on the front bench, I could see that he had tears in his eyes. Suddenly I felt like a traitor. I imagined my mother sitting next to me, rocking and looking down at her lap. I could feel her sense of betrayal and rejection. The whole thing was very confusing, and I told myself that my father, after all, had every right to marry again.

After the wedding I was surrounded by my new family. Everyone hugged, kissed, laughed, and shook hands. I only had a moment alone with my father.

"Are you coming to the reception?" he asked. There was to be a potluck wedding dinner at the condominium.

"No. I think I'd better get started. I've got a long drive."

My father looked down at the ground for a moment, then up and into my eyes. We held each other's gaze for a second. Finally, he patted me on the shoulder. "Okay, honey," he said. "Have a safe drive. Thank you for coming." He patted me on the shoulder again and disappeared into the crowd of his new family.

I felt oddly cut off as I watched him walk away. My father had chosen a new life completely different from his old one. My father, brother, and I—we were all still running away from our old lives. Every choice we made was a denial.

Before I could get away, Jenny came up and kissed me

on the cheek. "Thanks for coming," she said warmly. "I really appreciate it." She gave me a hug before she walked away. I left the chapel, got into my car, and started the long drive back to San Jose.

I was still bulldogging the police as to when they were going to arrest my mother's murderer. Then one day Officer Maler phoned me at work. "Richard Carrasco has finally been arrested." Officer Maler told me that I had Officer Mike Brown to thank for finding Carrasco. Officer Brown had been on the scene the day my mother's body was discovered. Brown had been investigating a series of unsolved rapes which he'd also connected to Richard Carrasco and called him down to the station to answer a few questions. Instead of surrendering, Carrasco fled to Texas. Officer Brown had been pursuing him relentlessly ever since, and now he'd arrested him not only for the other rapes to which Brown had linked him, but because I had linked him to my mother's murder as well.

The *San Jose Mercury News* picked up the story of my mother's murder. One line of the article read: "Lucia Rothwell's death passed with little notice." I was at work when I read the paper. I reread the article several times and then put the paper down. I shut the door to my office, closed the blinds, and sat in the dark for two hours. I didn't answer my phone. When my officemates knocked on my door, I told them to go away.

I sat in my dark office and thought about my mother. "My mother would have hated being called Lucia in the newspaper," I said into my empty office. I picked up a pen and a clean yellow pad and wrote: *Lucia Elaine Rothwell's death happened when she was crazy.*

When I got home that evening I powered on my computer and wrote for three hours. I wrote an article about my mother, whose life and death had passed with so much notice that my life had exploded. I felt very calm while I wrote. After I was done, I wrote a cover letter and mailed my article to the *Mercury News*. I received a telephone call from an editor for the Living section, telling me my article would be the lead in the Living section on Sunday, October 4, 1994.

The first line of my article read: "Elaine Rothwell's death did not pass with little notice." I kept in all the craziness, and I didn't once refer to her as Lucia.

I phoned Officer Maler the Monday after my article appeared in the paper. "So," I said, after the hellos, "Did you read my article in this Sunday's newspaper?"

"No," Officer Maler said.

"It was about my mother," I told him.

Officer Maler didn't reply.

"Okay," I said, "will the trial be soon? What happens next?"

"These things take time," Officer Maler said in his careful monotone.

"Ah. Hmm. Okay." I put the receiver carefully into the cradle of the phone. Since I consider myself an expert in the art of the silent telephone slam, I concentrated on putting the receiver down so softly and slowly that it didn't make the slightest click. I decided to phone Aunt Gayle. She had a right to know that there had been an arrest in her sister's murder. Perhaps there was some comfort to be found in relaying good news to her. I punched her phone number out on the telephone pad and listened to the ringing on the other end.

"Hello?" My aunt's soft southern drawl, so reminiscent of my mother's, came on the line.

"Aunt Gayle. Hi."

"Paula? Why, how are you, honey?"

"Fine." I drummed my fingers on my desk.

"Well, what a nice surprise hearing from you," my aunt said.

We were both quiet. I tapped my pen on my desk.

"Is there a reason for your call?" she asked.

I gripped my pen. *Fast,* I thought. *Say it fast.* "They arrested someone in Mother's case." I sucked in a deep breath. "I did research and made a connection between this man and Mother's murder. The police have just caught him."

My aunt was quiet for a minute. Two minutes. Three minutes. I began timing her. Five minutes. I began to wonder if she'd hung up the telephone. After all, if I could perfect the art of the silent phone slam, maybe it ran in the family.

"Well, Paula Jean," my aunt said, "maybe now you can forgive yourself for your mother's death."

CHAPTER 11

Selective Blindness

I mumbled "goodbye" to my aunt and hung up the telephone. I sat in my darkened office for a couple of hours after hanging up and was still sitting there when everyone else had gone home. I couldn't think of a safe place to escape other than staying there. At the moment, it seemed as safe a place as any. This was my first private office: not a cubicle, but a room with walls. If you are going to choose a place to hide, better make it one with walls and a door. That way you can keep everyone out but yourself. For better or worse, you're stuck with yourself.

My office had been a utility room at one point. It was an odd triangle shape. The window was too high up to see through without standing on the desk. Sometimes I did just that: stood on my desk in order to have a real good look outside. Doing this had the effect of making me feel more closed in, as if I'd been sentenced to jail. Still, this was my first office, and it was a badge of success, or at least progress of a sort. My mother would have been proud.

Though I considered my office comfortable and lived in, in reality it was merely cluttered. All around me were piles of papers and folders. My drawers were filled with piles and stacks of stuff I rarely looked at. When you looked at my office with objective eyes, it was all corners, sharp and forbidding to outsiders, who could never get comfortable in it. To me, however, the fact that it was private and could be closed against intruders and friends made me feel successful even if success came in a tiny triangle of an office with a window too high up to look through. My only problem with my office was that it could get quite dark when the daylight outside dimmed. This was darkness that no ordinary recessed lighting could deal with. I always used to think of myself as someone who was good at being alone, but I am really just good at being "in between" other people. I am fine being by myself as long as it is temporary. It's funny how you can feel alone and separate all your life and not grow to like it more.

My brother learned the aloneness lesson better than I did. He's been solitary all his life and doesn't much like or invite people to intrude on his aloneness. But even he's not entirely successful at it. My brother keeps the television on all night long, filling the hours up with someone else's script of what life should be like. The television set is his adult night light, which, I suppose, doesn't differentiate him much from lonely people finding solace in 3:00 A.M. infomercials.

When we were children, bedtime wasn't a pleasant experience for my brother and me. There was too much uncharted scariness waiting out there in the darkness. To combat the great, dark unknown, my brother used a night light until he was twelve. If something was going to grab him in the darkness, he wanted a chance to get at it first. My brother was one wary kid, always keeping watch. Now he's a wary adult. He remembers every wound and who inflicted it and has plans to get even. Once you injure my brother, saying "I'm sorry" is never enough, because he keeps the memory of the original pain as fresh as when it happened. The only one he forgives is his daughter. Maybe he wants to spare her all the lessons that those of us who go through life unforgiven learn early and never forget.

My father offered me a night light for my bedroom too when I was a little girl, but I told him no. I didn't need to keep the monsters at bay with a nighttime vigil, because by the time I was five years old, I'd perfected the art of selective blindness. If I didn't want to see something, it just wasn't there. I didn't want to see the monsters before they crawled out from underneath my bed and "got me," whatever "getting me" entailed. I just squeezed my eyes shut and refused to look.

Now, sitting in my quiet, dark, triangle office, I squeezed my eyes shut for a while and tried not to look. This began to feel like cowardice, and I opened my eyes and fixed my gaze on a spider web in the corner of my office. It was late, 8:00 P.M., and all my workmates had gone home. I could hear the janitor out in the hall vacuuming haphazardly down the hallways and through the center of all the offices, avoiding the corners. This was probably why the spider web, on which my attention was fixed, had survived. For a while, the janitor and I were comrades of a sort, lulled by the sound of his vacuum humming along through the empty offices. After a bit, the sound of the vacuum stopped, and there was a soft tap on my door, the tentative sort of knock that a child might make, afraid of reprimand.

"Ma'am," the janitor's voice came through my door, "may I clean your office?"

And as if some sort of spell I was under had been broken, I became an adult again, far from my childhood and all those ghosts I imagined still chasing me. I stood up, gathered my purse and briefcase. As a calm, reasonable adult, I could only sit in my dark office contemplating my guilt for so long. I had justice to pursue, at the end of which was someone else's guilt.

I'm of the television generation, so I'm always looking for a script to tell me how to behave. My television-watching experiences taught me that justice was swift. Murderers were arrested, tried and convicted within an hour, two at the most. Not only that, but the victim's family recovered from their grief before the credits rolled. With justice for my mother either creeping slowly along or perhaps even stalled completely, I needed some sort of signal so that I could figure out what to do, but none came.

Of course, I always had my memories.

However, since they can change with a mood or a whim, memories can't be trusted to tell you the truth. It's true that memories can surprise you from time to time, but it's what you've forgotten that shocks the hell out of you when you are alone in the darkness. When we're finally all grown up, we learn that those lessons about everything that went before have a price attached to them. The price is that we can never pretend that we don't know again. We are stuck knowing and remembering. At this point, I wasn't ready to learn anything more revealing about my mother than who had killed her. I wanted to solve the mystery of her murder. I still wasn't ready to solve the mystery of whom she had been.

Meanwhile, my business life rolled on. I was promoted, and the company I worked for was sold twice, during the end of 1994 and the beginning of 1995. Following the second sale, everyone in my division was laid off, and I began to start thinking about what I wanted to be when I grew up. In June of 1995, I chose to go back to college full-time and finish my degree. I also decided that I wanted to make my living as a writer. For years, I'd kept my intention to write quiet, keeping my ambition to myself and only whispering it into the mirror as if it were something to be ashamed of—sort of a Cinderella theory of ambition, where you wait to be discovered as beautiful among the ashes. But now, when people asked me what I did, I told them I was a writer. I repeated my ambition so often that it became a mantra of sorts. "Hello, I'm Paula Mints, writer." It became as much a part of my identity as the reality of my blue eyes and migraine headaches, and often as annoying as the latter.

Tom and I didn't spend much time together at this point. The fact that both of us were so busy was our excuse for allowing the distance between us that vacillated between comfortable and uncomfortable to grow. We were comfortable with it when it meant we could do what we wanted, when we wanted, and with whom we wanted. We had no friends in common anymore and spent holidays apart, me with my friends, Tom with his. On my side of the bed most nights, I was forlorn, longing for the comfort that comes between couples when they are in bed—an arm outstretched or the comfortable groove of your lover's shoulder, where you know your head is welcome to lie. Late at night, when I wanted to hold someone and be held, I missed the comfort of our relationship. The rest of the time, though, I was too busy to remember that I was lonely.

By May 1996, I had a year of study left before graduation from San Jose State University, and after that, I planned to pursue my MBA. I liked business and was good at it. I considered my business degrees an expansion of my goal to write. Also, I imagined that an MBA would imbue me with an aura of professionalism, and success would surely follow. The better to support myself, I thought, the lesson of a dead, homeless mother hanging over me.

I was also working part-time, doing contract writing for a small consulting agency in Sunnyvale, California. We handled overflow writing work from software and hardware companies throughout the area. I wrote "how-to-do-it" kinds of stuff for the high-tech crowd, manuals about how to install a motherboard or work with some obscure software tool.

The company I worked for was located on the first floor of a two-story white office building. We occupied two offices. There were five of us, four writers and our supervisor, who also functioned as the company salesperson. My boss had a closet-like office to himself, and the rest of us shared the other 300-square-foot office. We were a close-knit group, not because of any special affinity for each other, but because we spent our days crammed together. The desks and filing cabinets all butted up against each other. Leaving the office to go to the bathroom involved maneuvering through a maze-like corridor between desks. We all had bruises on our thighs from bumping into the corners and edges of the furniture.

With school and work occupying my time, I didn't have many hours left over to spend with friends. But I continued my homicide-nagging duties. In truth, I believe that my mother was forgotten by justice and that I alone remembered that there was something to atone for. To me, succeeding in my life was atonement for my mother never having the chance to see me become educated and successful. Occasionally, I closed my eyes and pictured her looking straight at me, instead of avoiding

eye contact as she did when she was her sickest. I imagined her approval, but I could not enjoy it, for in the recesses of my mind the fact that her killer had still not
been brought to trial loomed.

However, not even stalled justice stays that way permanently. One morning before I left for work, I received a
phone call from Officer Maler.

"Paula," Maler said, dispensing with the hellos and
other pleasantries, "I wanted to update you. It looks like
we're finally moving forward." I could tell that he was excited, because his voice kept jerking up a note and then
back down a note, as if he were taking his tonal inflec-
tion cues from sheet music. I imagined myself standing
at a podium conducting his speech. *Good staccato,* I'd say.
Now from the top.

Officer Maler cleared his throat and continued, "Assistant District Attorney Jim Shore will be giving you a call."

I dropped my mental baton. "Ah," I said. "Hmm," I
continued. "I see." At this point, having either nothing
clever or intelligent to say, I shut up.

Officer Maler continued, "Mr. Shore wants to talk to
you about your mother's case." He paused, and I thought
I heard the sound of papers shuffling. He continued,
"There's a deal on the table." Pause. "I've already spoken
to your brother."

Now this was a surprise. "My brother has always left
anything to do with our mother's murder to me. When
did my brother call you?"

"He didn't call, he was up here last week on vacation,
and he stopped by." Officer Maler paused again. Papers
were shuffled. Another pause. "Didn't he talk to you about
it?" he asked.

"No," I said. I bit my lip. I thought about explaining to
Officer Maler about the Rothwell family secrecy, but
thought better of it. Some family heritages are best kept

unexplained to those outside the family circle. "What do you mean, there's a deal on the table? I thought there was a trial in the eventual offing."

"Trials are expensive to put on." Officer Maler cleared his throat. "Not to mention painful for the victims. If we can arrive at some sort of accommodation, it's really better for everyone."

"'Put on' sounds like a musical," I said.

"Well," Officer Maler said, "it is, sort of."

"Also, it seems to me that a trial would be a piece of cake for a dead person," I continued.

"Dead person?" Officer Maler repeated.

"Yes, my mother was the victim. And she's too dead to be upset by the prospect of a trial." There was an awkward pause after I said this. At least, I felt awkward. Maler could have been picking lint off his shirt for all I knew.

"Mr. Shore will be calling you in the next day or so," Officer Maler said.

"Should I call him instead?" I asked.

"No, he'll call you. Just be patient. Should be a couple of days."

"I think I've heard the phrase, 'These things take time' once too often," I said.

"Excuse me?" Officer Maler asked.

"You know, these things take time. The murder happens real fast, but the investigation, arrest, and trial, they just take forever," I said.

Officer Maler didn't reply. I imagined him sitting there wondering what to say and hoping I'd end the conversation.

"Thanks for calling," I said. I hung up the phone. When my mother was alive, I'd had no control over what happened to her, but now that she was dead, I'd be damned if I had no control over bringing her murderer to justice. The requirement of remaining patient was beginning to make me feel ill.

"Screw it," I said to myself, and the sound lingered in the room. I picked up the phone, dialed Information, and asked for the phone number of the district attorney's office. Then I called Mr. Shore. "Hello, this is Paula Mints," I said, "Elaine Rothwell's daughter. I want to meet with you in the next twenty-four hours to talk about the trial of Richard Carrasco. I want to be sure everything is on track." Shore gave me an appointment to meet with him the following morning. Afterward, I called my boss and told him that I wasn't coming in to work.

That evening and all night long, I kept repeating, sometimes out loud but more often to myself, *Office of the District Attorney, Office of the District Attorney*. In my imagination, the district attorney's office was located in one of those huge, glass-covered edifices where the floors were impossibly shiny and the windows remarkably clean. Justice, I thought, would be done at a great and shining height.

Despite my sleepless night, I woke up feeling alert. My skin felt prickly. My heart beat faster than usual. I skipped breakfast, avoided drinking any anxiety-creating coffee, and dressed with care. I hoped to create a serious demeanor by means of costuming, so I wore severe black with no jewelry and only mascara for makeup.

Instead of the tall, clean building of my imagination, the district attorney's office had a second-handness about it, with cracks in the dirty floor and an unnerving ride upstairs in an ancient elevator. Apparently, justice was done at a medium, rickety height. I held my breath on the slow ride up to the fifth floor. Once there, the elevator doors paused, as if they were deciding whether or not to open, moaning and complaining as if I was asking too much of them. When they finally opened, a man was standing on the other side. We stared at each other until the elevator doors began to close. The man grabbed the doors to stop them from closing.

"Paula Mints?" he asked.

"Mr. Shore," I responded, stepping out of the elevator before it could swallow me up again.

"Yes," he said and then looked down at me kindly. "Call me Jim." Red-haired with a touch of gray, he was over six feet tall and well built, looking as if he had once been an athlete.

"Well," he said, looking me directly in the eyes, "my office is this way." He seemed surprised by my appearance, and I wondered what he had expected. He'd met my long-haired, bearded brother and seen pictures of my homeless murdered mother. He could have expected any sort of apparition to step off the elevator. Then again, perhaps I was overdressed for the occasion.

I followed him down a skinny hallway bordered on one side by a dirty wall and on the other by dirty windows. At the end of the hall was a door with a glass window in the center and a buzzer on the side. The whole place had an asylumlike feel to it. Jim pushed the button and turned to me.

"I apologize for our offices," he said. "We're going to be moving into the armory in about six months."

"Hmm," I said, wondering how long we were going to be kept waiting in the hallway. "So, you'll be acting as my mother's lawyer? I mean, I know that she isn't on trial, but you're acting on her behalf?"

Jim looked down at me. "Well, technically I'm not defending your mother. It's a little complicated. I represent the people of California." He paused, looking up. "Oh, here we go." Someone buzzed us through, and we moved from the dirty hallway into a disorganized office space filled with people looking through piles of file folders, staring blankly at computer screens, or leaning back in their chairs talking on telephones.

I trotted along behind him towards his office. "I realize that you're not exactly defending her. She's not on trial," I said again, "though it sometimes feels like she is." I said to his back, "But in a way, you are her advocate."

"Well," Jim said, continuing to walk and not turning around, "not really." He stopped, opened a door, and stepped aside so I could enter his office.

Jim's office was tiny and surprisingly neat. The books in his bookcase were arranged in alphabetical order. The folders, papers and notepads on his desk were arranged in neat piles. The stuff on his desk reminded me of the kind of toy furniture found in doll houses: everything placed "just so" for effect. There was a bulletin board on the wall behind his desk covered with pictures of his wife and children. Two chairs were arranged in front of his desk, and I sat in one of them. Jim and I addressed each other across the neat piles of folders and papers on his desk.

"Back to what you were saying. I don't understand— my mother may have been homeless, but she was still one of the people of California." I crossed my legs and folded my hands in my lap.

"No, now I know this seems a rough distinction." Jim leaned back in his chair. "But your mother was a *person of California*, and that's different from being the *People of California*."

I folded my arms and leaned forward. "Maybe I'm being dense, but I don't get the difference. Isn't a person of California also one of the people of California?" I asked.

Jim leaned back even further in his chair. I imagined it swallowing him up into some legal black hole where everything is either hypothetical or circumstantial, and nothing is easily explained. "Once again, I know this is difficult to understand, but technically your mother was one person of California, not the People."

"Oh," I said, "I see. So what you're saying is that you represent the mass of anonymous people who make up the State of California and not the individual who was my mother?"

Jim didn't answer.

My stomach was beginning to hurt from leaning forward on my arms and from the feelings bubbling up inside me, so I sat back in my chair and let my arms rest in my lap, palms down. I concentrated on letting my fingers dangle casually into my lap. I could hear conversations from the surrounding offices. "No," I heard someone say, "don't you understand me? No." From another office I overheard someone say, "He said what? He must be crazy." I decided to keep my voice low.

"Okay," I said, making my voice into a loud whisper, "I'm sort of stuck on this people, person thing. My mother was a person, she may have been homeless, but her homeless residence was in California. Doesn't that make her one of the People of California? Don't the deaths of individual people count?" I began tapping my foot on the floor. *Steady girl*, I thought and decided to change tactics. "Okay, let's forget about that for a minute. What's this I hear about a deal?" I asked.

Jim picked up a pen and tapped it against his teeth. It made an annoying little clicking sound. "As you know, a lot of time has passed since your mother's murder." Jim put the pen back on his desk. "And the county has spent, well, bottom line, a great deal of money keeping Carrasco behind bars. It's time to move on as expediently as possible." Jim picked up a pencil and began chewing on it. The pencil was covered with teeth marks. I looked around his desk and saw that all of his pens and pencils had teeth marks on them. Either the man had great stores of suppressed energy, or he didn't get out to lunch very often.

"Look, I know this is tough," Jim said, "but I have to consider what would be most expedient for the State, meaning the People, of California. And difficult as it is to hear, one person's wants and needs sometimes have a lower priority. I know how that sounds, and for what it is worth, I'm sorry."

The back of my neck began to feel tight, as if my hackles were rising. If possible, I would have growled. "I don't think you can imagine how that sounds to someone whose mother was murdered."

"Paula, it's not as if I don't understand how you feel or what your concerns are as a victim."

"Victim?" My body felt prickly and the tips of my fingers began to tingle. *Maybe I'm having a heart attack*, I thought. *I'll probably drop dead right here on the floor. That'll show them.* I continued, "Look, my mother is the victim here. She was the one who was raped and murdered. I'm just the victim by proxy. But I am the one speaking for my mother." I paused. My hands were clenched in tight little fists. I unclenched them.

Jim put a pencil into his mouth and began to chew furiously. Every now and then he took the pencil out of his mouth and spoke. "I don't know if you realize what a trial will put you through," he said.

"Are you seriously trying to tell me that the pain of sitting through my mother's murderer's trial will be worse than being told she was murdered? Or identifying her body at the morgue? Do you think sitting through a trial is worse than being raped and murdered in the first place? Or the fact that the murderer might not be brought to trial and could cut a deal instead?" My hands trembled in my lap, and the back of my neck was so tight it felt like it was going to break.

Jim put down the pencil and fingered a pen. Finally, he sat up, leaned his elbows on his desk, and began chewing on his bottom lip. "Hear me out now." He paused and chewed on his lip for a moment. "Look, I don't think you understand how difficult a trial will be on you and your family. Sometimes people think that a trial will bring them closure, but that's usually not the case."

"Excuse me," I said, "I hate to interrupt you again, but you do not know how I feel. Look, I am not fool enough to believe that this trial represents closure, but it is my mother's right. Or at least my right as her daughter."

"Unfortunately," Jim said, frowning, "it's not her right."

"Pardon me?"

"Richard Carrasco has a right to a trial. Unfortunately, your mother and his other victims don't have that same right."

"Oh, I see." I looked down at my hands. Then I looked up. "Actually, I don't see, but I can see where the 'justice is blind' thing comes from." I sighed. "Other victims?" I asked.

Jim sat back in his chair. "Besides the crimes against your mother, Carrasco is accused of raping two other women."

I thought back to the articles I had researched. I wondered if these women were the same victims I had read about.

"They've had a difficult time putting their lives back together," Jim continued.

"Not half as difficult as the time my mother is having," I said.

Jim cocked his head to the side and looked distressed "Excuse me?" he asked.

"My mother is dead. The point I am trying to make is that putting your life together after a violent rape is horrible, but putting your life together after being murdered is impossible." I glared at Jim over the neat piles of folders on his desk.

"Look," Jim said, "this isn't pleasant stuff. To be blunt, he raped, sodomized, and orally copulated these women at knife point in their own bedrooms. One woke up with him in bed next to her. You sure you want to hear this?" Jim asked, staring at me.

"Yes, I do," I said, staring right back.

"Okay. One of the women was elderly. Apparently, Richard had some problems penetrating her, so he used foreign objects to, I guess you'd say, gain entry." Jim put the pencil down. "Naturally, these women do not want to relive the experience if they don't have to."

"Richard's been very busy," I said. I looked over Jim's head at the pictures of his family. I stared at a picture of Jim's children. The picture was of two small redheads, leaning together and smiling big for the camera. "What can you tell me about him?" I asked.

"Carrasco?" Jim stretched in his chair, crossed his hands behind his head, and frowned again. "He had a pretty crappy life. His mother was a drug addict and a prostitute, homeless sometimes, sleeping in cars with her children. When Carrasco was seven years old, he watched one of his stepfathers rape his mother and then beat her unconscious—not a happy childhood."

I looked down at the floor. "So what's the deal?" I asked.

"Thirteen years for your mother's rape and murder and fifteen years each for raping the other women. That means he should be up for parole in about twenty-five years." Jim tapped another pencil on his desk. "He's twenty-two now, so basically he'll spend most of his life in jail."

"Twenty-two? That would make him sixteen when he murdered my mother. He was just a kid."

"He's a predator. The sooner we get him behind bars,

the better," Jim said. His tone took on an iron edge. "He's a serial rapist."

I looked Jim directly in his eyes and said, "Please understand. I'm not kidding myself. But justice, I have to believe, is something more than what people talk about at parties, even when it's only partial. For there to have been full justice in my mother's case, she would not have died on the streets a homeless schizophrenic." I paused. "And I am sorry, but taking the advice of *professionals* is the last thing I am inclined to do anymore."

I leaned forward in my chair and didn't retreat. Jim leaned back in his. "The last time I saw my mother alive, I tried to have her committed at Valley Medical Center. The *professionals* there advised me not to commit her, because she would be locked up with dangerous people and could come to harm." I frowned. I looked past Jim at the pictures on his bulletin board. "But I'll tell you something. If you want my okay to make a deal with Richard Carrasco, if my consent is important at all, you can't have it. Because thirteen years for my mother's entire life of pain plus the way she died is just not an acceptable bargain."

A banging sound came from the next office. "That's Marlene," Jim said. "She drops her books on the floor when she's frustrated." Another bang. "She must be having a bad day." Jim smiled at me. It was an odd sort of smile, as if trying to divert me from my point. The edge of his mouth didn't make a smiling curve. His upper lip just lifted up a bit and levitated above the lower. When I didn't return his smile, he cleared his throat and sat up straight, crossing his arms on his desk. "Look, I know you don't like this, and neither do I, but there is a good chance that everything will be settled by Monday."

"What do you mean?" I asked.

"Well." Jim looked down at his hands. "To tell you the truth, I don't like it either, but my boss has already okayed the deal. Carrasco is going to think it over and let us know on Monday." Jim's eyes met mine. He didn't smile.

I took a moment to consider this. Apparently, the only battle going on here had been within me. Updating me was really just a courtesy. "Well," I said, "nice that he has some choice in the matter."

"Oh, hell. I know it's not fair. But Carrasco wants to take the weekend and talk it over with his mother before he makes a decision." Jim raised his hands in the air and sighed.

"Talk to his mother?" I laughed bitterly. "Nice for him. That's something I can never do again."

"I understand," Jim said and stood up. I stood also, and he held out his hand for me to shake. "I'll call you Monday," he said.

Jim walked me to the elevator. After I got in, he stood waiting until the doors slid shut. *This is what happens to troublemakers,* I thought on my way down. *They get swallowed up in this elevator, never to be seen again.*

I tried to stay busy all weekend. I gardened. I housecleaned. I wrote an entire short story and then deleted it from my computer's hard drive. Tom and I went to the movies and for the first time in a long while held hands. I went to bed around midnight on Sunday night, but my eyes wouldn't stay shut, and my mind wouldn't stay quiet. By three in the morning, I was a wreck. I got out of bed, paced through the house, turned on the television, and picked up magazines. Night is the worst time for these kinds of thoughts. Oh, you can vacuum the rug, rewash the dishes, brush the cat, and mop a floor or two, but all the chores in the world don't override what you don't want to think about, your heartache. What you can't get by in the quiet moments is that someone you loved is gone forever.

By Monday morning, I was jumping at every sound

and overreacting at the smallest imagined slight. Still, it felt anticlimactic when Jim Shore phoned to tell me that Richard Carrasco had been advised by the jailhouse lawyers to refuse the deal.

I found out from Jim that in jail, an inmate who chooses to defend himself is called a *pro se*. *Pro ses* study law books and write briefs; they're sort of like paralegals and are allowed to spend more time out of their cells and in the prison libraries, researching case law, and are allowed more visitors. They spend time thinking and talking about legal matters and are considered knowledgeable. Since a *pro se* doesn't wear a suit and isn't connected in any way to "the Man," a *pro se* is considered more trustworthy than an inmate's real attorney. Carrasco had been convinced by some of the *pro ses* that if he pled guilty without insisting on a trial he wouldn't survive his sentence. Once incarcerated, rapists—particularly rapists of old women and children—are unpopular, and Carrasco might well be convicted by a jury of his jailhouse peers and murdered.

Richard Carrasco refused the deal and wanted to go to trial. I didn't ask what his mother's opinion on the matter was.

CHAPTER 12

Confrontations and Configurations

A covered overhead walkway spans the street between the parking garage and the Santa Clara County Courthouse. Waiting to drive into the garage leaves plenty of time for pedestrian watching at the stop light, which forces you to sit in your car for about five minutes before it changes. A person can either concentrate on feeling their anxiety build or count the overhead pedestrians. As I'd had plenty of prior practice with anxiety, I chose to watch pedestrians. Finally, the light changed, I pulled into the garage, and stopped my car at the automatic ticket dispenser. "Please take your ticket," said a feminine-sounding mechanical voice. "Thank you. Have a nice day." I checked my watch. 11:30 A.M., July 22, 1996.

The real trial wasn't starting. You get a lot of dress rehearsals before the real show starts. Everyone just keeps getting all gussied up for the trial, while things are put

off one more time. After a while, you learn only to antic-
ipate more waiting. This way, you stave off disappointment and at the same time keep hope alive. The point
of today's court date was to set the actual trial date. This
would be done at one-thirty, in Department 24, with the
Honorable Harold Tolman as presiding judge. The district attorney had advised against my coming to court.
"Nothing to be gained by it," Jim Shore told me. "Nothing's going to happen. I'll call you. Really, I'll keep you
informed."

I was tired of being kept informed. Years of staying in
the background while people kept me informed had only
served to frustrate me, making me feel helpless. Every
time someone told me to be patient, I felt my mother die
again. The only way we had gotten this far was that I had
not been willing to be patient. I might not be able to
change anything by being in court, but I could at least
make my presence felt. The act of watching would make
me a participant. I had, after all, inherited my mother's
eyes to watch the world through. After many midnight
conversations with myself, I was convinced that I was here
to monitor justice, to make certain there were no delays
that I could ameliorate, or at least find out the real reasons if there were delays. I told myself these lies so that I
wouldn't think about how much I needed to look in the
face of the person who killed my mother.

I am a nervous car parker, having trouble with tight
spaces and other boundaries, so it was noon when I finally
parked my car. I didn't get out. Instead, I stayed put for an
hour staring at the newspaper I had brought. Unable to
concentrate, I found myself reading the same few articles
over and over.

At 1:00 P.M. I got out of my car, and having given up on
the newspaper, I left it behind.

When I arrived at the courthouse steps, there was a

line waiting to go through a metal detector. I stood behind a man wearing a gray suit who carried an over-flowing briefcase in one hand and held a newspaper in the other. Behind me were two Hispanic women. They held babies and spoke to each other in Spanish. I was in a hyper-aware state, noticing everything and curious about it all. The little details of being in line were com-forting, delaying as they did what awaited me inside. I kept myself busy, looking around at everyone. I wanted to remember every impression so I could carry with me how it felt to stand in this line, on this day when the timetable for the trial of my mother's murderer would fi-nally be set.

The crowd inched forward. I glanced back over my shoulder and was surprised to see that the line now stretched down to the sidewalk and along the street. A hot-dog vendor stood on the corner, selling his wares to the people waiting. The man in front of me shook his paper and checked his watch. Two children played hide-and-seek around my legs, and three people stepped out of line and lit cigarettes. Line-dwellers all, we shuffled slowly forward. After a while part of me began to wish the line would move faster, but thinking about my desti-nation, I found I didn't mind that much that it seemed to move in slow motion. Finally I was inside the door of the building. I obeyed a sign instructing me to place my purse on a conveyer belt, and I stepped through the metal detector, which buzzed.

"Step back," said a bored looking sheriff. I stepped back. "Step forward." Same bored looking sheriff. I stepped forward. The detector buzzed. "Step back. Step forward." Buzz. "Step back. Step forward." Buzz. "Step back." He motioned me back with a wave of his hand.

"Step forward." The sheriff motioned me forward. Buzz.

"Anything in your pockets?" he asked.

"I don't have any pockets," I said.

"See the officer." He motioned to the woman in back of me. "Next."

Behind me the metal detector buzzed again. I walked forward to the sheriff at the end of the line. He ran a metal bar around my body and motioned me to proceed.

My destination was Department 24, which, according to the directory on the wall, was in the basement. I took the elevator down and found the basement crowded with the afternoon's grouping of the accused, their lawyers and observers. I assumed there was probably a smattering of my fellow victims also, but I didn't know how to pick them out of the crowd. We weren't wearing name tags. A clipboard hung on the wall by Department 24, listing docket numbers followed by names and then more numbers. I looked down the list until I found Carrasco. His name appeared next to numbers 13 and 14 and had two different docket numbers. I touched his name with my index finger.

"That's our boy," I heard from behind me.

I turned around and looked up. Jim Shore stood there, looking down from his great height.

I took my finger away. "Why is he listed twice?" I asked.

"Last month he assaulted a fellow prisoner. They're setting the trial date for that today too." Jim leaned forward and looked at the list. "Docket one-seven-three-zero-six-seven. That's us."

"How long will it take to get to number thirteen?" I asked.

"Depends on how behind they are." Jim put his hand on the small of my back and nudged me towards the double doors. I allowed myself to be propelled forward into the courtroom.

Jim excused himself and went to talk with his fellow

district attorneys, leaving me with the beginnings of a panic attack. I fought back my anxiety by memorizing the details of the courtroom.

It was divided in half: on one side the people and on the other, the law. It was noisy, and I didn't know where to look. Between us was a waist-high wooden barrier with a swinging gate in the middle. Bailiffs stood on the other side, scanning the courtroom. I had sat in an uncomfortable chair in the second row when I noticed two signs in front of me:

FIRST TWO ROWS RESERVED FOR ATTORNEYS ONLY, and ALL COMMUNICATION WITH PRISONERS, VERBAL, WRITTEN, OR SIGNAL, IS UNLAWFUL WITHOUT PERMISSION OF DEPUTIES. SECTION 4570 PENAL CODE.

I got up and moved back a row.

Jim came back and sat beside me. "They're going to be bringing the prisoners in soon," he said. "They'll be in different-colored uniforms. Orange for the main prison population, green for prisoners who are mentally ill, and red for those accused of violent crimes."

"You'd make a good tour guide," I said to him, trying for humor. I gathered that I'd failed in my attempt, as he didn't answer me and just looked at me sideways from the corner of one eye. Unfortunately, the more anxious I am, the stranger my remarks become. I seem compelled to try for wittiness to ameliorate stress. "What color will he be wearing?" I asked. At this point, I couldn't bring myself to call my mother's murderer Richard, or even Richard Carrasco. There was something unnerving about the intimacy of using his name. I tried saying the name in my mind, *Richard Carrasco, Richard Carrasco.* The effort made my head hurt.

"He'll be wearing red, because he's considered violent and dangerous," Jim said and began looking through a manila folder. "They'll come into the courtroom through that door." He motioned with his folder towards the left side of the courtroom. Across the barrier and against a wall were three rows of seats.

"Is that where they sit?"

Jim glanced up from his folder. "Yeah," he said, "and Carrasco will sit in those chairs." He motioned with his free hand. Against the same wall were six chairs, separated from the others by glass. The violent criminals had their own in-court cage, like game show contestants that are kept separate so that they won't hear the answers to the questions they'll be asked.

After a bit, a door on the other side of the wooden barrier opened, and a bailiff stepped into the room. He held the door open, stood to the side, and gestured. Fifteen men in orange uniforms came through and sat down. The bailiff shut and locked the door and waited for them to get settled. Then he unlocked and opened the door again. Three men in red uniforms came through. They wore shackles and shuffled their feet, and their chains made rattling sounds. One man was tall and blond, and another was tall with a dark complexion. The man in the middle was Hispanic. He stood about five-feet-six-inches tall. Most of his hair was shaved into a crew cut, but there was a long pigtail hanging from the top, and he had a long, thin mustache. He didn't relax into his seat like his two companions but leaned forward in his chair, glancing around the courtroom. He looked into every corner and at every face but didn't seem to be looking for anyone in particular. His expression was curious rather than anxious. When he looked at me, he stopped. He didn't look away. As we held each other's gaze, I thought, *I'll bet this is him.* My heart began to pound, and I felt a little nauseous.

Jim nudged me, and I turned to look at him. Turning

put the scene momentarily out of focus, and I blinked to clear my vision.

"That's our boy. That's Carrasco," Jim said.

"Who?" I asked.

Jim pointed, "The man with the pigtail."

I looked at the floor for a moment. There was a smudge on the end of my shoe. I concentrated on it. The conversations around me merged into one loud hum, and I could feel my heart beating faster and faster. "Wow," I said, "this is a strange feeling."

Jim gripped his folder. "Are you all right?" he asked. "I told you this wasn't going to be pleasant." He looked at me while he spoke, but he didn't look directly into my eyes. He seemed nervous, and I wondered if he expected me to collapse or have a fit. Probably after our conversation in his office he'd been led to expect the possibility of hysteria. The right to be emotionally vulnerable is always suspect and often denied.

"I'm not going to be ill," I said, realizing as I said it that this was true. "It's just an odd feeling. Nothing more. Just odd." That odd feeling then became physical, spreading from my shoulder blades, down my back, and around to my stomach. I felt as if I were being squeezed in a vise. I wanted to either throw up or faint, neither of which would have been appropriate in court. Instead, I squirmed and felt guilty for it.

Jim relaxed into his chair and began reading his file, freeing me to look back at Richard Carrasco.

Carrasco was talking to the man next to him now, so I could study him more closely. He had a wide, smashed-looking nose and beard stubble on his chin. He began to laugh. Finally, he turned and looked at me again. He stopped laughing, and his smile faded away. I looked into his eyes, which were less friendly now. They had a harder look to them, as if he were daring me to look away. I stared

at the sign in front of me: ALL COMMUNICATION
WITH PRISONERS VERBAL, WRITTEN, OR SIGNAL, IS
UNLAWFUL WITHOUT PERMISSION OF DEPUTIES.
Then I looked at the clock. When I looked back at Carrasco, he was still staring at me. He leaned forward in his
chair with his hands on the seat, staring at me. I was
shocked that I didn't see a rapist and murderer in his face.
He didn't look crazed, angry, or even especially violent. If
it is true that our lives are written on our faces, then the
writing hadn't begun on Carrasco yet. Or maybe anger
and violence are meant to be invisible, hidden parts
of our experience and potential. If we could ever see the
potential for doing harm written on the faces around us,
we would likely never leave our houses. The realization
that I didn't know what was going to happen next was
sobering.

I looked away from Carrasco at a spot on the ceiling
tile.

"I'll see you in a few minutes." Jim got up and walked
to the front of the room where he began talking to the
other attorneys. It seemed to me like court was an "us
and them" club: the attorneys in front of the courtroom
beyond the barrier, and us, sitting in uncomfortable
chairs, waiting to get on with things.

I looked at the clock again. It was now 1:40. The judge
was ten minutes late. Of course, after six years, what was
another ten minutes? I asked myself. I was there, after
all, to claim control for my brother and my mother, and
for myself. At least, that's why I thought I was there.

Once again, my thoughts fixated on the man in the red
suit behind the glass. It was ironic and more than a little
bizarre that at that moment I had more in common with
Richard Carrasco than with anyone else in the courtroom. What we had in common was my mother, except
that he owned the rights to my mother's last minutes.

Aside from being responsible for her death, he was also guilty of another crime: the theft of her last moments on earth—how she looked, what she thought. I wanted to take back from him that experience. I looked at Carrasco and tried to harden my face.

It didn't work, and I felt a headache begin at my right temple and move slowly across my forehead. I was invisible and unimportant here. Even my mother wasn't a party to these events. Carrasco had placed us all in the middle of a system that lumbered along at its own pace. Resolution, in the process, was not really the point. Right now, Carrasco was waiting to go back to his cell, and I was just an observer, waiting for some acknowledgment. This wasn't really about my mother.

"All rise," the bailiff said as the judge, an imposing man in his sixties, came into the courtroom. "Department Twenty-four is now in session, the Honorable Harold Tolman presiding."

"Thank you, and please be seated," Judge Tolman said. He folded his hands in front of him. "Now, what do we have today?" he asked, as his clerk handed him a stack of files.

Jim stayed in the front of the room while cases were called. One after another, busy-looking attorneys and their humble clients approached and were given dates to return. After a while, I realized that the point of the afternoon seemed to be postponement.

"Docket number one-seven-three-zero-six-seven, the People of California versus Richard Carrasco," the court clerk finally read aloud from her list. I leaned forward in my seat. I had trouble seeing around the people in front of me and raised myself a bit out of my chair.

"Are the People present?" asked the judge.

"Yes, Your Honor," Jim said.

"The defense?" the judge asked without looking up. He leaned his head on one hand.

"Yes, Your Honor. Brent Mathews with the public defender's office here for the defense." A stocky man in a gray seersucker suit walked to the front of the courtroom and stood next to the violent criminal section. Richard Carrasco stood up also. Brent leaned over to Richard and said something. Richard smiled and nodded. Brent turned back to the judge. "May we approach?" he asked.

The judge nodded. Jim and Brent Mathews moved towards the judge. They talked for about five minutes, Jim gesturing with his folder, wearing a disbelieving look on his face. Mathews wore a sincere and serious expression, and the judge's face was softened into paternal benevolence. Finally, everyone returned to their places.

The whole thing had a staged look to it, as if the judge and two attorneys were playing out a familiar scene, made dull by repetition. My headache moved from the front of my head to the back, and from there traveled down my spine.

Judge Tolman said, "I get it. This matter is reset for one week."

Jim came over to me. "Okay," he said, "that's it for today."

I gathered my purse and followed him out into the hall. Brent Mathews was behind us. Once in the hall, Jim led us a bit away from the other people standing around. "Brent Mathews," he said, pointing at the public defender, "meet Paula Mints. Her mother was one of the victims."

Brent looked me in the eye. His gaze began and ended with my pupils. "I know," he said and turned back to Jim. "Look, I'm sorry about this," he said and shrugged.

"Hey," Jim said, "what can you do?"

Brent shrugged again.

The foreign language I heard in the courtroom had

apparently extended itself to the hallway. "Tell me," I asked Brent, in an effort to direct the conversation, "what's he like?" I paused and bit my lip. "Richard Carrasco, I mean."

Brent took a long time to answer. When he finally looked at me, he wrinkled his forehead and stared intently, as if he was trying to classify my interest. Though, as the daughter of the deceased, I imagined my interest in my mother's murderer to be obvious; as a victim, I realized I had no real place in the justice system. Victims create a roadblock in the smooth processing of cases.

Finally, Brent said, "He's a kid." He said it in an almost belligerent fashion, making eye contact with me and seeming to dare me to disagree.

"A kid?" I said, "A kid who rapes and murders elderly homeless women." Thinking of Richard Carrasco as a kid was a stretch for me. The problem was that after seeing him in court, I didn't know how to think about him. I had been expecting a more defined monster. Now I felt separated from both my mother and my equilibrium.

"Is he sorry?" I asked. The problem was that, in my mother's case, we were all to some degree the bad guys. I sensed, however, that to keep the conversation going, I would have to pretend not to care. I needed to pretend to have no feelings so that Carrasco's attorney would talk to me. If I showed him my pain, guilt, and confusion, I would become the enemy. Still, I really wanted a hallway confession.

Brent looked directly into my eyes. He wore a hard, closed-up expression that I imagined must take a great deal of practice. "Is he sorry? I would say so." Then he walked away, down the hall.

I turned to Jim. "Okay, what does that mean?" I asked.

"It's kind of a complicated story," Jim said.

"Try."

"Okay." Jim looked away for a moment. "Well, Brent Mathews is Carrasco's second public defender. Carrasco fired the first one. But before he did that, Carrasco's ex-girlfriend told the first public defender that Carrasco had confessed your mother's murder to her."

"Isn't that a good thing?" I asked. My insides felt compressed, as if a weight had been placed on my stomach. *Here it is*, I thought, *the confession. Now it can end.*

"Sort of," Jim said. "Sort of good in that we can go to the girlfriend and get her to give us a statement, which will be useful." Jim rubbed his chin. "Sort of bad in that the first public defender didn't pass this information on to Brent, and now there is a conflict of interest in the public defender's office."

"Excuse me," I said, "but all I can think of to say is, 'Huh?'"

"Hey, I know, I know," Jim said, "but basically, the court needs to appoint a new attorney, and I'm sorry to say that puts us back to square one."

"What does that mean?" I asked.

"It means that a new attorney will be appointed next Monday, and after that, the case will be delayed anywhere from six to nine months."

Another long week passed. We went back to court on July 29. I wore severe black once again, toned-down makeup, no jewelry, and low heels for court. Before I left the house, I looked in the mirror and noticed a new wrinkle between my eyes, a little furrow just deep enough to give me an annoyed appearance. I looked like an angry nun. When I arrived in the basement of the courthouse, I went straight to the bathroom and sat in a stall on the toilet seat with my head in my hands. There would be another delay, or things would finally move forward. Either way, I didn't know how I felt other than numb.

In the courtroom, I sat in the third row near the aisle,

saving a seat for Jim. Next to me, three nervous women compared notes on their arrests. They apparently all knew each other from past court appearances and incarcerations. As they waited for court to be called into session, they discussed rehabilitation stays and new boyfriends. I leaned over a bit and listened to their conversation.

"This time wasn't as bad as the others," one said. "The cops were nicer for one thing, and since then, I've been working my program."

"Bless you," the second said. "I just don't know what'll happen to my children if I get sent away again."

"Mine are on the streets," the third one offered.

It must have become obvious that I was listening to them, because the woman next to me turned and gave me an unpleasant stare. Then they all got up and moved to seats on the other side of the courtroom. Up until then, I had felt like an invisible observer, so I was startled when my eavesdropping was discovered. The truth was that coming to court brought back painful memories of my life with my first husband. I had pushed that period of my life into the recesses of my mind. My escape from the sort of despair the women exhibited had been a slim one, and I was grateful for the reprieve. Yet, my mother's murder brought me into contact with those times again. In a way, my mother's fate made me face who I no longer was, as well as what I was now.

The prisoners were brought into the courtroom. The moment Carrasco sat down, he began to look around. He conducted a systematic visual search, beginning with the back rows and sweeping forward. When his gaze came to rest on me, he leaned forward in his chair and looked me in the eyes. His expression was serious. I stared back, waiting for him to blink.

"How are you doing today?" Jim asked as he sat down next to me, and I broke my stare to talk to Jim.

"Fine," I answered. "Listen, does he know who I am? Does Carrasco know who I am now?" Referring to him as "Carrasco" allowed me to erect a barrier against the unwanted intimacy of murderer and victim's daughter. He had, after all, raped my mother and had forceful knowledge of her body, her most intimate feminine self. The thought of his knowledge made me shiver, and I could not allow myself to think about it for long.

Jim's face wore a pensive expression, and I wondered if he could read my thoughts and if so, what warning he wanted to impart. "Well, you felt you needed to come," he said grudgingly.

"Not really an answer to my question. Yes, I did. So, does he?"

"Yeah. Brent Mathews told him," Jim said. "Look, can I see you in the hall for a minute? Something's come up."

I looked back at Carrasco. He was still staring at me, but this time his expression had gone past intent all the way to angry. Looking at him made me feel quiet and still, as if I were a small animal in the forest trying to avoid detection by a larger predator. I felt afraid, and I began to be angry with myself and then with him. What right did he, a murderer of homeless women, have to make me feel afraid? Still, when I imagined meeting him in a situation where I would be helpless, my fear was palpable.

I got up and followed Jim to where he was waiting for me outside the double doors. We were surrounded by anxious looking people. Their anxiety made them seem helpless, and I didn't want to give the same impression, so I smiled.

"Yes?" I said, forcing the corners of my mouth to remain upright in a sort of smile salute. Even my teeth felt stiff.

"We have a problem," Jim said. He motioned for me to follow him and then walked towards the elevators.

"Yes?" I asked, feeling my smile fall away and trotting after him. He walked very fast. "Problem?" I said to his shoulder blades.

Jim stopped walking and turned to me. "The court appointed Phillip McGuire to defend Carrasco."

"Why isn't that a good thing?" I asked. "Now we can move forward. You know, have an actual trial. What a concept." Years of frustration and waiting for the justice I had helped bring about made me sound both impatient and difficult to deal with.

"Last night Carrasco dismissed McGuire as his attorney. He wants to defend himself." Jim stopped talking and looked down at me. He didn't smile and neither did I. Silence filled the space. After a while, Jim continued, "This means a couple of things for us. First of all, Carrasco will need more time to prepare than Phillip McGuire would have, so the trial will be delayed for . . ." Jim paused and looked down at his well-shined oxfords. He stared at them for such a long time that I looked also. They looked like fine, comfortable shoes. "About a year," Jim said to his shoes.

"What?" I completely lost interest in his shoes. "A year?" I felt dizzy and angry to the point of rage. "My mother has been erased. She lived her entire life as an invisible woman—the more she needed help, the more she was ignored. As a murder victim, she was still invisible, and now, in a way, I have been erased with her. How long does he get to play these games? When does this end?"

Another attorney tapped Jim on the shoulder. "Excuse me, I'll be right back," Jim said and walked away.

I stood in the courthouse hallway, my thoughts thrashing about in my mind. It wasn't enough that Richard Carrasco had raped and murdered my mother. Now he would get to assault her memory again and again. A numbness started at the top of my head and worked its way down to my feet. All I could do was stand and stare at the wall.

"Paula?" Jim stood before me again. "He could change his mind. Actually, he probably will. Don't get upset."

"Jim, I am tired of hearing really bad news and then being told not to get upset."

"Okay, okay." Jim held his hands up level with his chest in a placating manner.

It's interesting that if you remain calm no matter what happens to you, people think that you don't care. If you get upset and show emotion, people think that you're falling apart. Emotional middle ground must be signified by some graceful lifting of eyebrows or other small gesture.

"Is there any more bad news?" I asked. I tried to make my face expressionless but felt a tic start at the corner of my eye.

"Well, we still need to talk about your status as a witness."

"What could I possibly be a witness to? I didn't see my mother for three years before she died," I said. My voice was beginning to rise, and I fought to control it. I learned from my mother that shrill people are never taken seriously.

Jim made another placating motion with his hands. "We need someone to testify to your mother's mental state and her ability to consent to sex."

"What?" My voice rose several octaves, so I shut up and took a deep breath. "My mother was schizophrenic. Part of her paranoia was a fear of men and sex. She would never have consented to sex with any man."

Jim looked at me, then back at his shoes, then at me. Silently, we held one of those I-know-what-you-know-and-you-know-I-do exchanges. Of course, I realized, he must know that not only had I searched for her murderer, I'd read the autopsy and other reports. For a moment, neither of us said anything.

I was the first to give in. "Okay. I know about," I made my voice into a whisper, "the genital warts." I took a deep breath. "She must have been raped other times before her death, because she never would have consented to have sex with anyone. Look, she didn't even have sex with my father after my brother was born." I looked down at Jim's shoes. I didn't want to look away from them. "Up until now, I never wanted to closely examine my mother's pain. I didn't want to think about her life as a homeless schizophrenic." I looked into Jim's face. "But I'm ready now. If you think I can help as a witness, I am ready."

"You need to think it over, because if you act as a witness in this case, you cannot attend the trial." Jim paused and sighed. "And if Carrasco defends himself, he'll be the one to cross-examine you."

So, I wouldn't be able to watch the trial of my mother's murderer, and he would get to question me about her. I must have looked like I was going to pass out, because Jim suddenly reached forward and grabbed my elbow.

"You mean he gets to ask me questions about my mother?"

Jim nodded. His face was as bleak as my thoughts. "He can ask you anything he wants. Unfortunately, judges tend to bend over backwards to make certain that a *pro se's* rights are not violated." Jim shook his head. "Carrasco has a massive ego, and he's going to play this to the hilt." Jim gave me a minute to absorb the news. "Come on, we better get back."

Court was already in session when we returned. I tiptoed to my seat, which miraculously had been saved for me. Jim went to the front of the room and began talking to one of the bailiffs.

I looked over at Carrasco. He was talking to another

red-suited prisoner. They laughed together. I hated him. I could see the word *hate* in my mind. The letters were all capitals. I felt my upper lip curl. Feeling this way didn't leave any room for fear. It made me feel invincible. Carrasco turned and looked at me. He leaned forward in his chair and stared. It was an intimidating look. *What a coward you are*, I thought and grimaced. It was a "fuck you" sort of grimace. I didn't want to hate him. It gave us too much in common. Then again, I sure as hell wasn't going to like him either.

Carrasco looked away. Suddenly, I realized my ability to look at him without looking away made him uncomfortable. I felt exhilarated. I kept my gaze on his face. There was no longer a connection between us. I was the owner of the memory of my mother, not him. All he had was his hatred. I felt freer than I had in months.

The court clerk called our case. Carrasco stood up, and Jim moved towards the bench.

The judge took a moment to read from a file. "I understand the defendant wishes to take on *pro se* status?" He said, "Mr. Carrasco, do you understand the ramifications of this choice?"

"Excuse me, Your Honor." A man with salt and pepper hair walked swiftly by me to the front of the courtroom. He paused by Carrasco, spoke to him briefly, and then walked towards the judge. "Philip McGuire here," he said and then opened a file he was carrying and looked down. I noticed that he had a very large head for his body size.

"Yes, Mr. McGuire," Judge Tolman said. "I came to understand you are no longer representing Mr. Carrasco."

"That changed as of this morning, Your Honor." Philip McGuire looked up from his file. "The defendant has agreed to be represented by counsel."

"Good decision," the judge said. "How long will you need to prepare?"

"Just a minute," McGuire replied. He spoke to Jim for a moment. They nodded their heads and smiled. More nodding. More smiling. I looked at Carrasco, and he was smiling too. Everyone seemed very pleased with themselves. Finally, McGuire spoke. "This is a complicated case, Your Honor. Frankly, I'd like about eight months to prepare."

"That's not acceptable to the People, Your Honor," Jim said.

Good for you, Jim, I thought.

"Your Honor." McGuire cocked his head to the side, turned to look at Carrasco for a moment, and then addressed the judge. "We're talking twenty-eight counts of rape here, witnesses with poor memories, not to mention other problems. I need time to put on a proper defense."

Judge Tolman didn't say anything for a moment. He folded his hands. He pursed his lips. Finally, he said, "Trial date will be set on March fifth, nineteen ninety-seven at nine A.M. in this courtroom."

Jim and Phillip McGuire moved to one side of the courtroom and spoke briefly. Afterwards, McGuire spoke to Carrasco and then rapidly left the courtroom. Jim came over to me.

"Let's go," he said.

We didn't talk as we walked to the elevators. And we didn't say anything as we rode upstairs and walked out to the sidewalk. Jim walked me to the stairs leading to the parking garage.

"I'm sorry for the delay," he said.

"I'm not afraid of Carrasco or testifying," I told him, "but I want to attend all of the trial. I want to be there for my mother. I need to be there for myself."

Jim looked down at his shoes again. Between munching on pencils and staring at his shoes, the man was filled with stress-relieving habits, but, having been so close to him in these days, I was beginning to see that the veneer of complacency he erected to deal with people like me was just that. Jim Shore cared a lot more about right and wrong, justice and injustice, than he wanted to show. Nevertheless, as time went on, I was seeing his real feelings emerge from beneath his guard. After a moment, he looked down at me and smiled. "I'll see what I can do," he said.

"Look," I said, "I spent most of my life hating my mother for being crazy. And that's not an easy thing to admit to a stranger."

"I know," he replied.

"Do you know what the real crime here is? The real crime is that she had to die for me to realize that I loved her all along. I loved her my whole life, and I didn't know it until now. Until today."

CHAPTER 13

Without Passion or Prejudice

There were a series of delays before the trial actually began. Justice, it seems, prefers to plea bargain. According to Jim Shore, 60 percent of murder cases are resolved in deals between the state and the defense. This saves the state the cost of the trial and the accused the uncertainty of that trial's outcome. I waited through the pretrial maneuvering, hopeful that the man who murdered my mother, Richard Carrasco, would not make a deal. I wanted him to face my mother's ghost in the courtroom, and I wanted to face her too.

First, there were pre-trial motions, all of which I attended. Most of these were held behind the scenes in the judge's chambers, with the district attorney and the defense attorney supposedly arguing fine points of law, but probably talking about their golf games. Judge Ball was the presiding judge on the case. His courtroom walls were covered with frames exhibiting his collection of American flags from different eras. While waiting, I walked through the courtroom counting the flags and studying the aging patriotic symbols of our American democracy.

While the behind the scenes stuff went on, I sat in the courtroom along with the bailiff, the court reporter, the clerk, and Richard Carrasco. The court reporter, clerk, and bailiff gossiped and told jokes to each other. Carrasco and I were quiet. I usually read chapters from my textbooks. If justice took any longer to proceed, I would be the best prepared person in my MBA classes. I was finally a graduate student. I didn't know how I felt about that, or how I felt about the trial for that matter. I seemed to be in a state of suspended animation. My insides felt quiet and still, and nothing inside me seemed to be moving. For all I knew, I'd finally become invisible just as I'd imagined earlier, and indeed, this time in a way I had. I'd become an observer.

Finally, the pre-trial motions concluded and, eight years after I identified my mother's body, the trial of her murderer began. As the lawyers and witnesses assembled, I was reminded of a stage play. All the main actors were present, and they rarely got their lines right the first time. However, the show was live, and since it had to go on, it did. In the beginning, it seemed sloppily done, and I wished for more rehearsals so that nothing could go more wrong than it already had since my mother died.

My brother, Michael, had chosen not to attend the trial, and I asked my father and husband to stay away. Truthfully, I didn't want to share or explain my pain to anyone. I didn't want someone to hold my hand during difficult testimony or talk to me during the breaks. I couldn't cope with sympathy or understanding and believed it would be better to remain self-contained. Those were the reasons I didn't want my father or husband with me. As for my brother, I was afraid of what I'd find if I looked into his eyes. I was afraid that he'd loved our mother more than I had and that his raw emotions would force mine into the open and destroy the calm exterior I was trying to maintain. Also, I was afraid of the force of his reaction against Carrasco, sitting every day in the same courtroom with the person accused of raping and murdering our mother.

In any case, Michael decided not to attend and I was left to find my own way alone.

Even a murder trial develops its own bizarre plot line. Every day the scene is set, the actors take their places, and the play starts. The routine fashion in which my mother's murder trial unfolded forced me to maintain detachment, at least when it began. Otherwise, the horror of casual discussion of her rape and murder would have overwhelmed me. So, during the beginning, I concentrated on the little details, avoiding the impact of the events and what they meant for as long as possible.

I watched as Jim Shore, the DA on the case, sat hunched up and then slumped in his seat. Since he was such a big man, I wondered if he sat that way so that he looked less intimidating. While he listened to testimony, Jim chewed on the pens and pencils he brought with him to court. I wanted him to impress the jury with his passion for justice, his passion for convicting my mother's killer. So, sitting behind him each day, I concentrated my mental energy on willing him to fight. Detective Mike Brown sat next to Jim. When I'd met Mike for the first time at the trial, I was struck by the inadequacy of the words "Thank you." I knew that without Detective Brown, my mother's murderer would never have come to trial. Yet, when I met him, I merely said "Thank you" and numbly shook his hand, letting the moment of gratitude, for which I had waited so long but had no means of expressing, pass.

A modest sort of hero, Mike always sat looking straight

ahead with his hands folded on the table in front of him. The back of Detective Brown's neck was so rigid that it implied a certain fragility to me, strange as that may seem. There was something breakable and compassionate in Detective Brown's neck, as if he had to maintain that artificial posture so as not to convey all he was feeling inside.

Every day, the villain, Richard Carrasco looked clean-cut and nicely dressed for his appearance at his trial. He was freshly shaven, and often his attorney helped him knot his tie. From a distance, he appeared a young, eager college student. Sitting behind him every day, I memorized the contours of his back. As the trial went on, I knew and could describe the shape of his head better than I could my own. From the back, his head and neck had a vulnerable appearance, but I knew this to be an illusion. Carrasco's victims were the vulnerable ones, and I doubted that if I met Carrasco outside the courtroom he would appear clean-cut to me.

Carrasco's family came to court every day. Aunts, uncles, cousins, and friends—they filled up one whole side of the courtroom. Though they didn't introduce themselves to me, I knew immediately who they were, just as I'd known who he was the first time I'd seen him in court. Carrasco's expression when he looked at his family was grateful, even loving. Every time he turned toward his family, the tender expression on his face shocked me. When Carrasco looked at me, however, his face hardened and closed up until I could see the anger and the promise of violence there. But he didn't scare me anymore. I was here for my mother's sake, not his.

Phillip McGuire made up Carrasco's one-person defense team. He was one of those people who always seem to be in a hurry. He hopped, he bounced, he rummaged through his briefcase; even standing still, he gave the impression of being a man on the move. Watching him in court wore me out. He put more energy into unpacking his briefcase than I put into my morning run. Would his excess of energy make the truth invisible to the jury? I hoped it wouldn't.

Methodically, Judge Ball presided over the case. He'd wanted to settle it out of court and spent much effort and time trying to get Richard Carrasco to come to terms. He was a grandfatherly looking man, large, serious, and determined looking. The first time I saw him in his judge's robes, I imagined him at home in his paneled den, sitting in an expensive and comfortable leather chair, smoking a cigar and genially expounding on an eternal truth of some sort.

Judge Ball generally wore two in-court expressions. He either looked intense or bored. When he wore his intense face, he looked straight ahead into the courtroom, leaned on his elbows, and usually gripped a file folder. His bored face was more difficult to describe, since he wore it when he faced away from the main courtroom and hid his expression by leaning his head on his hand. With the jury, Judge Ball was jovial and courteous. With his booming voice, strong opinions, and semi-famous collection of United States flags dating back to pre-Civil War days, Judge Ball presented a distinctly judicial presence.

Sitting in the courtroom through months of pre-trial maneuvering, I was reminded on a daily basis of Americans' constitutional right to justice and a fair trial. I didn't deny Richard Carrasco his right to due process. However, confronted every day with my mother's murderer, I was occasionally overcome by a "what about my mother's rights" feeling. I could see myself slipping over the edge and becoming one of those people that others are uncomfortable around. I was reminded of the lessons of my childhood and kept my thoughts to myself. Better to sit invisibly in Judge Ball's courtroom and quietly study my surroundings, from the flags on the wall to faces in the jury box.

The twelve jurors and four alternates were a mix of ethnic groups, young and old, but only two were female. There was one Asian person and one African-American. Hearing all the charges read for the first time was a somber, solemn, weighty moment, but a bit surreal. Even as well-acquainted as I was with the reality and the pain of so many rapes and one murder, it was a bit hard to believe. As the stark facts were read out loud, I leaned forward so I would not miss a word.

Count 1: 187, First degree murder, April 2, 1990, in the County of Santa Clara, of Lucia Elaine Rothwell, a human being

Count 2: 261.2, Rape by force and violence, April 2, 1990, in the County of Santa Clara, of Lucia Elaine Rothwell

Count 3: 261.2, Rape by force and violence, May 8, 1990, in the County of Santa Clara, of *Jane Doe with use of force and fear, namely a knife

Count 6: 286. Sodomy, May 8, 1990, in the County of Santa Clara, of Jane Doe, with the use of force and fear

Count 20:261.2, Forcible Object Rape, August 8, 1990, in the County of Santa Clara, of *Sara Smith

And so forth. . . .

Finally, the day came when Jim Shore rose from the prosecutor's table to begin his opening statement. Almost loping, Jim made his way to the front of the room and began to address the jury.

"Good morning, ladies and gentlemen of the jury."

The jury murmured a response.

"Elaine Rothwell was often seen seated at the foot of a light post on North First Street near Highway 880. Her campground was underneath some bushes and was separated from an office complex by a chain-link fence. The occupants of the office complex had known Elaine for three years. They called her 'Little Elaine.' Elaine was sixty-three years old, weighed seventy-nine pounds, was about five feet tall," Jim began. While he talked, his eyes focused on the jury faces one at a time.

"There were a series of sexual assaults that occurred in the City of San Jose, all of which occurred not far from this very courthouse. They occurred basically from January of nineteen eighty-nine until March of nineteen ninety-three. What you're going to hear in this trial is evidence of the commission of those sexual assaults, rape, sodomy, forced oral copulation, and penetration by a foreign object.

"Now, mixed in among those sexual assaults, was a murder.

"In April of nineteen ninety, a woman was found dead with a severe laceration in her vaginal area. The laceration was so bad, ladies and gentlemen, that the victim of that brutal crime, Mrs. Elaine Rothwell, bled to death."

Jim paused, but his gaze never wavered from the sixteen faces before him.

"The evidence will show, ladies and gentlemen, that she was in very, very poor health to begin with. Mrs. Rothwell's body was found in the bushes that separate an on-ramp to Highway 880 here in the City of San Jose. The on-ramp is accessible from First Street traveling north-bound on First Street. Again, not very far from here.

"And in the bushes that separate that on-ramp from an office complex adjacent to that on-ramp, Mrs. Rothwell's body was found. She was basically nude from the waist down, save and except for a pair of pantyhose that was found somewhere between the knee and her waist on one leg. The rest of her body, upper body, was clothed.

"Mrs. Rothwell," his voice was quiet now, almost respectful, but his words stabbed my heart, "well, Mrs.

Rothwell lived—she actually lived in that area of trees and bushes that separate that on-ramp from that office complex. Mrs. Rothwell, the evidence will show you, lived in that area basically under a tree for some three to four years.

"The people that worked in that office complex got to know Mrs. Rothwell to some extent. One of the witnesses particularly will comment that he helped her out, gave her some money from time to time, brought some clothing, and the evidence will tell you when he's asked, why did you do this thing, and he said because Mrs. Rothwell, unlike so many other people that he characterizes as homeless, never had a hand out. Apparently, she didn't talk to very many people and, if she talked at all, it was very short."

"She was a teacher," I whispered into my lap. When I looked up, the bailiff was looking at me. He looked away when I met his eyes. I felt exposed as the sort of daughter that would let her mother die all alone on a cardboard box, weighing only seventy-nine pounds.

Jim was still speaking. "There was an encampment of homeless men near where Little Elaine lived. They were mostly alcoholics. The men always got up early so that they could be at the soup kitchen in time for breakfast. They always said hello to Little Elaine when they passed her. She never responded or acknowledged them in any way."

Of course not, I thought, *if she didn't acknowledge me, why would she acknowledge strangers?* I wanted to stand up and say, *That's not who she was. Let me tell you about her beautiful voice and how good she was with math.* Instead, I concentrated on the American flag to the left of me, counting stars and stripes while Jim continued.

"Now, Mrs. Rothwell, as I said before, was in very poor health, and the evidence is that she was living in these bushes, as I said. She was about sixty-three years old and

some days at the time of her death. And as I told you, she
was about five feet tall, and at the time of the autopsy by
the coroner, she weighed only seventy-nine-and-one-half
pounds." He paused and studied the ceiling for a
moment and then said fiercely, "She basically looked like
a survivor from a concentration camp."

Tension hung in the air. Jim eyed Carrasco with a hard
stare and went on. "And the evidence will show you that
there was, during the autopsy, swabs done, and the swabs
were looked at under a microscope by the coroner, and
he detected semen and sperm.

"That evidence was taken by the coroner, was shipped
off to the crime laboratory, and it was frozen, saved for a
day when there would be some evidence of who committed this vicious crime.

"Well, that day came," Jim waved a hand towards Mike
Brown, "and the man seated next to me and now stand-
ing, Detective Michael Brown from the San Jose Police
Department, got involved. He was, at the time, a sexual-
assault investigator in the Sexual Assault Investigation
Unit for the San Jose Police Department.

"Michael Brown had many cases that were assigned to
him, and a case came across his desk that led him to
make contact with, by phone, the defendant in this case,
Mr. Carrasco, and I'm going to fast forward you now to
nineteen ninety-three.

"During that phone call, Officer Brown told Mr. Carrasco, and it's very important that you understand what
he said. In essence, he said, 'Mr. Carrasco,'—this is by
phone—'I'm investigating some things that are going on
in your neighborhood, and I need to talk to you about
it.' Basically, that was it. No 'You're under arrest.' No
'You're forced to come down here.' Officer Brown didn't
even say what it was. Didn't say it was a sexual assault.
Didn't say it was murder. Didn't say it was about anything.

"Mr. Carrasco—you'll hear evidence from Mr. Brown—told Mr. Brown, 'I'll be happy to come and talk to you,' made an appointment to come and talk to Detective Brown at the San Jose Police Department, and, lo and behold, didn't show, and in fact fled.

"Well, Detective Brown scratched his head, and you're going to hear exactly why he did that and what he did after that. But it's because Detective Brown searched so hard for him that Richard Carrasco was finally apprehended in and about El Paso, Texas, within days and weeks of that initial phone conversation between these two men. And he was brought back to San Jose, and he had his blood drawn, and that blood was analyzed for its DNA properties by the crime lab here in Santa Clara County.

"The crime lab in Santa Clara County has the capability to do different types of blood tests. Those blood tests include what we'll call conventional markers, things as simple as the type of blood you are: O, A, et cetera. There's also something that's a little more sophisticated than the conventional, and it's called DNA typing, and that allows a specific type of evidentiary sample. It can be saliva, can be sperm, can be in some cases even hair or sweat, but in this case it was blood.

"At the time of the autopsy, there was blood drawn from Mrs. Rothwell, and that blood was compared by the crime lab to the blood drawn from Mr. Carrasco at the time he was arrested and brought back to San Jose from Texas after he fled the area. And, yes, the evidence will show you that he fled, ran away from this area.

"The crime laboratory will tell you, based on the type of DNA they did, and it's called PCR—some people call it alphabet soup because there's all these initials and acronyms—and the initial PCR test merely gave the analyst the type, a certain type to analyze someone's DNA in the blood. Like I said, you're going to hear a lot about DNA, and by the time we're done, you will all be experts.

"Suffice it to say that the lab personnel, the experts that do this for the Santa Clara County Crime Laboratory, compared these two blood samples, and what they will say is they cannot exclude the defendant as the donor of the sperm found inside Mrs. Rothwell.

"Let me make a little aside here about experts. You're going to find that experts, the scientists that you hear from, are very, very meticulous and very careful people. That's their business. Sometimes we'd like them to come in here and make statements like, 'Yes, for certain, that sperm came from that man.' In the case of the Santa Clara County Crime Laboratory, what they're going to be able to say is that the evidence cannot exclude that he, Richard Carrasco the defendant, cannot be excluded as the donor of that sample of that sperm, and we didn't stop there.

"Shortly after the Santa Clara County Crime Laboratory got involved, the suspended evidence, if you will, from nineteen ninety in Mrs. Rothwell was sent to a lab back in Baltimore, Maryland. It's perhaps the number one, premiere DNA analysis unit in the country. It's a private organization. It's not run by any government, any government function. It's run by a couple of doctors, two women. The company's called Cellmark Diagnostic. They're in, I believe, Germantown, Maryland. And these people do a test that's known as RFLP.

"Now, this test, this is another DNA test, and unlike PCR, this test is very precise and exacting. They have developed a way basically at Cellmark to look at a piece of DNA and to determine whether someone gave the donated, the supplied, item or not.

"So, basically what we have is Cellmark Diagnostic, the scientists from that group are going to come in here, and they're going to show you what we call a pattern of the DNA that was swabbed initially from Mrs. Rothwell, and you'll see. Then they'll show you the pattern that was taken from Mrs. Rothwell's blood sample that was drawn from her vein at the time of the autopsy, and, yes, there is blood in the vein at the time of the autopsy. And they compared the sample of Mrs. Rothwell's blood to the sample taken from her at the autopsy, and they found that there was indeed a match."

Shore's voice was a monotone as he went over the scientific material, but as he came to the end of it, his voice charged with a sort of suppressed excitement.

"But they also found something else, and that is, they found something that was foreign to her. They found something that was different than her, and what they found, ladies and gentlemen, was the defendant's sperm. And the scientists from the Cellmark Laboratory will come in here, and they will tell you that what they, in fact, found is a match, that it is basically a genetic fingerprint of the defendant, inside Mrs. Rothwell. Sixty-three years old, found partially clad, seventy-nine-and-a-half pounds." He paused now and once again surveyed the jury to be sure his words were impacting them. Then he looked back at me. I was sitting forward, half-leaning my head against the wooden rail in front of me. I returned his gaze and he went on.

"You're going to hear two types of evidence in this case. You're going to hear evidence of charged crimes. Those are the crimes that His Honor just read to you: murder, rape, robbery, sodomy, burglary, et cetera. You're also going to hear what's known as uncharged crimes.

"The importance of uncharged crimes is, if you find those to be true, that you may infer that the defendant also committed the charged crimes. It's the old adage: once a thief, always a thief. So I'm going to break down for you the charged and the uncharged today, right now, so that you're going to have a sense of what's coming to you. I'm also going to attempt, and as I say, underline the word *attempt*, I'm also going to attempt to keep each of these cases and each of these incidences in a nice little package for you to consider.

"You're going to try to keep straight in your minds all of the witnesses that pertain to any particular case, and there are many of them charged and uncharged in one group, but I already know that that's going to be impossible. If I were writing a novel, that's how I'd hopefully be able to present it to you, but I can't because of the way the world works and the way the witnesses work.

"Now, Detective Brown and I are going to attempt to try to keep these vignettes separate and distinct for you so that you can consider, but there are going to be times that we take witnesses out of order, witnesses are going to be late, witnesses are going to get sick, and I apologize to you for that purpose, but the opening statement right now gives the opportunity to look at these things as a whole.

"If I could direct your attention to the overhead projector and what I've prepared—is it possible to dim the lights a little bit at this time? That would be great. Thanks. That's probably even better.

"Ladies and gentlemen, what you have before you is a map showing you the areas in question. Most of the criminal activity occurred, as I said, from nineteen eighty-nine through nineteen ninety-three. There are several points on this map that are very important to remember, not the least of which are the three places that the defendant, Mr. Carrasco, resided during this time period.

"I'd like to point those out to you now. I have in my hand a laser pointer that will put a dot on the screen, but it won't remain there, so bear with me here, but if you see the dot here, let me give you some orientation. At the top of the page which is somewhat facing north, in essence, and towards the left is a major line here, which is Highway 87, commonly known as the Mexicali Expressway. Intersecting that and proceeding both south and north is Highway 880. You can see that here and a little bit further north of Highway 87 is the intersection of Highway 880 and Highway 101, which is 101 not marked on the map.

"We are currently in the area known as the Civic Center, which I'm highlighting now. The Civic Center area, basically you can see very barely the word 'jail,' and to the left of that on Hedding Street are the words, 'muni court.' When this map was put together, this building didn't exist that you're sitting in now. This is a rather new, recent addition, and anyway, we are sandwiched currently between the muni court and the jail currently."

The thoroughness of his presentation in tying Carrasco to the area of the crimes was another telling piece of evidence. Though, when we'd first met, I had been nervous about Shore's commitment to my mother's case, my earlier suspicions were laid to rest now. He was doing a masterful job.

"The area of concern basically is bounded here by Sonora that you can see and Baler that you can see here, Baler intersecting with the Mexicali Expressway as well.

"The defendant resided in several different locales during this four-year period. It was at a time when he didn't live with his father. His mother was apparently in and out. You're going to hear from her, get to see her. But basically, he's either living with his mother, he's living with uncles and aunts—he had many of them—a grandmother, and on one occasion, even his older brother. But we know that the defendant resided at the corner, and his family—some of his family still do reside—at the corner of Sonora and San Juan, and my hand is not as steady as it should be, but basically you can see that. There's a house there.

"He also resided at the apartments that exist at Kerley, which is here, and the intersection of Gish, which is here.

"And, finally, on First Street, adjacent or in between Hedding and Younger, he lived in an apartment here with his brother for a very short period of time but, basically, from nineteen eighty-nine through at least nineteen ninety-one and nineteen ninety-two, he's living in this general area.

"Now, why is that important? It's important because what we have is that in that same area the very first of the sexual assaults occurred."

Shore spoke of first one and then other women—some old, some young—whom Carrasco raped. I looked searchingly at the man in the red suit and then around me at his family. Their heads almost uniformly were cast down as if they were trying not to hear what was being said. I looked over at a woman I assumed was his aunt; her face was still, but her hands twisting a handkerchief seemed to have a will of their own.

Shore began to sketch each rape, adding ugly personality traits to the portrait as he went along.

"The first victim of sexual assault of a rape by the defendant is one of the uncharged crimes, and this is January of nineteen eighty-nine, uncharged crimes that occurred at the apartment building in which Mr. Carrasco lived. That apartment building is actually a set of buildings. It's actually a complex, and that complex which I will describe is somewhat like a motel in that there's a string of doorways that all open into either one corridor or out into the street.

"And you're going to hear that Mr. Carrasco lived during that time with relatives in an adjacent building to the one that the first victim, and I'll call her Mrs. T., lived. Mrs. T. was a fifty-two-year-old woman who lived alone in apartment number four, there at the corner of Gish and Kerley. In apartment number two, which is two doors away, resided an uncle and aunt of Mr. Carrasco, who from time to time would spend nights sleeping on their couch or on their floor. That's the very first assault that occurred.

"A sixty-nine-year-old woman living by herself was also raped and sexually assaulted. She lived about right here on a street that is called Mexicali Parkway. Although the street physically still exists, the houses have all been torn down by Caltrans, who bought them out in the early or mid nineteen eighties and early nineties and slowly has gotten rid of them to make room for the expansion that is going to take place on Highway 87.

"In August, at North Second Street almost at the intersection of Baler, which is right here, a single woman, living alone in an apartment, was raped and sexually assaulted.

"And the one on which we'll concentrate in this case was the murder and the sexual assault of Mrs. Rothwell, which you'll see on the diagram, occurred basically, again, right here, in nineteen ninety.

"Finally, what brought attention to the Rothwell case is a case involving a woman by the name of Ellen Lopez. Ellen lived on this same Mexicali Parkway, not many doors down from some of the other victims I've told you of. Hers is a very pivotal case, and I'll tell you why."

In order to cement Richard Carrasco as a monster, for three days the jury and I watched the district attorney lay out a "map" of testimony about Richard's whereabouts and past violent behavior.

"During March of nineteen ninety-three, Richard Carrasco, the defendant in this case, was living at 314 Sonora.

"Unfortunately, near there is where Ellen Lopez moved."

Judge Ball interrupted. "I was just going to say—you understand that the clock is fifteen minutes wrong?"

Jim Shore, his mind still on Ellen Lopez, was taken aback. He looked at the clock and said, "Slow."

The judge nodded. "It's three minutes to twelve."

Shore, his mind back on the present now, looked at the judge. "I'd be happy to break now and. . . ."

Judge Ball had his hand up. "I think this would be an appropriate time. We'll take the noon recess at this time, ladies and gentlemen. Once again, you're reminded of my previous admonition that you're not to form or express any opinion concerning the matter, discuss it among yourselves or with any other person. We'll reconvene at one-thirty. I wish you a very pleasant lunch. Thank you so much."

Leaving the courtroom I went to a small coffee shop nearby and sitting at the counter, ordered a chicken salad at which I barely picked. Around me I heard snatches of conversations. I watched idly as some of the male reporters hit on their attractive lunch companions, making dates for later. Others, not constrained by the judge's instructions to the jurors, chewed over details from Jim Shore's opening statement, but I, feeling almost invisible again, neither thought of this day's beginning nor the events to come. It was as if time and my life had paused, and there was only now, and I had to hold onto it tightly so I could move forward.

The court reconvened for the afternoon session.

Judge Ball stated, "The record will reflect that counsel are present, the defendant is present, all members of the panel are present. You may proceed, Mr. Shore, with your opening statement."

Once again, Jim Shore began his sonorous delivery.

"Thank you very much, Your Honor. May we dim the lights one more time, Deputy Carter, please? Thank you.

"Good afternoon, ladies and gentlemen. When we left off prior to the lunch break, I was about to tell you about the episodes that occurred on the third and fourth of March, nineteen ninety-three, and these are among the uncharged crimes. And I had explained that the defendant at the time was living at the corner of Sonora and San Juan Avenue at 314 Sonora Drive, or maybe it's Sonora Avenue, excuse me.

"Anyway, Ellen Lopez, shortly before March, within maybe six months or so, moved into a duplex down the road from where another of Carrasco's victims, Margaret Carroll, lived.

"Ellen had twin boys who were five years old, and those boys attended a nearby elementary school.

"Now, the importance of the Ellen Lopez incident to this case goes to what the defendant was doing on and about the days and evenings of nineteen ninety-three that led him to Detective Brown's attention in the first place.

"As I said, Ellen lived alone with her two twin sons, and the defendant apparently hung out in the neighborhood quite a bit. In other words, he was around, and on one particular day he was actually in the driveway of Ellen Lopez's duplex, and the defendant was—at the current time, I believe, the defendant is twenty-three years old—and at that time he would have been nineteen years old or so. And he struck up a conversation with this forty-five-year-old, Ellen Lopez, who lived alone. Among other things, he said to her that he's nineteen, she's forty-five. He says to her, 'You're looking pretty good. You're looking pretty good. And by the way, do you live alone?'

"A few days later, Ellen Lopez on March third was

walking back from school with her children, and as she passes the corner at San Juan and Sonora where the defendant was living, she noticed that a side gate where that house is was open, and Ellen had been living in the neighborhood for quite a number of months at least and noticed taking her children out, in March to school, that that side gate was always closed at 314 Sonora, always remained closed, but on this particular day it remains open. As she's walking back from the school and the defendant is standing there, keep in mind that he's already said, 'You live alone? You're looking good,' and he's standing there in the gateway, if you will. The gate is open to the side of the house, and he's exposing himself.

"This is a pretty upsetting thing for Mrs. Lopez. As you can quite imagine, she knew who he was. She knew what had been said, and she went, and she'll tell you this, but she went and she called a neighbor, and the neighbor called the police. This is on the third of March, and she said the police asked her should they send a patrol car out. And she said, 'No, I'll just give the report on the phone.'

"So she gave a brief report of that to the police, she'll tell you, and along comes the next day, and she's walking to pick her children up from school. Apparently, they were in the morning session in kindergarten, so it's some time before noon, and she's walking by the defendant's house, and not by coincidence, the defendant walks out around noon in his bathrobe, and he walks from the front towards the sidewalk. He bends down, crouching down, and exposes himself once again to Ellen Lopez, who, by this point, is literally beside herself.

"On March the eighth, Michael Brown went out and talked to Ellen Lopez. She recounted these events that I've told you about, and thereafter Brown went to find Mr. Carrasco. And no one was home. So Brown left his business card, which again, does not identify him in terms of what the business is that he wanted to talk to Mr. Carrasco about, and Mr. Carrasco called him, as I've detailed for you earlier this morning. They had this conversation, they set up this appointment, and Carrasco fled. The next time they talked, Detective Brown was accompanying Mr. Carrasco back from Texas after he had been arrested and later linked to the murder of Mrs. Rothwell.

"Now, what you have before you now on the overhead is a summary of the charged crimes, the charged crimes. Later, we're going to take a look at these in a little bit more detail than we've talked about already, but it is to the rape and ultimate murder of Mrs. Rothwell I now turn.

"This case occurred—there are some of the people that are going to come in whose memories are going to be better than others, that's the case in any trial. It's certainly going to be so in this trial where the events happened some time ago. Not everybody is going to have a perfect memory of everything. Some people are going to come in and say things a little differently than they might have said to a police officer back in nineteen ninety. But back in April of nineteen ninety, which was the month, by the way, when two women who worked at a business next door came to work and noticed the lifeless body of Mrs. Rothwell. They called the police. The police responded to the scene and initially labeled it a suspicious death.

"We actually have a videotape. It was just the start of the time that the San Jose Police Department videotaped crime scenes, and so we have a videotape about ten minutes long. We're going to see that. If the equipment cooperates, you'll even get to see it on this big screen here so it won't be a small television set.

"But there weren't a lot of clues at the time. There weren't a lot of clues. The body of Mrs. Rothwell was removed, as it is supposed to be by law, by the coroner's office, and they took the body to the coroner, who's a medical doctor, and it's the job of the coroner to determine in any suspicious death case the cause of death, and it was later on that afternoon of the second of April when the coroner called the San Jose Police Department and said that this woman died of a laceration.

"Now, what basically happened here is that Mrs. Rothwell suffered an episiotomy at the hand of the defendant.

"The laceration to the vagina was very severe, over six inches long, and extended from and through muscle and skin. It extended posteriorly below the perineum and basically adjacent to the anus."

Jim Shore waited for the impact of his words to register. The seconds ticked away. My thoughts raced wildly, until I heard him continue.

"At seventy-nine-and-a-half pounds, malnourished, living under a tree for the last three years or so, Mrs. Rothwell lost so much blood that it caused her system to shut down. This is what the coroner is going to testify to, that eventually caused her death."

Jim spoke his next words softly. "How fast she died? We don't know. How much she suffered? We don't know. We do know that the coroner will testify that there was a lot of pain associated with her death.

"The evidence we are going to present in this case is and will be overwhelming. There's going to be a lot of sad parts to it. There's going to be parts that are going to be hard to stomach. I'm going to have to show you some photographs of things that are going to be rather unpleasant. The judge alluded to those during the time that you were all selected. But it is necessary for you to see and understand.

"The trial and the evidence should take us—we're going to try to keep it going as fast as we can, but it should take probably the better part of five or six weeks.

Thank you in advance for the attention that you give to this case. After you hear the overwhelming evidence on the guilt of Richard Carrasco, I'm going to stand here again before you, and I'm going to ask each one of you to render verdicts of guilty on all charges. Thank you very much. And thank you, Your Honor."

The judge turned to Phillip McGuire, the attorney for the defense. "Mr. McGuire, did you wish to make an opening statement at this time, sir?"

"Yes, Your Honor," McGuire said.

"All right. You may address the jury."

"Thank you, Your Honor."

As he strode forward, McGuire drew a deep breath, paused to look at the defendant, and then turned to the jury. "Good afternoon, ladies and gentlemen," he said. "As you know, now is my opportunity to give you my opening statement. At the end of the case, like the district attorney, I'll be able to give arguments concerning the evidence and the interpretation of it at that point, but right now I'm going to tell you what I believe the evidence will show.

"Now, part of the problem is, as the district attorney explained, these events took place a long time ago, so memories have faded. We can't be positive of what people are going to say. We have reports and what these people said before, and we assume that probably they will say the same, but there are certain things that are known.

"For example, one victim will not say someone grabbed her and pulled her by the neck as was demonstrated by the prosecutor. To the contrary, I believe the evidence will say, by her, will say that the arm was around her waist. I don't know if there's any true significance, but that's an example of the differences both the prosecutor and myself look at. Arguably, it is the same case, and I feel it's my honor to be here representing Richard Carrasco, to show you a different view of the case.

"There is other evidence, other than what Mr. Shore has said, that you're going to find out. I'll give you just a few examples, as the case develops. Also, you're going to see a lot for yourself. One of the examples is that the prosecutor says, once a thief always a thief. Well, that is not alone always true and in others you will see there are fingerprints on some occasions that don't show this because there will be no evidence that these are fingerprints of the rapist."

McGuire was doing his best to maintain a rational defense, trying to pin his opponent to the wall by nitpicking. I wondered where it would lead.

"Another example is that reference to Mrs. Rothwell. And then you're going to hear about evidence, about possible suspects. Contrary to what the prosecutor said, there were suspects back in nineteen ninety. Why they weren't pursued I don't know, but that's the problem. Why did they lose some evidence? Why did they order things destroyed? I don't know. That's not—that wasn't our doing.

"In terms of the—what we call, what they refer to as the uncharged crimes, the uncharged offenses, what is before you to decide as the jury, are the cases that deal with the period nineteen ninety which the prosecution is going to be allowed to show under the law is that the events that took place in nineteen ninety-two, nineteen ninety-three somehow assist you in determining that my client committed offenses in nineteen ninety.

"Well, the evidence will show, the people in nineteen ninety-three will say, 'We know Richard Carrasco. He flashed or exposed himself,' or 'asked if I was living alone.' Where he is positively identified, there's no ifs, ands or buts about it, the identity. None of those are charged offenses. None of those are here for you to determine whether he's guilty or innocent.

"The ones that you are going to determine, not a single victim, and there's no dispute Elaine Rothwell, Margaret Carroll, and Denise Willard are all victims. That is not disputed. Their homes are broken into or some event took place. No one denies Elaine Rothwell bled to death under the bushes next to the Cyclone fence on the on-ramp. No one disputes that. That will not be challenged. What will be challenged is, who did it?"

I strained to hear every word, wondering if the jury thought him credible. Anxiety further raising my fears, I prayed that they didn't.

"We don't have a witness saying, 'I saw that person; he did it.' There are specific people that see it, but the evidence will show that Elaine Rothwell certainly will not show it, the other people that—whose houses were broken into, they're not going to get there. They're going to tell their very emotionally upsetting stories about what happened to them. Not one, not one will point to the defendant and say, 'That's the person that did it.' That's what the evidence will show, that they do not identify the defendant."

McGuire began to go through the cases one by one. "Basically," he said, "there are a lot of different crimes being committed, and we're not challenging whether they were committed. What's the issue is, who committed these offenses. And that's what it's going to come down to." He stood motionless for a minute, looking as if he felt he had made his case.

My head ached with the unfairness of the way he had twisted the facts. I shook my head in disbelief.

"I ask that you just sit through this, listen to all the evidence, and see what the evidence really does establish in this case. Thank you."

McGuire was finished. The judge said, "Thank you, Mr. McGuire."

At the end of that day, Jim spoke to me about his strategy. "I'm laying out the case," he said, "but Judge Ball doesn't think I'm making a clear statement. He says the jury looks bored." Jim chewed on his bottom lip for a minute. "You've been watching the jury. What do you think?"

I thought about the jury: twelve strangers tasked with judging the truth of my mother's death. At this point of the trial, Carrasco was almost an afterthought to me, because this was more my mother's trial than his.

There were sixteen jurors, ten men and two women faced with deciding Carrasco's guilt or innocence, plus four alternates, should one of the main jurors drop out or be dismissed. In setting a high number of alternates, the judge hoped to avoid a mistrial. Our jurors were a serious looking bunch, as befits those sitting in judgment at a murder trial. None of them smiled. Since I'd been in attendance all through jury selection and every day since, they also paid attention to me. They probably didn't place me yet as a victim's daughter, but I was obviously an interested party.

I watched the jurors, partly because I hoped to imbue them with my passion to see the trial finished and Carrasco convicted, and partly because I considered this jury my mother's advocate. I wanted to know which way they would vote. I wanted to learn how to read their minds, or maybe more importantly, their hearts.

District Attorney Shore's early days involved prying testimony from a parade of witnesses about crimes for which Richard had already been convicted, but that were uncharged at this time. He was doing this in order to draw a portrait of a violent and evil young man and present a pattern of criminal behavior to the jury.

On one long day of testimony, Jim and I were standing

in the anteroom between the courtroom and the hallway. The last witness for the day had been a man named Bart Gomez, a former continuing education teacher. Richard Carrasco was a fourteen-year-old dropout when, through a friend, he became acquainted with Gomez. Together, Carrasco and his friend provided Gomez with drugs and sex in exchange for a place to hang out and access to a car. Gomez, a recovering addict eager to confess, offered testimony acknowledging a lifetime of drug addiction and debauchery and asked the courtroom at large for forgiveness. Listening to his testimony, I felt more like an eavesdropper than a witness to the details of Carrasco's capacity for crime. Some of the jurors shook their heads as if in disbelief while he testified.

Another of the early witnesses, Susan Podell, knew my mother and was one of the first to find her dead.

Jim asked her, "Can you tell us when you first came in contact with Elaine?"

"I don't know the exact date or even the month. It was a few months before she died."

"Can you tell us the nature and circumstances of the contact?"

"Usually she was in between the on-ramp and our parking lot in a wooded area when I would pull up to work early in the morning, and I befriended her, started talking to her periodically, and came to where I would check on her in the mornings to make sure she was okay."

"Were most of the conversations that you had with her then in the wooded area and you on the parking lot?"

"Most of them, yes."

"And was there a typical time you would arrive for work?"

"Somewhere between six-thirty and eight, depending upon the day."

"And typically you would find her there in that wooded area at that time?"

"Yes."

"Was there a particular place you would find her?"

"Much closer down towards the corner. There's a steep incline as you come up to the freeway, up to the raised area, and she stayed lower down towards the corner of First Street."

"Is there a sidewalk on First Street there?"

"Yes."

"Was it—how far away from the sidewalk would you say it was, approximately?"

"Forty feet or so."

"And when you would see her, when you would come to work at six-thirty in the morning or eight o'clock in the morning, whatever time it was, was she typically doing something or was she in a particular place?"

"She usually was right around that area. Once in a while, if the sun had come out, she would move closer down where it wasn't so wooded so she could get warm. The sun would hit her earlier."

"When you arrived at your location, typically was she sitting, standing, lying down?"

"Usually sitting. She was sitting upright and kind of huddled over. I don't know if she was reading anything. I seem to remember she had a book or something that she would go through a lot."

"And was she—can you describe in the area that you typically saw her, what was on the ground in that area?"

"She made almost like a little bit of a home for herself. You could tell that she stayed there a lot. There was usually some cardboard around, there were eating utensils, bits and pieces like of bottles, plastic bottles, water or soda, and some articles of clothing."

I felt my heart contract.

"And when you found her typically sitting upright, huddled or whatever she was doing, was it typically sitting on the ground or on a cardboard box or on some other object?"

"She wasn't sitting on the ground. In fact, I don't ever actually recall her sitting on the ground. She was always doing something. She sat on, I don't know if it was a little stool or like a carton."

"Did you ever come upon her while she was in, one of these mornings while she was lying down?"

"No."

"So is it fair to say you never saw her asleep?"

"Not lying down, no."

"Did you ever see her what appeared to be sleeping when she was sitting up?"

"It looked like she would doze off. I don't know if she was daydreaming, but she was either sleeping or had her eyes closed."

"This period of time that you got to know her a little bit, did you ever give her anything?"

"Typically I gave her food, especially on Monday mornings, and I don't know why it was Mondays. It was just, I guess, when I put together a care package or something. It was usually fruits and crackers."

"And would you hand it to her?"

"I would go up, start a conversation. 'How are you? How are you doing?' You know. 'It's cold out.' Just very casual. Sometimes she would respond, sometimes she wouldn't. Sometimes I would just kind of place the food on the other side of the fence. There was an area where the fence had kind of been pulled up a little bit where you could put things through. Sometimes I would hand it to her."

"So, all of the times that you had contact with her, how

many times would you say she responded to you by speaking?"

"About half, maybe less."

"And the times that she did not respond by speaking, could you tell that she acknowledged that you were there?"

"Yes. She didn't necessarily make eye contact. Maybe just a slight nod of the head, something at least. I always felt that she knew I was there. Sometimes she wouldn't turn her head or even open her eyes, but she just would kind of rock a little bit or make a movement."

"Did you ever give her anything besides food?"

"No."

"Did she ever refuse to take the food?"

"No."

"In the area that you've described that you saw her that she sort of made this makeshift—and I don't want to put words in your mouth—but was it sort of a makeshift campsite?"

"That would be accurate."

"Was there a tree in the vicinity of that campsite?"

"It was a bush that had gone wild, so it looked more like a tree. So it was very large. It had a very thick base. It was away from the fence a number of feet, about six feet or so."

"And where was the campsite in relation to the tree or was this a bush?"

"In between the fence and the bush, in that area. She stayed up closer to the fence area."

"Now, when you came to work on the second of April, nineteen ninety, do you remember that date?"

"Yes, I do."

"That was a Monday morning, correct?"

"Correct."

"About what time did you arrive at work?"

"Probably around seven-fifteen or seven-twenty."

"Did you park in your normal parking area?"

"Yes, I did."

"Did you see Elaine?"

"I went to find her. I didn't see her sitting up."

"So, when you arrived, the first thing, had you prepared like a care package or something that Sunday or that morning?"

"I don't believe I had that day. I don't recall that I had."

"But when you arrived at the location there at the office, you didn't go inside the building first?"

"No. I always checked on her first on my way into the building."

"And did you see her?"

"Yes, I did."

"Okay. And were you in the parking lot when you saw her?"

"Yes."

"And where was she?"

"She was on the ground. Laying on the ground."

"Could you see her entire body?"

"No."

"What parts could you see?"

"From her waist down."

"Can you describe how that looked?"

"Her clothing had been either removed or pulled down quite a bit."

"Was the lower half of her body exposed?"

"Yes, it was."

"And that is, you could see her skin?"

"Correct."

"Could you see her face?"

"No."

"What was blocking your view?"

"There were articles of clothing over her face. I

don't—I had the feeling it was a scarf of some type, but I don't know for sure."

"Can you describe generally how she was dressed day in and day out?"

"Usually with a lot of layers on, a lot of clothing. I remember, like, she had a sweater, a button-up, cardigan-type sweater. I believe she had a windbreaker. It wasn't a winter jacket—it was more of a shell-type thing, and she normally was wearing pants, I believe. And, I believe, a scarf."

"Did she wear it in any particular way, this scarf?"

"She would pull it real tight down around her face so you would just see this little face showing out and then kind of wrapped around."

"You said she was lying down?"

"She was down on her back."

"Okay. And what was she—what was under her, if anything?"

"I thought there was cardboard."

"What did you do when you saw her there? Did you attempt to call out to her or . . . ?"

"No."

". . . attempt to touch her in any way?"

"No."

"Why not?"

"It was very obvious that she was dead."

"What led you to that conclusion?"

"Her body wasn't in a natural position. Her legs were skewed, kind of just not normal. And she just—it was obvious to me that she was dead. There was another gal who had arrived at about the same time—she may even have gotten there a couple of seconds earlier. But I went into the building, and I believe I called the police."

The images of her testimony still floated in my mind at the end of the day when Jim and I talked together as usual in the hall. "Who is the next witness?" I asked.

"I'm putting Carrasco's ex-girlfriend on the stand."
Jim watched for whatever effect his words were going to
have on me.

Now that I'd seen him in action, examining and cross-
examining, I recognized that it was important to Jim that
his actions and words bring forth the right response from
the audience. I raised my eyebrows but said nothing.

Jim went on, "She's the one Carrasco confessed to
about your mother's murder."

"And you're hoping she'll talk about that on the
stand?" I asked. Jim nodded.

That night, I had a hard time falling asleep. Bits of what
I'd learned about my mother's last years kept coming into
my mind. Every time I was about to fall asleep, I remembered something else that I'd heard from the witness
stand or that Jim had told me. Strangers had offered my
mother comfort at the end, while I'd lived only fifteen
minutes away. The knowledge stung me.

Carrasco's ex-girlfriend, Patty Rodriguez, took the
stand right after the noon break the next day. Dark haired
and nervous, she was attractive though she looked hardened by life. She was twenty-seven and Carrasco was sixteen when they became lovers. She was thirty-five now,
and the circles under her eyes were so dark that she
looked like someone had blackened her eyes. Her voice
was so low that I had to move up to the front row in order
to hear what she was saying. Now and then she giggled,
then hiccuped, then snapped her chewing gum. I kept expecting that any moment she'd light up a cigarette. *After
all, what could be done to her in this courtroom that would be any
worse than the life she has led?* I asked myself. Patty had the
demeanor of someone who expects to be arrested or
punched and who is waiting for the world's next blow.

I sat alone on one side of the courtroom. Carrasco's family took up every seat on the other side. They were everywhere—in the bathroom, the hallway, the elevator. I couldn't escape their eyes and their curiosity. They kept their distance from me, and I thought it was somewhat ironic that they considered me their enemy. I didn't hold them responsible for my mother's death, but I didn't want to know them personally either.

"How are you today, Ms. Rodriguez?" Jim's manner with witnesses was polite and low key. Already I knew that he liked to ask the important questions quietly so that the answers would have more impact. He did not upstage the witnesses. Instead, he gave them something to react to.

"I'm fine," Patty whispered.

"Speak up, Ms. Rodriguez," Judge Ball said, and Patty looked as if she were ready to either cry or spit.

Her eyes widened, and I could see her nostrils quivering. Finally, she said, "I said, 'I'm fine.'"

"Are you afraid of being here, Patty?" Jim asked quietly, softly, his tone coaxing, his manner gentle. Yet, despite Jim's manner, it was possible to make out the edge of his distaste for Patty Rodriguez and her life and times. Though his manner was gentle and deferential, his mouth curved slightly, giving his remarks a slightly ironic flavor. He had never been this nice to me. But since he seemed to offer up contempt with a smile, I realized that he must like me more than he let on.

"Yes," she said softly. Patty crossed and uncrossed her long legs and leaned back in the chair as if she wanted to get away. Her face wore a strained look. "I forgot all about this stuff. I have a new life with someone new."

Jim asked, "Why are you afraid, Patty?"

McGuire objected and was overruled. Phillip McGuire had none of Jim's soft manner with witnesses. The prosecution witnesses, no matter how hostile, were enemies of the defense, and McGuire treated them with a swaggering discourtesy, a put-up-your-dukes sort of attitude.

"Is there someone in the courtroom you are afraid of?"

"Objection. Leading," McGuire interrupted,

I glanced at the jury. They all leaned forward in their chairs, fascinated with Patty.

"Why are you afraid?" Jim asked.

For a moment Patty didn't answer. Despite her silence there seemed to be a collective courtroom conviction that something important was about to be said. The room was quiet. The jurors stopped taking notes. The judge stared down at Patty. I leaned forward in my chair, and Carrasco's family members were halfway out of their seats. Patty curled up inside the witness chair. She didn't look at Carrasco, her one-time lover, murderer of my mother, rapist of helpless women, abused child and monster. Carrasco, however, kept his eyes on her face. He leaned forward like the rest of us and stared; he didn't look away. All his attention was concentrated on his ex-lover. Patty's lawyer had asked in one of the pre-trial hearings if the judge could block eye contact between the defendant and her client during Patty's testimony. I remembered this as Patty stared at the microphone in front of her. The power of the oppressed to confound authority is unsurpassed. Patty Rodriguez, the meekest in our little tableau, held us all in her thrall.

"I feel nervous to see Richard again." Patty held her hand over her mouth while she talked.

"Please put your hands in your lap and speak clearly," Judge Ball interrupted again.

Patty complied and went on, "We had a relationship for two years. We stayed at each other's places, but we didn't live together." Her voice lowered with each word, becoming almost a whisper. The courtroom was one big ear.

"Did there come a time in your relationship when

Richard asked you to go away with him?" Jim stood before Patty with his hands folded and his head cocked to one side.

"Yes, he done some crime."

"Objection."

"Overruled."

"And he wanted me to go with him, so I did."

"Where did you go?"

"Texas. Richard had family there."

"Why did you come back to California?"

"Richard got arrested. They came and took him away."

"Did you know why?" Jim was downright paternal, a *Father Knows Best* of the courtroom.

"No, not until we got back to California. We were still together, so I went to the trial."

"What was he on trial for?" Jim asked.

"Raping a woman when he went to rob her apartment."

"Did this upset you?" Jim asked.

"Yes. I knew he had to get money, you know, but not like that I felt like he betrayed me. I couldn't take that."

"Objection. Hearsay."

"Overruled."

"What did you do, Patty?" Jim asked, willing confidence into his voice, but his gaze never wandered from the sixteen rapt faces before him.

Patty began to cry. "I went to the jail, and I asked him if he did this thing. And he cried and said that he might have. So I asked him if he'd done it before. And he said that he did." She paused, and for a heartbeat there was silence. When she went on, her voice became very quiet, yet distinct. "He said that once he raped an old woman under a bridge and that he might have killed her."

A collective gasp sounded from the courtroom.

"Objection." McGuire was up on his feet. "Permission to speak without the jury present."

The jury stared at Carrasco as they were led out of the courtroom by the bailiff.

"I'm leaning towards allowing the objections," Judge Ball said.

"Your Honor, this goes directly to the Elaine Rothwell matter," Jim pressed.

"It's hearsay," Phillip McGuire said. "She is repeating what was said to her."

Jim looked at McGuire with a look of disgust. "She is testifying to a conversation she had with the defendant."

"I'll allow it," said Judge Ball. "Bring the jury back."

The bailiff brought the jury back into the courtroom, and the case continued.

"What happened after this conversation?" Jim asked.

"I went home and ripped up his letters to me. I had them all over the walls of my room like wallpaper. But I went home and ripped them all up."

"So you were upset?" Jim asked.

"Yes. I felt like he lied to me doing that."

Over and over at different points of her testimony, Jim sought the details which fleshed out Richard Carrasco's predator personality.

"Did you believe what Richard said about raping and maybe killing another woman?"

"He said something like that to me before, and he used to say a lot of things to me that scared me. So it could have been he was trying to scare me or something at that time for some reason or another."

"Did you tell Detective Brown on July third, nineteen ninety-six that Richard said he was out walking one night when he came upon a woman, raped and possibly killed her?"

"I think so."

"Did Richard ever threaten your life?"

Her face closed off like a cornered animal's before she answered, "Yes, I think so."

"Now, a few moments ago you told us one of the statements the defendant made to you was that he had killed someone before, and he would do it again or words to that effect. Is that true?"

"Yes."

"Do you remember when that was said to you?"

"I think when we were at the pizza place."

Jim wanted her to spell it out. "What's the place called?"

"Jack's Pizza."

"Was that at a time when you were dating Mr. Carrasco?"

"Yes."

"Okay. So the two of you are at Jack's Pizza. Is that correct?"

"Yes."

"What was going on?"

"He was flirting with some other girl."

"And what happened? What did you do when you saw that?"

"I got mad. I confronted him."

"Confronted him with words?"

"Yes. Then I think I hit him in the stomach."

"And then what did Mr. Carrasco do?"

"Well, after that I walked away and sat back down at the table, and he came up to me and grabbed me by the back of my neck"

"He grabbed you where?"

"Behind my neck. Like this."

"And what did he do?"

"He wanted me to leave him."

"What did you say?"

"'No.' I didn't want to go."

"And then what happened?"

"He just kept putting his nails into the back of my neck and telling me, 'Let's go,' and I believe that's when he said something about killing somebody, and he would do it again, and I still refused to go, to leave, and he just said something like I wasn't worth it and just—he left."

Finally, Patty Rodriguez added, "Look, I don't want to talk about this. That part of my life is over. I don't want to remember anymore—it scares me. I don't remember no more."

"You don't want to remember your life with Richard Carrasco, do you?"

"No." Again, the struggle showed in her face. "Not ever."

After Patty Rodriguez's testimony, I felt emotionally and physically exhausted. The jury looked wiped out too. Testimony was done for the day, and they all filed past me out of the courtroom, heads down, no conversation among them.

I realized the next ordeal would soon come. I prepared to be my mother's silent witness to her rape and murder. The realization startled me, and I went into the bathroom and sat for a while in a stall with my head in my hands.

The next morning, Jim and I met in the hall. "What will you do now?" I asked him.

Jim chewed on his lip. "The judge wants me to put a victim on the stand."

For a moment, I felt dizzy, wondering how my mother could possibly testify. The problem with wanting something so much and waiting so long is that you tend to feel disoriented when it happens. Much of the time now I felt invisible, as if I were floating along unseen, helplessly observing events and wanting to scream, "Don't screw it up!" I thought about my mother's fellow victims, who were strangers to me and whose assaults at the hands of Richard Carrasco would bring me closer to the truth of what happened to my mother. "Is the information about my mother going to be last?" I asked.

"Yep." Jim chewed on his lip some more. "That's the big gun, that's what'll put him away for a long time."

"I think Judge Ball is right," I said. I knew this was the right time, but through my mind passed the fact that now would come my mother's fellow victims' experiences with her murderer. "A victim will have most impact at this point. Also, you'll give the jury a reason to care."

Jim paused and nodded.

Margaret Carroll, the first victim Jim called as a witness, was sixty-nine years old when she was raped eight years before. At the time of the attack she lived by herself with three cats.

I winced as I listened to her testimony. "I woke up about 4:00 A.M. on May eighth, nineteen ninety. There was a man straddling me. I could see him fairly clearly, because there was a full moon. So I'm certain he was young. I could tell that even though he wore a mask or something over his face. And a wig. I remember the wig gleaming in the moonlight." Mrs. Carroll paused. "I remember the wig." She paused again. "I was tired from work, so I'd left my kitchen window open. I was working as a chef at a restaurant. Anyway, I was tired, so I forgot to shut up the house when I went to sleep around nine o'clock."

"Excuse me, ma'am," Jim said, his voice respectful, his manner somber. "Tell us about your work at the restaurant."

"I was a chef." Mrs. Carroll smiled. "I was a very good chef. Of course, I haven't worked since that night, but then I was the meat chef at my son's restaurant."

"Did you take pride in your work, ma'am?" Jim asked in a soft voice. He stood before her, head bowed, hands crossed; he could have been her grandson asking for forgiveness after tracking mud on the carpet.

"Yes, I did. And I kept my knives just as sharp and clean at home as I did at work." She paused and put a hand to her throat. She looked every bit of her seventy-seven years. She looked tired. "I really don't like remembering this. But I remember now that he had a knife, and he said, 'I got a knife here and I'll kill you.' He made me take off my clothes, and then he took off his pants and underwear. I really don't like to remember this." Mrs. Carroll coughed and drank some water.

"What happened then, ma'am?" Jim asked. I looked at the jury. Their heads were all turned towards the witness box. All their necks were twisted in that stiff, unnatural way that you know will cause kinks later.

"He made me lie on my stomach, and he pushed himself in where it didn't belong."

I noticed that two of the male jurors looked away. The female jurors did not look away, and their necks remained kinked at that odd angle.

"I cried and begged him to stop, and eventually he did. Then, he turned me over on my back and tried to push himself inside me." She stopped talking for a moment, and when she resumed, her voice was loud. "It was painful, and I knew I was bleeding. He kept trying to kiss me, but I told him I wouldn't do that, not that." She shook her finger at Jim. "Don't ask me to explain this pain. You can only understand this pain if you have a vagina. To think that something like this could happen to me, I thought I was strong, but I wasn't. After a while, he stopped trying to get inside me. Then he yanked all the phones out of the wall, took my purse and my kitchen knives, and left. After that, I bled for a long time. It was as if something broke inside me."

Later, after Margaret Carroll's testimony was finished,

I was left alone in the courtroom. The jury and the judge were gone. Jim always allowed me to stay until Carrasco's family was out of the building. I imagined my mother sitting beside me, rocking herself and patting her head. She was like a ghost here, a silent witness, and it was in her memory that I could stand to stay in court and listen to these terrible stories.

When I left the courtroom, despite the late hour, Carrasco's mother, Francie, was still in the hallway. I had overheard her call her son "Richie," a name for innocent little boys playing pranks and going fishing, not for men accused of causing this much blood and pain. I was a bit in awe at how a mother's love can bring forth the little boy from the rapist, the child from the monster.

I looked at Francie's back. From the way her shoulders shook, I felt that she must be crying. Outside, it was raining hard. Two days this week, the streets in front of the courthouse flooded, and I supposed they were a mess today. But after sitting in the courtroom all day, the weather mattered not at all.

Had she lived, my mother would not have talked about her rape. Actually, if my mother had survived Carrasco's attack, I would never have known about it. Alive, my mother most likely would have remained lost to me.

Looking at Carrasco's mother standing at the window, I was somehow drawn towards her. I felt compelled, as if my mother were pushing me forward. After all, if I were on trial, my mother would have stood in the hallway crying too. I realized what mothers must suffer for their children and for the lives their children both lead and don't lead. I was shocked to find this small edge of forgiveness within me. Francie and I had something in common: she found her son again in the rapist, I found my mother in the victim.

"Excuse me," I said to Carrasco's mother, and she

turned towards me. There were circles underneath her eyes and a sagging of the flesh on her face, more indicative of a long, tiring life than just a long, tiring day. "I am sorry for your pain," I said softly.

"I am sorry for yours also," she answered even more softly.

Early the next morning, the first witness of the day, Denise Willard, took the stand. With her dark hair and eyes, she looked a bit like Demi Moore.

"It was August, nineteen ninety," Denise said. "I came home from work and decided to do some exercises. It was real hot in my apartment, so I opened up some of the windows. After I finished exercising, I was tired so I lay down on the couch. I don't know how long I was asleep, but something, some noise, woke me up."

Denise was Carrasco's youngest victim, a single mother. Twenty-seven when Carrasco broke into her apartment and raped her, she was thirty-five now but looked younger. She wore a tan sweater and black skirt and her brown hair in a ponytail. She didn't look at Carrasco and spoke with a monotone voice.

"A man was sitting next to me on the couch. He put his hand over my mouth and said, 'Shut up, bitch.' Then he made me go into the bedroom. He told me to undress. I was crying and couldn't get my bra undone, so he put the knife against my chest, between my breasts, brought the sharp edge underneath my bra, and cut it off. When he took the knife away, he cut me and I started to bleed."

As she spoke, instead of imagining my mother, I imagined myself standing before Richard Carrasco. I imagined the knife against my chest and felt the trickle of blood on my stomach afterward. I stood with my mother now, a rape victim in my mind, feeling her pain, letting anger bubble up for both of us. "He will answer for all this pain," I whispered. The bailiff glanced at me.

Judge Ball's chair was turned towards the witness stand. He leaned his face on his hand. I imagined that he'd heard a million stories in this courtroom, testimony that would make your heart break. *Eventually*, I thought, *the heart must just refuse to break anymore.* As I listened, I always hoped I'd gotten to that point. However, something always came along to prove me wrong. I don't think hearts have much choice whether they break or not.

Denise's eyes were like saucers, but her voice was crystal clear. Only the trembling of the hand with which she gripped the rail in front of her betrayed the emotion she obviously felt as she told what happened. "After I was undressed, he took off his clothes too. Then he lay down on the bed and made me get on top of him. He didn't think I was moving enough, so he put his knife against my stomach and cut me by my bellybutton. He kept making me change positions. I don't know how long he stayed. After a while, he finished on my stomach, I mean he came. Then he rolled me over so that I was face down on the bed, and he tied my hands. He asked me if I had any money, and I said no. He looked around and found some change and jewelry, and then he left."

Though it almost felt like a violation, I kept my eyes on her face, drawn and taut.

"After a while, I got my hands free. Then I got dressed and went outside into the street. A patrol car was driving by, and I motioned to the policeman to stop. When he pulled over, I said, 'Help me, I've been raped. Help me.' And he took me to the hospital."

After Jim thanked Denise Willard, McGuire stood up and introduced himself. This was a different incarnation of the Phillip McGuire I'd come to expect. He moved slowly and kept his voice low and soft. He'd left the elderly victim-witness alone, but this one got questions. "I just have a few questions. One really. Do you think your memory is as clear today as it was eight years ago?"

Denise didn't answer for a moment but continued to stare straight ahead at some invisible point on the courtroom wall. I felt my heart contract as I thought of what she must be going through. Finally, she turned and looked at Carrasco. "My memory is fine. I've forgotten nothing."

Later, standing in the anteroom together, Jim asked me, "How do you think it went today?"

"Very moving," I responded, trying to keep my voice steady.

"Do you think Willard made a good impression on the jury?" he asked. "You know, I've begun to rely on you to gauge their reaction to what's going on."

I looked down at the floor and felt dizzy. It was hard to get the words out. "She got to them, they couldn't keep their eyes off her." It was four o'clock in the afternoon. After talking with Jim, I went straight home, got into bed, and fell asleep. Just like a dead person. No dreams and no thoughts, just oblivion and the weight of discovering my mother again in this place where hope had evaporated, and all that remained was the opportunity for justice or another injustice.

I awoke at around 3:00 A.M., thinking about open windows and knives. Tom was asleep next to me. The house was filled with the kinds of night noises that you don't notice in the daylight. The creak of a door, the refrigerator motor humming, even the sound of the cat scratching in her litter box was loud and oppressive.

I suffered from nightmares as a child, often dreaming that the house was on fire. When I was ten years old, after my mother came home from the hospital and we moved to our house in Hayward, I woke up in the middle of one of those nightmares, certain that our new house was burning down. I could feel the heat from the flames and smell the smoke. I screamed until my mother came to get me and took me into bed with her. But I still had trouble sleeping. Both my parents smoked then, and I could smell it in their room—stale cigarettes and sulfur from matches. I must have fallen asleep, though, because I woke my parents up with my screaming two more times that night.

After that, no matter how scared I was or how much my mother pleaded with my father, he made me stay in my own bed. The poor man did have to wake up at 4:00 A.M. to go to work.

Now a murder-trial-attending adult, I still didn't want to go back to sleep for fear of what I'd find hiding in my imagination. I decided to get up and phone my brother in Los Angeles.

"Michael, were you sleeping?" I asked, when he answered the phone.

"Sister," he said. My brother's greetings were more like announcements. "Sister," "Father," "Daughter"—he gave us titles instead of names. This seemed to fulfill some need within him to classify things. "Nah. I'm awake. Never do sleep much. What's up?"

One interesting thing about my family, we can begin or end conversations at any time of the day without feeling uncomfortable. "I just couldn't sleep," I answered. "I was thinking about what it was like when we were kids."

"You think too much," he said quietly.

His words hung in the air.

Finally, I said, "Maybe so. I was thinking about when I used to have nightmares, how Dad made me stay in my own bed no matter how scared I was. You're lucky. I don't think he was as hard on you."

"Oh, really?" my brother said. "Don't go there, Sister. I tell you, don't go there."

"Why?" I asked.

"Okay. Let me tell you about Dad. Remember when I was in the fifth grade, and I was having trouble in class because I was shaking?"

"No."

"The teacher kept sending notes home with me. I would just sit in class and start shaking. Couldn't stop. Well, finally Mom made Dad take me to the doctor. But the day he took me to the doctor, I was fine. And this really pissed Dad off, me being fine and all. So when the doctor left the room, Dad started screaming at me. And he screamed at me until I started shaking. Then, he says to the doctor, 'See, the kid's nervous. I don't know why.' So the doctor prescribed tranquilizers for me. All the way home in the car, Dad kept saying to me, 'Now you're like your mother. You're gonna be on pills your whole life, just like your mother.' So don't go telling me that he was nicer to me. Dad just wanted things the way he wanted them, and you better get it right the first time. I remember, so I try real hard with my daughter not to do that to her. I tell her when I'm proud of her, and I don't tell her she could have done better."

"I guess we had the same childhood after all," I said. I closed my eyes and thought about my mother locking herself in the bathroom with my baby brother and me. I heard my father asking me to unlock the door and then felt the wall against my back and doorknob against my chest when he opened the door hard. I could see my mother lying in the bathtub curled up around my brother while my father kicked her. I felt surrounded by my childhood trauma. "You must hate him," I said.

My brother didn't answer, and we let a pause develop and sink in. Except for the night noises, the creaks and groans of a lived-in house, it was very still around me.

"Nah," Michael said, "I don't hate him. I stopped hating him years ago."

"Why?" I asked.

"Because he's my father," Michael answered.

"I love you, Michael," I said. It was the first time I'd said it since he was a baby.

"I love you too, Sister," he answered.

My brother had reserved his resentment for our father, just as I hated our mother for the things she couldn't help. In the end, all of it mattered and at the same time didn't matter. Family is what you escape from and what you return to, but it's love that saves you.

CHAPTER 14

By Force or Fear

Watching the trial every day, I no longer had a good definition for the words "crime" or "judgment," and even the word "commit" held a different connotation for me than it had before. Every day, I walked down the hallway past the jurors, all of us waiting for the day's session to begin. I always stood for a while, listening to the jurors talk amongst themselves. They talked about their lives, their jobs, the weather, and how long the line to validate parking was. They formed little cliques, like kids in high school, and sat in little intimate clumps, though certainly this intimacy would vanish after the trial. I'd served on a jury myself and knew how fast a promise to keep in touch could fade, much as real life promises that we make when the truth of a final goodbye seems too harsh. Years ago, when I put my mother on the plane and sent her off to live with her sister, I'd told her that I'd see her soon, when what I really meant was, "I can't help you,

Mother, so I'm sending you away." In the end, "I'll see you soon" may be kinder than saying goodbye.

Usually, I found that I couldn't stay in the hallway for long, so I went into the courtroom early or hid in a bathroom stall. Sometimes I went to another floor and hid out in a new bathroom. And sometimes I got my exercise by walking up and down the stairs. I'd lost three pounds since the first day of trial. It wasn't the presence of the jurors that bothered me. It was Carrasco's family, especially his younger relatives. I couldn't stay in the hallway under the scrutiny of their curious expressions. The second day of the trial one of his younger relatives had asked me if I was a reporter. I gave her a curt "no" and disappeared into the bathroom away from her baffled expression. Observing the signs of affection between Carrasco and his family every day was too confusing. On one hand, Carrasco sat in court every day, shackled to the floor, doodling on a yellow pad, and occasionally glaring at me. Then there was his family, telling him they loved him during breaks and calling him "Richie." To me, Carrasco seemed to be two people. He was the son who loved his mother and family, and he was also the accused rapist and murderer of helpless women. Sometimes I had to get away from it, and during breaks when the courtroom was off-limits, I hid in a bathroom stall with my head in my hands.

Never in my life had my powers of observation been so keen and yet so detached. Each day they seemed to sharpen more. Monday through Thursday each week, I watched from my seat in the courtroom everything that happened around me, scribbling notes in my journal. I paid particular attention to small reactions, those sudden expressions and gestures we normally take for granted or simply don't notice. Such as the way a woman grips her purse or puts her hand over her chest or mouth, or the slow movement of a mother's hand as it slides across her child's cheek on its way to tucking a strand of hair behind an ear. Or the way Carrasco watched every witness that took the stand and the way that the jury never once looked in his direction. I spent entire afternoons watching the way the judge lay his cheek against his hand, wondering if he were asleep, and if he was, who would know if justice was being abused. I watched everyone in the courtroom for signs of life. Honing my skills as an observer and listening to painful testimony was exhausting but riveting.

The trial had been going on for several weeks, and by Thursday night of each week I felt so weary that I went to bed as soon as I got home and was sound asleep immediately. On Fridays, which were reserved by the court for sentence hearings on other cases, I woke up in the morning groggy and had to lie in bed for a couple of hours trying to de-fog. Once I got up, I was busy with all the work I didn't have time to do during the week.

One of those groggy Friday mornings, the phone rang at ten o'clock, interrupting my de-fogging and forcing me out of bed earlier than usual. The caller was Jim Shore, warning me about what testimony was coming up the next week. "Tuesday morning, Richard Carrasco's mother is going to testify, and Tuesday afternoon, testimony about your mother will begin."

I thought of nothing else the entire weekend.

That Monday, January 20, 1998, we had a surprise witness before Richard Carrasco's mother took the stand. Alex Cavello, Carrasco's uncle and one of the last people to see my mother alive, was to testify. I remembered reading about him:

Every Sunday for the past two months, Lucia Elaine Rothwell sat on the curb across the street from Alex Cavello's house. After Alex and his daughter, Alicia, came home from church,

Alex would send Alicia across the street, in order to ask Elaine to Sunday dinner. Elaine never answered the girl's invitation, or looked up to acknowledge her presence.

Alex Cavello, a stocky, thirty-seven-year-old man with horn-rimmed glasses and a well-trimmed mustache, walked slowly to the witness stand and was sworn in. He was married to Francie's sister and thus was related to Carrasco by marriage. While he testified, Alex didn't look at his nephew, nor did he look at me.

"Did Richard stay with your family often?" Jim asked.

Staring straight ahead the witness replied, "Off and on, but if he'd ever felt the need he wouldn't have been denied."

"Were you acquainted with the victim, Elaine Rothwell?" Jim asked.

"Yes, I would see her on Sundays when I came home from church." Alex looked down at his hands and didn't speak for a moment. "She was always either standing or sitting by a stoplight. I never knew her name until after she died, but I talked to her every Sunday. I invited her to go to church with us on the way to church, and afterwards, I asked her to come home with us for dinner." Alex said all of this very fast, as if he'd rehearsed it before the bathroom mirror, much as I rehearsed my expressionless in-court face.

"Did she ever accept?" Jim asked.

"No, sir. She wouldn't talk to us. It was pretty obvious that she was in a bad way."

Jim looked down at the floor for a moment. "You spoke to her on the morning of April second?" he continued.

"Yes. As usual I asked her to join us for church and dinner, and as usual she didn't answer. My daughter, Alicia, gave her some fruit finally, and that's the last I saw of her. When I heard on the radio that she'd been killed,

I called the police. I wanted to attend her funeral, but I couldn't find out where it was."

"Were you sad?" Jim asked. "About Mrs. Rothwell's death?"

"Yes, sir, I was. She was a quiet, shy lady."

Jim finished with his questions and Phillip McGuire had none, so Alex left the courtroom. As he passed me, I wanted to reach out and touch his arm. I wanted to thank him for caring, but he was moving too fast and he didn't look at me. The words "thank you" stuck in my mouth with no place to go. I closed my eyes and pictured my mother refusing the invitation to dinner without even looking up. It was possible she hadn't heard the offer, but instead had been listening to a number of other anonymous voices inside her head. I wondered now what her voices said to her, and if they'd kept her from being lonely or just terrified her.

As the next witness, Carrasco's mother, came to the witness stand, she moved slowly, with her head down. Once on the stand, she seemed to want to talk about her own life.

She began, "I am forty-one years old, and I have three children, all born in El Paso. We sort of moved back and forth between El Paso and San Jose three or four times. It's hard for me to remember. I was on drugs then, and things were pretty unclear." Francie sat very straight in the witness chair, looked the district attorney right in the eye, and smiled. "I was on drugs most of my life, but I'm clean and sober now."

"Congratulations," Jim said, the tone of his voice indecipherable.

"Thanks," Francie answered and smiled. "Richie was a normal kid. You know, it wasn't an easy life what with me on drugs. Sometime we lived in cars, sometime we didn't have nowhere to go."

As I watched and listened to her, things I'd read about her son echoed in my mind.

The defendant, Richard Carrasco, was interviewed by a clinical neuro-psychologist in May 1993, shortly after his arrest. According to this psychologist, Richard outlined the particulars of the charged rapes and further outlined his family history and involvement in the use of alcohol, hallucinogenics, and crack cocaine. The doctor's conclusions indicated anti-social personality disorder and described Richard as a chronically anxious and angry individual. In his report, the doctor noted that the circumstances of Richard's upbringing gave him ample reason to experience this anger. The doctor further noted that unfortunately, Richard had developed a pattern of expressing the underlying rage that he felt via the domination of others.

Instead of looking at Francie, one of the female jurors wrote on a pad of paper that she had in her lap. Her body was turned away from the witness stand. All the male jurors watched Francie. None of them wrote down her testimony. The other female juror bit her lip and held her pen suspended in the air while she watched Francie testify.

"I don't remember much. We were homeless sometimes, you know, off and on. I can't blame my family for not putting up with me when the drugs and booze had me."

The words of another report on Carrasco came back to me:

Richard Carrasco's first rape occurred when he was sixteen years of age. At that point he had been thrown out of the family home. His Uncle Manuel, aunts and mother were drinking to excess and smoking crack. Carrasco stated, "No one cared what happened to me." He was living in cars or staying with friends. This is when he started breaking into houses.

"Was Richard home with you at night, Francie?" Jim asked.

"I'm sure he was."

"You're certain he was at home with you in the evenings during the spring and summer of nineteen ninety?"

I looked at the back of Carrasco's head. Each day, the bailiff brought Carrasco into the courtroom neatly dressed in a shirt and tie before the jury was seated, so that they did not see him shackled to the floor. All the jury saw was a neatly dressed man who never stood up. Carrasco must have been well coached by his attorney because he was attentive to all the witnesses. He sat with his hands folded, occasionally talking to his attorney. Often he looked at me, and then his expression was not friendly. At the beginning of the trial, he would stare at me until I looked away. Now, I was never the first person to look away. I didn't know if my mother fought for her life against Richard Carrasco. She certainly wasn't equipped to put up much of a defense. But I was fighting for her now. And her murderer was no match for me. After eight years of waiting, after finally identifying her killer, I'd learned never to give up.

"Francie," Jim repeated, "were you aware of Richard's whereabouts during the spring and summer of nineteen ninety?"

"I remember that he was there sometimes. I don't remember much about that time." Francie looked at the jury. "I'm clean and sober now," she said again. "I'm working my program."

I looked searchingly at her. Something else I'd read about her son floated up from my subconscious:

Sixteen-year-old Richard Carrasco's first rape occurred while in the process of one of his break-ins. He climbed in the bathroom window of one of the apartments in the building next to his uncle's house. Once inside, he saw a woman in the bedroom. She woke up and started screaming. Richard jumped on the bed and tried to shut her up. He began slapping her and while he slapped her he became aroused. He removed her pajama bottoms and top and raped her. Afterwards he was shocked at what he'd done and stopped breaking into houses for a while.

His next rape was in 1990. Richard was always either drunk or stoned at this point. He'd been living on the streets for a while and had no means of support other than breaking into houses. He felt remorse after this rape, but not enough to stop him from raping again and more often.

I refocused on the testimony.

"Thank you, Francie," Jim said.

"No questions," Phillip McGuire said.

"I've been clean and sober for six months now," Francie said yet again to the jury. She looked over at Carrasco and smiled. "I love you, son," she said.

"I love you too, Mom," Carrasco answered, even though he wasn't supposed to speak.

Although Francie's memory of the early events in Richard Carrasco's life appeared hazy now, they had been clearer when she spoke to Officer Brown, as he testified when Jim Shore recalled him to the stand after Francie stepped down.

Shore asked, "Now, did you ask her about Richard's habits in nineteen eighty-nine and nineteen ninety in terms of where he was spending the nights?"

"Yes." Brown nodded.

"Did she indicate that he was spending some nights sleeping in cars?"

"Yes."

When the court recessed for lunch after Brown's testimony, I just sat there in the courtroom, thinking of my own family.

With my mother, the loud, crazy years were either before my brother was born or when he was too young to remember. Since he missed all that, he was freer to love her than I was. For me, loving my mother meant overcoming my childhood and then coping with a present that was no less confusing and painful than the past had been. After shock therapy and institutionalization beat my mother down, she was crazy in a quiet way. Now, instead of the wild, crazy expressions she often had when I was three or four, it is the look of betrayal in her eyes that I remembered. I used to think I put it there, and my own guilt made me hate her. But it was life that betrayed my mother and put the hurt in her eyes. People took advantage of her because she wouldn't fight back. I think that our dreams keep us alive, keep us fighting back against the odds. Even nightmares serve some purpose. First, my mother dreamed of being a teacher. She made that dream come true. After her time at Agnew's Psychiatric Facility, my mother gave up on teaching and just got quieter. She tried to hide her breakdowns from my father. Mostly, she just kept her dreams to herself and slept away as much of the day as she could. I don't know what she dreamed in her sleep, or if the fantasies she had when she was awake exhausted her so that her sleep was dreamless. Maybe sleep was further torment or her only peaceful place. At the end of her life, when she was homeless and living fifteen minutes from my house, I believe that it was her dream of being with her children again that kept her alive. And that's what kept her alive for me now.

I looked around me; mostly everyone else had gone to lunch. I stood up and stretched my legs, wondering where I should go until the afternoon session began.

The only other observer left was a neatly dressed woman, about fifty years old, who seemed intensely preoccupied and was sitting directly behind me. Jim Shore and the court clerk were at the front of the courtroom gathering things to leave while at the same time sorting through pictures for the afternoon's proceedings. Every now and then the clerk held up a picture and said, "How about this one, Jim?"

I gasped. They were pictures of my mother taken while she was on the autopsy table. In some of the pictures she was dressed, and in some she was naked. The clerk held them up so that they were facing me, and I had a clear view of my mother's naked body on the metal coroner's table. In one picture my mother was wearing clothes. This picture was mainly of her face. There was a shirt wrapped around her head, and her mouth and eyes were open. This picture was particularly difficult for me, because looking at her face, I didn't feel a tug of recognition. I came here, after all, to find my mother, not to lose her all over again.

As Jim and the clerk finished up and left, I walked out behind them. The only other person left in the courtroom, the strange, intense woman, followed me. I felt a tap on my shoulder.

"You're her daughter, aren't you?" the woman asked.

I spun around and looked at her. There was an eagerness about her. She wore an expression that promised news or truth of some uncommon sort. "Excuse me," I said, "who are you? How did you know my mother?"

I was gripping the courtroom door with one hand. I could see that my knuckles were turning white. The woman placed her hand on mine. "I knew her when she was homeless," she said with a smile. "I'm an attorney for the district attorney's office—that's how I knew about the case. I was hoping to meet you. You are her daughter, right?" The woman leaned forward.

I slid my hand out from under hers and stepped into the hallway. "Yes," I said. "How did you know?" I felt uncomfortable under her scrutiny. She looked me over as if I were on display.

"Your eyes. I recognized you by your eyes. They are exactly the same color as your mother's." Even though I felt uncomfortable under such scrutiny, I couldn't help smiling. "She had very unusual eyes." Taking my hand she said, "Your mother wasn't like other people."

"I know," I said, taking my hand back. "She was mentally ill." Thinking back, I remembered the odd telephone call I'd received after my mother had died. The call had been from a woman in the district attorney's office. Somehow I was sure this was the caller. "You called me, didn't you?" I said. "Right after my mother was killed. Why didn't you call back?"

The woman shifted her weight from one foot to the other, finally taking her gaze away from my face. "I didn't want to intrude," she said. "I thought it would be best to leave you alone. But," the woman persisted, "I kept track of the case. I didn't think it would ever come to trial. I'm glad it has. Your mother was special. She was obviously very intelligent and kind. You could see in her eyes that she knew things about life."

"What things?" I asked. I felt drawn into the conversation by the fact that this woman had known my mother at the end of her life, when I had lost her.

"Well." The woman grabbed my hand and patted it. "She was very quiet the last time I saw her, lost in her own thoughts."

"Perhaps she was hearing voices. My mother was schizophrenic."

The woman dropped my hand. "How do you know that?" she asked in a sharp tone of voice, loudly enough to cause a passerby to look our way.

Tired of explaining, I merely said, "I grew up with her. Trust me, she was mentally ill. May I know who you are?"

The woman smiled. "My name is Sharon. I saw your mother about three mornings a week. There was a time I thought about taking her into my home." Sharon leaned closer to me. "Your mother was a wise woman."

A lifetime filled with frustrated explanations of my mother's mental state welled up in me, erasing any pretense of remaining polite in the face of this intrusion into my privacy. "My mother was a sick woman," I replied. "She was paranoid. She thought people were out to get her." I smiled after I said this. The woman had tried, after all, to be kind to my mother.

"Well," Sharon said, "she was right, wasn't she? Considering what happened." She patted me on the shoulder, and having said what she'd come to say, left me standing alone in the hallway.

A few minutes later, Jim Shore returned from lunch. I followed him into the courtroom and took a seat. The final witness of the day was to be a man who worked in the office building next to my mother's campsite, and he arrived to meet with Jim before his testimony. He was a tall man and another fast walker like defense attorney McGuire, so he created a slight breeze as he walked past where I was sitting. Jim moved forward to greet him, and they shook hands in the firm, dueling fashion of tall men. Jim began showing him pictures from the pile on his table, and I could overhear them as they talked.

"Yep," the man said, "that's her all right. That's Little Elaine. Boy, that sure was a shame." He looked down at the floor, shaking his head.

Jim glanced in my direction, then placed a hand on the man's shoulder and led him towards the corner nearest where the jury always sat. Jim lowered his voice, but not enough so that I could fail to overhear. "That's her daughter."

At that the man's head snapped up, and he turned in my direction. His mouth opened, and he stared at me for a moment. "My God," he said, "I didn't know. Little Elaine's daughter?"

Finally, the jury filed in, and the afternoon session was about to begin. The man settled himself in the witness box.

The clerk asked the witness during the process of swearing him in, "State your name for the Court."

"Bob Pritchard."

"Be seated."

Jim asked Mr. Pritchard to draw a picture of my mother's encampment. The witness obliged, drawing quite an accurate picture and providing us all with a visual aid for the afternoon. Then Jim asked him to describe how he came to know my mother.

"Well, I became aware of a little homeless lady living on the other side of the fence pretty quickly after I opened my business. I guess that was in nineteen eighty-seven. So, I knew her for about three years," Mr. Pritchard answered.

"Is this the woman you knew?" Jim asked, holding up a photograph of my mother.

"Yes, that's Little Elaine." Mr. Pritchard looked at the jury. "That's what I called her. She was so tiny." He looked at me then, with an apologetic half-smile on his face. It's just the way it was, his expression seemed to be trying to convey, just the reality of the situation.

"So, she told you her name?" Jim asked.

"Yes, Elaine Rothwell." Mr. Pritchard sighed and looked at his lap for a moment. Before he began testifying again he looked over at Carrasco.

This afternoon Carrasco's shirt was wrinkled. His hands were folded on the defense table, and he rested his forehead on them.

Mr. Pritchard continued, "She was pretty quiet, but eventually she told me her name. I wouldn't exactly call her talkative. I don't think we ever had a real conversation."

"Did she panhandle?" Jim asked.

Mr. Pritchard shook his head. "What I liked about Little Elaine was that she never panhandled. She was just a quiet little lady. She lived in a box with sleeping bags, a pink blanket, and a coat. As a matter of fact, she always wore a coat, no matter the weather. And jeans and a hat. I never saw her without something on her head. A ski hat or a hood, or something. Once I noticed that her shoes were getting kind of old, so I bought her some new ones."

"Was she clean?" Jim asked.

Mr. Pritchard looked over at me for a moment. "No. She looked homeless. I don't think it's possible to stay clean living that lifestyle."

"Did she keep to herself?" Jim asked.

Pritchard nodded his head. "Yes. I never saw her with anyone else. Anyway, I got to work around six-thirty in the mornings about six days a week, and she would be asleep in her box. A little later on every morning I would bring her some coffee and a roll. She'd be up then, sitting under a lamppost. Every week I gave her twenty dollars. She took it, but she never asked for anything. She was a nice, quiet little lady." Mr. Pritchard said this last sentence directly to me. I nodded in response.

"What happened on the morning of April second, nineteen ninety?" Jim asked.

"Well, I got to work and looked, as usual, for Little Elaine. Instead of sleeping in her box, she was laying on the ground outside her box."

"Was she on a blanket or sleeping bag?" Jim asked.

"No, she was laying on the ground."

"What condition was she in?" Jim asked.

Mr. Pritchard looked into his lap for a moment. He sighed. "Her pants were down and her legs were spread."

"Did you think she was hurt?" Jim asked.

Mr. Pritchard was silent for a moment. Finally he

blurted out, "No. She looked dead. I knew that she was dead."

After Mr. Pritchard's testimony was over and court was dismissed for the day, I waited in the courtroom until everyone but the district attorney left. I didn't look up at the jury as they passed by. Jim had stopped to speak with the judge, then he joined me and we walked to the elevator.

"Look, about tomorrow," he said. "There's going to be a video of the crime scene. You might want to skip the morning session and just come in the afternoon."

"What happens in the afternoon?" I asked.

"We start hearing DNA testimony." Jim turned and looked at me.

"I'll be here all day," I said. "I am here for my mother. Don't worry about me."

"Think it over," Jim said as the elevator doors opened. "There are some memories you don't want to have and some things a daughter shouldn't see."

"I understand all about bad memories," I said, "believe me." I got into the elevator and turned around so that I was facing the doors. Putting my finger on the *Door Open* button, I said, "If she had to suffer it, I can stand watching it." Then I took my finger off the button and the elevator doors closed. Feeling very brave, I rode down to the bottom floor. When I got to my car, I sat with my eyes closed for quite a while. I'd purchased a month's pass for the parking garage. I thought, *I can sit here as long as I want.* I waited until the garage was almost empty before leaving. Inserting my parking ticket into the machine, I retrieved it and waited for the gate to open while the mechanical female voice said, "Thank you for coming. Please come again soon."

CHAPTER 15

An Important Day

The next morning, Officer Mike Brown was already sitting at the prosecution table when I came into the courtroom. He turned and smiled at me.

"Good morning, Paula," he said, and then got up and walked over to me. Tall, dark, and blue-eyed, Officer Brown was the best-looking man I had ever seen with the exception of the occasional movie star.

"Hi," I said and sat down. Then I stood up again. "So, an important day."

"I think you should reconsider sticking around this morning. It is going to be rough," Officer Brown advised. His brow had concerned-looking crinkles running across it.

"I'll be all right," I said and felt my determination stiffen. "I'm here for my mother."

Officer Brown smiled, patted me on the arm, and returned to the front of the courtroom where he became engrossed in the contents of his briefcase. I sat down.

There isn't much of a chance for casual conversation during a trial. Apart from the jurors' opportunities to chat during breaks, the rest of us just passed each other in the hall or shared the courtroom in not quite companionable silence. Today, I had a book with me, but as usual I didn't read it. I opened to the middle and lay it across my lap as a prop. Looking around the courtroom, I tested my memory of the judge's flags on display and tried to relax. This trial, this pause in my life, had come to represent eight years of missing my mother. Every day, sitting in the courtroom, I experienced what I'd put off feeling for eight years. I saw my mother's face again and heard her life described by people who had not known her when she was young, when her illness was under control. They never heard her sing or saw her soft hair bounce when she turned her head, and most of them thought her eyes were gray. I don't know why it was so important to me that everyone know her eyes were blue, but it was. I looked over at the bailiff. He was watching me. I smiled.

"Sorry to stare," he said, "but you have the most beautiful eyes I've ever seen."

"Thank you," I replied. "I got them from my mother. My eyes are exactly like hers."

From the bench, Judge Ball signaled that he was ready, and the bailiff called the court to order.

The first witness of the day, Frank Stubbs, was a squat little man with a hunched-up quality about him. Frank Stubbs told how he had been homeless off and on since 1970. He was my mother's neighbor under the freeway ramp during the last three years of her life. Listening to this witness testify might be the jury's first opportunity to listen to a homeless citizen speak about their life on the streets.

Mr. Stubbs made a not exactly clean and not exactly dirty appearance. He looked like someone who had forgotten what it was like to be well-groomed and was making his best effort based on what he'd observed around him. There were deep grooves on his forehead, probably from years of drinking, worrying, and living outdoors. He was missing his front teeth, so opening his mouth or smiling made him look even odder. His hair was combed back with either water or gel, and the tracks of his comb were visible. He wore an off-white shirt that was just a bit too big for him, baggy pants, and new tennis shoes. Agewise, I thought he could have been anywhere from forty to sixty-five.

"I'm fifty-three," Frank said in answer to Jim's question, "and I'm working down at Saint James Senior Center. In the kitchen. I ain't always been working, but been doing this pretty steady."

"Were you working in nineteen ninety?" Jim asked.

Frank sucked on his gums. Doing this made the front of his face shrink a bit. After a minute his lips popped forward, and the furrows in his brow became deeper. "No. Pretty hard to work when you're drinking all the time. Pretty darn hard." Frank's hands formed fists. He made a belligerent "dare-you" impression.

"Did your days follow any particular pattern?" Jim remained seated while Frank testified.

"Yep. Me and my friend Alan got up every morning if we wasn't too sick and had breakfast down at the Mission. Then, if we had any money, we got ourselves some malt liquor. I don't panhandle. Never have. Sometimes people gave me money, but I didn't panhandle. If we wasn't too drunk, we ate at the Armory, and if the weather was bad we slept there too."

"What was your campsite like?"

"It was just behind some bushes. You know, we had some cooking stuff, a couch, and some sleeping bags. We tried to stay pretty quiet, because we didn't want to get run out. Usually it was just Alan and me staying there. Sometimes we had guests. You gotta kinda stay on guard when you carry everything you own with you." Frank sucked in his lips and blew them out again. "It ain't no way to live."

"Did you become acquainted with Mrs. Rothwell in nineteen ninety?" Jim asked.

"Who? I never knew her name. If you mean that little lady, her camp was about fifty yards from ours. I passed her every morning on the way to the Mission. Sometimes I said hello, but she never answered. Sometimes I saw her at the Armory, but she kept to herself. I never saw her speak to anybody. Saw her a lot sitting under a streetlight. She was always alone, kinda bundled up, always had her head down."

"Do you remember what happened on April second, nineteen ninety?"

"Don't remember anything about that night. I was drinking pretty heavy, and when I was at home in my campsite I usually wore earphones and drank beer until I fell asleep. Kind of hard to hear anything with the traffic anyway. But in the morning, man, I woke up early because there was cops everywhere. They was all over our campground. They took me into the station and talked to me for a couple of hours, and then when they let me go, I couldn't go back home. Matter of fact, we couldn't go back for a couple of months. It was a bummer, man."

"You didn't hear any screaming that night?"

"Nah, man. I was pretty drunk. I'm working now. I work down at the Saint James Senior Center in the kitchen. I ain't had nothing to drink for six months."

Defense attorney McGuire asked Frank a few questions: how often was he drunk, how many visitors came through the campground. While McGuire cross-examined Stubbs, I looked over at the jury. The youngest juror, a blond man

in his late twenties with a smooth, boyish looking face, was
watching me. He stared right at my face. I looked away,
but when I turned back, he was still watching me.

After Mr. Stubbs finished testifying, there was a short
break while Jim set up the courtroom for the video of
the crime scene. I looked around. Richard Carrasco's
family was not in court.

During the break, the other side of the courtroom
began to fill up with a gaggle of district attorneys. They
trickled in until finally there were twelve of them sitting
across from me. Eight men and four women, they made
up an unofficial law enforcement jury. When the last of
these observers came into the courtroom, he introduced
himself to me as Gary Sholes, a part-time investigator for
the district attorney's office.

Mr. Sholes was a retired police officer. He was huge,
standing about six-feet-eight-inches tall. A solid, muscular
man, he had a serious expression. I couldn't help thinking I would have been very nervous if he pulled me over
for a traffic violation. As it was, sitting next to him, I felt as
small as a young child sitting beside her father in church.

Finally, the jury came back in, and Jim called Officer
Frank to the witness stand to explain to the jury what
they would see in the video of the crime scene. The
lights in the room dimmed and the video began.

At first there was just a scene of yellow tape, chain link
fence and bushes. I wasn't listening to Officer Frank,
who was describing the physical aspects of the scene.
Then I noticed something that looked like a white tree
branch lying on the grass. The camera pulled closer, and
I realized with a shock that I was looking at my mother's
body on the grass, naked, with her legs spread. *Her legs
are so thin that they don't look like they belong to a human being,*
I thought. The camera panned over my mother's naked

body. Behind it, there was a cardboard box with what appeared to be a pink blanket spread out next to it.

I was looking at my mother's last home.

"Oh, no," I heard myself say but didn't realize that I was speaking out loud. My voice sounded like it was coming from somewhere deep inside me, near my stomach. It felt like a groan working its way up and out. "Oh, no," I repeated and gasped. I felt the air stop in the middle of my throat I brought my hands up to my face, as if covering myself from view as I watched would somehow keep the awful truth from finding me. But it found me anyway. A moan snuck out from my mouth, and I began to sob. I cried until I couldn't see the front of the courtroom.

Officer Frank continued narrating the video. As the camera focused on my mother's body, he explained why they did not try to revive her. "Visually, she was obviously dead," he said. "Rigor mortis had set in."

Once again, the camera panned over my mother's body, ending at her head, which was covered with her shirt.

Unable to muffle my feelings, I cried out again, "Oh, no."

Officer Frank described to the jury the amount of blood found and where it was found on the ground in relation to the body.

The camera panned to the area on the ground next to my mother's hip. It was possible to make out the blood on the leaves in the video. One of my mother's knees was up, while her other leg stretched out on the ground. I looked over at Richard Carrasco's back. His head was down on the table with his hands on the sides of his face as if he were hiding.

I could not stop myself. "Oh, no."

More reports I'd read flooded through my mind.

On April 2, 1990, at approximately 9:00 A.M., investigating officers responded to the Highway 880 on-ramp at North First Street on report of a found dead body. It was subsequently

ascertained that the body was that of victim Elaine Rothwell, a
transient, who had been using the area under the on-ramp as
her makeshift camp. Her body was found semi-nude with her
legs and vaginal area exposed. She was wearing a panty on one
of her legs. It was subsequently ascertained that the victim had
been raped and had lost a substantial amount of blood to the
point where she went into shock and died. The officers discov-
ered an area of blood consistent with where the victim had been
lying which penetrated the ground by approximately four inches
and a diameter of approximately eight inches.

Even my thoughts were against me, enlarging this real
nightmare.

"Oh, no," I sobbed.

"Come with me." Gary Sholes took my elbow and led
me from the courtroom. We walked down the hallway to
the elevators and sat on the benches facing them. "You
don't need to watch any more of that video," Mr. Sholes
said as he handed me his handkerchief. "Your mother
isn't in there."

"I want to be here for her. No one else is," I answered,
wiping what remained of my makeup from my face.

"You are here for your mother. You don't have to sit
through that video to prove it. Please go home. Later
this afternoon we are beginning the scientific testimony.
Come back then if you want, but go home now." He
patted me on the hand.

I knew he was right. I went home, got into bed, and
went immediately to sleep. I didn't wake up until the next
morning. Tom had already left for work. When I walked
into the courtroom at around nine, Carrasco was already
there. It was just the five of us, Carrasco, McGuire, the
bailiff, Detective Brown, and me. I looked at the back of
Carrasco's neck.

Detective Brown came over and sat down beside me.
Placing his hand on my knee he said, "I want you to

know that I admire you. Yesterday, listening to you crying in the courtroom during the video broke my heart." He patted me on the knee again and then returned to the prosecution table.

"I'm here for you, Mother," I said, quietly but out loud. Carrasco turned around when I said it and looked at me. I stared back, and he turned away. "I'm here for you, Mother," I said again.

For perhaps the first time in my life, I was both proud and in need of the Paula Jean in me. It was the tough little girl I used to be that was stubborn enough to look Richard Carrasco in the eyes and not turn away. A person can't escape their childhood, their history. It's a mistake to try. Your past chases you if you try to run away, and it'll keep running after you until it runs you down. If you turn and fight, all that haunts you will back down and set you free to face what's in front of you.

CHAPTER 16

The Finale

Richard Carrasco's family was present in the courtroom for the scientific testimony. For four days, experts testified about DNA and blood typing. Half the scientific testimony was educational, and half went directly to the rapes and murder. All the results matched Carrasco's genetic makeup. Before they testified, each expert offered a summary of their education and work history as proof that they were capable of performing the test and drawing a valid conclusion.

Defense attorney McGuire had no experts of his own. His cross-examination tactics were based on trying to refute the various experts' credentials. Failing that, he resorted to sarcasm. At one point, McGuire began to draw his own expert conclusions from the DNA, blood, and hair samples. Jim responded to this tactic by saying, "Perhaps Mr. McGuire should be sworn in as an expert witness."

I was as lucky as a murder victim's daughter can get. Despite my mother's homeless state, the County ordered the two most sophisticated DNA tests performed on her sample. If anything convicted Carrasco, it would be this evidence. As Jim had outlined in his opening statement, Richard Carrasco had left his genetic fingerprint inside my mother's body.

During the two days of DNA testimony, Carrasco, in contrast to his clean-cut appearance earlier in the trial, was unshaven and sat slumped in his chair. He didn't smile at his family or talk to his attorney. He didn't look at me. Mostly he leaned his head on one hand, held a pen in the other hand, and doodled. For most of the trial, even during the most horrific testimony, the jury didn't look in his direction. Now they watched him. Every time a piece of scientific evidence identified him, they turned and scrutinized his face. It was as if they expected the capacity to commit violence to become apparent in his demeanor. And in a way it did, as every day Carrasco's appearance became increasingly disheveled.

The last prosecution witness was the coroner, Dr. Cochran, Sven's boss and the person who'd performed my mother's autopsy. I learned now he had presided over more than 6,000 autopsies. He described the facts of my mother's condition at the time of her death. I'd heard it before. I'd read it before. I had the details of my mother's murder memorized. Watching the jury, I couldn't tell if they sympathized, though I was certain they must. They all nodded at me in the hallway now.

I could almost feel my mother's hand in mine and hear her laughter, like in the early days when I was a very little girl before the screaming and the pain.

"Doctor Cochran," Jim asked, "what killed Mrs. Rothwell?"

Doctor Cochran cleared his throat, looked down at his notes, and said, "Mrs. Rothwell died of what I would refer to as an episiotomy, which is an incision made at the vagina, moving towards the anus, to enlarge the vaginal opening. In this case, the laceration was made by a blunt instrument."

Dr. Cochran finished testifying, and the prosecution rested.

McGuire did not call any witnesses for the defense.

The day that final arguments were to be presented we had a late start because Carrasco was in solitary confinement. On the trip from the jail to the courthouse, he had been caught with a homemade knife.

Judge Ball spoke with authority. "Ladies and gentlemen, you have heard the entirety of the evidence at this time. Next in order will be what are called closing statements.

"Now, you've been reminded previously, and I will remind you again, that statements of lawyers aren't to be construed as evidence. The purpose of closing statements is for the attorneys to attempt to have you recall that portion of the evidence that supports their position, but it's your recall that controls, not theirs.

"The format is that Mr. Shore is allowed closing argument. Mr. McGuire is entitled to respond, and then Mr. Shore is given another, final opportunity for a rebuttal.

"And, at the conclusion of all the arguments, I will then instruct you in that applicable law, and due to the time that we've taken this morning, I'm sure that those instructions will be tomorrow.

"So with that, Mr. Shore, you may address the jury."

Before Jim began talking, he stood very still for a minute facing the jury, as though he was thinking about where to begin. Their eyes were fastened on him.

"Thank you, Your Honor. Good morning, ladies and gentlemen. It's been, I think, five weeks to the day since I got a chance to actually talk to you directly."

As Jim began to speak, I tried to block out my intrusive thoughts and what I knew and hear only what the jury was hearing. What were those on the jury thinking? All I could tell was that they were listening intently. Their expressions, though, were blank and unreadable.

"When we started this trial," Jim began, "I told you at that time what I believed the evidence would show each one of you, and I told you at that time that at the conclusion of my opening statement that I was going to ask each one of you at the conclusion of the case to render a guilty verdict as to each count that's presented to you. I'm going to renew that charge to you today.

"The most important job in this case is to determine the true facts and combine the facts with the law. Facts can be derived from the evidence and from no other source. The evidence can be either direct or circumstantial. Circumstantial evidence, if you believe it, is every bit as good as direct evidence. What I've tried to present to you is a portrait of a young man who had a disposition to commit sexual offenses. This is a portrait of a sexual predator." Jim's voice had a razor edge, and now the depth of his concern was apparent.

For the next three hours Jim painstakingly reconstructed the case for the jury. When he talked about my mother's death he asked for the maximum verdict. "Regarding the murder of Elaine Rothwell, if in the commission of a rape, the victim dies, the perpetrator is guilty of first degree murder. If you find that the assailant still had control of Mrs. Rothwell after the rape and that a fatal blow was struck, it is still first degree murder." Jim paused.

"Let us consider Mrs. Rothwell, living under a tree for two to three years prior to her death. She was always awake when people arrived for work at the building next to her campsite. She kept to herself. People tried to help her because she never had her hand out. She never panhandled

even though anyone could see, even Richard Carrasco's
uncle, that this was a person who needed help. So we have
Mrs. Rothwell, living underneath a tree, weighing seventy-
nine pounds, looking like a concentration camp victim,
found with the bottom half of her clothes off and her
panties down around one knee. She was very frail, very
fragile." Jim paused, to let what he had said sink in. After
a minute he continued, "Mrs. Rothwell was helpless. She
could not have put up a fight. When he became frustrated
and more violent, using a bottle, she died during the commission of the rape."

His portrait of my mother and her murder was now
complete. Shore moved on to draw a portrait of Richard
Carrasco and his behavior in the other cases in the trial.
"Sometimes Mr. Carrasco is cunning and attempts to
hide and attempts to conceal [himself] by wearing gloves,
by wearing a mask. You've heard evidence of that in this
case, and at other times, for seemingly no reason that
we can put our fingers on, he doesn't care.

"Like the Ellen Lopez case, like this woman who has
known him, he's had conversations with, he's flashing
himself at her. And like the Margaret Carroll case where
he just happened to be at the wrong place at the wrong
time. He was upset. He was humiliated at the time. And
so the—what the portrait—what I'm getting at here is
where the evidence is showing of a young man who is
sorely troubled, and certainly, without a doubt, is a sexual
predator. He preys on women, and he assaults women."

Shore picked up a pencil from the defense table,
wrote something on his note cards, clenched the pencil,
and then dropped it on the table hard.

"Mrs. Rothwell, what do we know about her? We know
that for at least two or three years prior to her death, she
was living under a tree. By the time Mr. Carrasco comes
upon Mrs. Rothwell, who's been living out on the street

for at least three years and who knows how many more, who is not nourished well, who is, the evidence shows she wouldn't even talk to anybody. She weighs seventy-nine and a half pounds. She basically looks like someone who has barely survived a concentration camp. She is severely malnourished with basically skin on her bones. She is living, like I said, under the tree. She doesn't talk to anybody, and her body is found with the bottom half of her clothes off, her panties on one leg down almost to her knee on that left leg."

Shore took a few steps back and surveyed the faces of the jurors. He still had their attention, so he pressed on.

"And police receive a phone call and go out there and rule hers a suspicious death. It wasn't called a homicide at first.

"Mrs. Rothwell is taken to the coroner's office. The coroner does the autopsy, and he determines that she died as a result of a laceration that is one-and-a-half inch diagonal along the bottom of the vaginal wall, backwards. So you have this laceration that's basically six inches by one-and-a-half inches."

I had been listening to him for more than an hour before I realized there were tears streaming down my cheeks.

"You heard testimony from the coroner about that injury.

"Now, what's the importance of what caused the injury that led to her death? Well, the importance is that, if the act that caused the laceration was done in the attempted commission or the commission of rape, remember, this is the expanded version, this time frame," his voice rose, his passion echoing my thoughts, "then it's first degree murder."

The jury greeted his words with respectful silence. He paused a few moments, then went on. "If the fatal blow occurred some other time then, and you find it was done by Mr. Carrasco, then it would be what's known in the law as involuntary manslaughter. I'm not going to talk about involuntary manslaughter, because it doesn't apply here. This laceration was caused during—the evidence has shown you—the commission or attempted commission of the rape. And, looking at the evidence, it occurred in this way.

"Mr. Carrasco knew very well where Mrs. Rothwell was at all times, day and night, or most times day and night. He had lived down the street on First Street in an apartment at the time set up by his uncle. He lived on Gish and Kerley. He lived on Sonora. He knew the area very well, very well, and everybody in that area, including Mr. Martinez, who went by that First Street exit, knew Mrs. Rothwell, and I don't say knew her, knew who she was.

"And I don't know that the evidence has shown us what drove Mr. Carrasco specifically to do what he did. The law does not require me to prove motive. What his thinking was, what was going through his mind when he decided to victimize this defenseless, seventy-nine-and-a-half-pound woman. . . ."

McGuire stood up, steely-eyed. "Your Honor, I'm going to object. That actually misstates the law, because under the felony murder rule it requires specific intent to commit rape at the time, and so he does have to prove what was going through his mind at that time."

Judge Ball, waving his hand, had on an intense look. "Well, to that extent, the objection is sustained. Once again, the jury is admonished that counsel's statements are not to be construed as evidence as to the law, nor with recall of the facts," he said sharply. "With that, you may proceed, Mr. Shore."

Jim nodded. "Thank you, Your Honor." He went on, "We do not know, nor do I have to prove what went through Mr. Carrasco's mind as he went to that location.

"We know that Mrs. Rothwell's body is found off of the cardboard box which another witness says she always was on. That she never even saw her sitting on the ground in the leaf-covered area.

"So, whether or not Mr. Carrasco got angry that night at somebody like he did the night that he was punched and pushed away by Patty Rodriguez that led to an excruciatingly painful evening, we don't know. But for whatever reason, he made his way to that location at that time, and he had one thing on his mind when he got there, for sure." I looked over at Carrasco. He was staring angrily at Shore like he wanted to snap him like a twig.

"And it wasn't a very—it wasn't a very big consequence whether or not a knife was used or not. We don't know. Mrs. Rothwell, due to her condition—the evidence is pretty clear—couldn't have put up much of a fight.

"Ladies and gentlemen, I have now presented my evidence. The veil of the presumption of innocence is not quite lifted yet until you hear all of the evidence, all the arguments from the defense as well as the prosecutor as well as the judge's instructions, but I am going to ask you, when you finally get this case submitted to you, that you, of course, carefully look at all of the evidence, it goes without saying, and that you convict the defendant, Richard Carrasco, on all counts."

Jim stopped talking, and his back stiffened as he turned to look at Carrasco with a scowl. Carrasco stared back. But there was an anxious look in his eyes. Then Jim turned back to the jury, and with a quiet moral authority, said, "I want you to think about the case piece by piece and then as a whole. Nothing that has been presented excludes the defendant. Lastly, I want you to remember the pictures I have shown you of Elaine Rothwell. The look on her face describes the horrific nature of her end."

As it was past five o'clock, court was adjourned until

the next morning. One of the jurors was isolated by the flu, and he was replaced by an alternate.

"Now, we're ready to proceed this morning," the judge announced the next day when court reconvened. "Mr. McGuire, you may address the jury, sir."

Phillip McGuire stood up to give his own summation. It was a difficult case with so much evidence against his client. The tension showed on his usually animated face, and the confidence he had shown earlier in the trial was now subdued.

"Good morning, ladies and gentlemen. This is my chance to tell you how I viewed the facts and how I think you may be able to interpret them based on what you've seen and heard so far for the last four weeks."

He spoke of a few of the crimes, finally reaching my mother's murder.

"This issue is, who did it?" he said, directing a hard glance at the prosecutor. There was a hum of voices in the courtroom. "I have told you at the beginning, none of these victims are going to come to court, point to Mr. Carrasco, and say, 'That's the person.' Not one did that. So we have to look at the circumstantial evidence and decide whether that is sufficient to show beyond a reasonable doubt that my client is guilty.

"And in terms of the circumstantial evidence, what Mr. Shore left out is when he says that, if it's two possible interpretations, one is reasonable and points to guilt, another that's reasonable and points to innocence, he's correct in saying you must—this is mandatory under the law. You as jurors have to follow the law. You must adopt that interpretation that points to the innocence. You have to. It's not even an option. As jurors, you've sworn to follow the law. In fact, there's an instruction that tells you you have to follow the law whether you like it or don't. That's the law. That's your task as jurors.

"Well, that law is kind of technical. I don't agree with it or that's really hard to do. That's beside the point. When you took the oath as jurors, you said, 'I'm going to follow the law.' And you're going to follow the law no matter what the consequences are. And that's what I'm going to ask you to do, to follow the law no matter what the consequences are," he said grudgingly.

A hush had settled in the courtroom. I looked over at Carrasco. His face was drawn and taut. McGuire went on, "I'm not going to tell you which way you have to vote. I'm not going to tell you to do your duty as a juror. In terms of circumstantial evidence, when you find an interpretation, an inference that can point to guilt, you have to look and ask yourself, are all the factors that would complete that inference, are each of the factors proved beyond a reasonable doubt?"

As he had not put Carrasco on the stand, he began to defend that decision. "One of the other instructions I think applies is that a defendant has a right not to testify. That is the law. There's no ifs, ands, buts about it. If the defendant chose, after talking to me, not to take the stand, we rely on the state of the evidence. You cannot draw any negative inference. You can't say, 'Well, gee, I never heard him say anything about . . . Why isn't he telling us? He has something to hide.' The law doesn't allow that. That's not even permissible."

From out of the corner of my eye, I saw Carrasco squirming in his seat. He shot Jim Shore a hostile look, and Shore returned it full force.

"In terms of the reasonable doubt, presumption of innocence instruction," McGuire continued, "it says in relevant part in terms of defining this reasonable doubt, because again that's not something we use every day. Maybe if you're—now get into the cherry pie thing. Let's say you have two kids about the same age, and a cherry pie is missing. Unfortunately, neither one had cherry stain on their cheeks, and you're wondering which son or daughter did it. You as a parent have to decide based on quizzing, whatever, but you don't use beyond-a-reasonable-doubt standard. I mean, there are other things that come into play, because it's not, you know, crimes involved.

"And so this beyond-a-reasonable-doubt is not something we do in our everyday lives. No matter what it is, you don't use that kind of a standard. And so it's very important to look at the words of the actual instruction when they define it, because, as I said before and the judge has said, it's not a possible doubt, because everything relating to human affairs is open to some possible or imaginary doubt. It is that state of the case which, after the entire comparison and consideration of all the evidence, leaves the minds of the jurors in that condition that they cannot say they feel abiding conviction of the truth of the charge.

"Now, abiding conviction, obviously, that's something that's not just today, tomorrow, or next week, but it would be a year from now, two years from now, and say I made the right decision based on the evidence presented. I made the right decision."

Shore signaled his displeasure: "Your Honor, that's a misstatement. That's not the standard. The question is. . . ."

McGuire: "I'm defending abiding. . . ."

Judge Ball's face tightened as he interrupted. "The Court will instruct the jury as to the applicable law. Once again, the jury is admonished that statements made by counsel are not binding on either the facts or the law. You may proceed with that admonition."

"Thank you, Your Honor," McGuire said. He continued on a new tack: "I would like to talk about a few things in terms of—in light of this burden of proof. The prosecutor has to prove it beyond a reasonable doubt. I don't have to prove anything."

Carrasco was nodding now, and he was punctuating his lawyer's words by jabbing his hands.

"We don't have to prove anything. The prosecution has to prove it. In terms of dealing with Mrs. Rothwell and actually all the victims, I want to point out one thing, and the law is clear too, that you have a beginning instruction, not that it's the most important, it's just a practical side of the first instruction, tells you you have two duties to perform.

"First, you must determine what facts have been proved from the evidence received in the trial and not from any other source.

"Secondly, you must apply the law that the judge states to you to the facts as you determine them and in that way arrive at your verdict. Okay. That's your obligation. You must accept and follow the law as the judge will tell you.

"You also must not be influenced by pity for or prejudice against the defendant. You may think Mr. Carrasco was a flasher and, you know, all sorts of bad things about him. He's a thief and hangs out with the wrong people. You may think all of that, that's fine. I'm not going to convince you otherwise. But you can't let that influence the decision-making process as a juror.

"Another thing you're going to have is sympathy. You're going to have passion. You're going to feel sorry for the victims that all testified, both the uncharged and charged ones, and that's a given. I mean, when Margaret or Ellen or Denise gets up and describes these horrible acts that were performed on each of them, I mean, yes, I mean no one can say, 'I don't care, I'm indifferent.'

"That will arouse sympathy, that will arouse passion. Poor Mrs. Rothwell. She didn't deserve that. She seemed to have no enemies in the world. She just kept to herself.

There's a lot of sympathy that's there, but again, as jurors, and the judge will tell you, whatever you have in terms of the sympathy, don't let it influence your duty as a juror. Have the sympathy, recognize it, okay, but realize now my role as a juror is to do this. Afterwards, you can feel sorry and express it, that's fine, but don't let it influence your duty as juror to look at what the facts are, look at the evidence that's been presented, and base your decision on that.

"In terms of the charges, there are twenty-eight. Count One, the first one, being what we call—well, it's murder, but basically it's what we call the felony murder rule. It's an artificial piece of the law saying if during the commission of the certain offense you cause the death is something—we're going to call that murder, and again, whether you agree with that or not is besides the point. That's the rules." He walked to the jury box, and his voice rose as if the force of it alone would convince the men and women in front of him. "You have to follow that. So what the district attorney has to prove to you beyond a reasonable doubt is that Mrs. Rothwell died during the commission of a rape.

"Now, we know she died."

Shore was on his feet objecting again. "Well, that misstates the law, clearly misstates it, because that's not what the law says."

Judge Ball looked tired and testy. "Again, counsel is admonished, the jury is admonished that statements of law will be given by the Court. Proceed."

McGuire nodded and gave a mocking sidelong look at Shore. "Thank you.

"In terms of the actual instruction," he went on, "it says every person who unlawfully kills a human being during the commission or attempted commission of a crime is guilty of the crime of murder.

"Okay." He looked at Shore, as if expecting another objection, but Shore stared straight ahead. "So, the elements are a human being was killed. Yes, sir, unfortunately, Mrs. Rothwell was killed. The killing was unlawful. I don't know anyone claiming it was lawful. And the killing occurred during the commission or attempted commission of rape."

Next, McGuire tried to call into account every aspect of the coroner's verdict, even the time of my mother's death. Once again, I studied the jury. Their mood was serious but their faces inscrutable. I was perspiring. I put my hand to my forehead to wipe it and saw myself visibly trembling. I prayed they understood the truth. Prayed that McGuire had not stirred up doubt.

His words wound in and out of my fears.

"What has the district attorney proved beyond a reasonable doubt about that? What about the problem of time? When was the blunt instrument inflicted? Well, Dr. Cochran was the only one who testified in terms of time. He said between twelve and thirty-six hours. Excuse me, and actually it's not from the autopsy, it's Mr. Shore who misunderstood and questioned him. 'Oh, you're talking about, that's from the time of the autopsy?' 'No, no. That time from the autopsy is not going to deal with it.' Which is the correct way.

"What Dr. Cochran is referring to is in relation to when the body is found. The body is found nine A.M. So, we're talking nine P.M. Friday to nine P.M. Saturday is Dr. Cochran's best guess as to when death occurred.

"That's when death occurred, and in terms of the blunt instrument, he didn't really know how long it would take for someone to bleed to death going into shock. Definitely, I believe, now, again I may be mistaken, but you can always have it reread, but I believe it was ten, fifteen, twenty, probably thirty or so minutes. I don't have the magic words.

Don't necessarily hold me to that, but I believe that's what he said.

"Okay. So, basically its nine P.M. Friday night to nine P.M. Saturday night time frame when cause of death was inflicted. That's when death occurred, and plus thirty more minutes for the blunt instrument to inflict its damage.

"The prosecutor assumes that the events occurred at the same time. Did anyone say that? Do we have evidence that shows clearly beyond a reasonable doubt that the deposits of the semen and the whatever-it-was that was inserted, this blunt instrument, occurred at any time within even hours of one another?

"Again, I don't have to ask the question, 'Excuse me, Doctor, I have this pressing point I just want to know.' I don't have to ask that question. I can sit and rely on the state of the evidence. The failure of proof. I think you can say, 'Oh, clearly it had to, it had to.' Why? Because he says so. I'd like to—can anyone point to the record anywhere that says they were deposited at the same time? He will say, 'Well, it can be deposited before, during and after.' There's only, timewise, three possibilities. If the rape is consummated before then you have to make a determination. Well, what proof is there that even assuming Mr. Carrasco did the rape, what proof is there that he, at a later time, inflicted the blunt instrument trauma that led to the death?"

I could not help it. A deep sigh escaped my lips. Though I hated to admit it, McGuire was an effective advocate.

"Well," he pushed on, "the prosecutor believes so. Okay. So. Just keep that in the back of your mind."

How strange, I thought as I listened to the obtuse content and the strong presentation, that the truth should take second place at times to mind games. McGuire was repeating his thoughts, covering and recovering the same ground. I looked over at Shore. He smiled sympathetically at me. McGuire's speech dragged on and on. I clamped my lips and narrowed my eyes, willing myself to look at the jury. My emotions and thoughts were in such a state of disorder at this moment, I didn't know what to expect. I could not predict their response. I had to pull myself together to put my rational self in charge again. I looked over at Judge Ball who had a Lincolnesque air of fairness. I sighed. Somehow this calmed me, and my eyes returned to the jury. Would they know the truth? Would they see that Carrasco was guilty? Completely guilty?

McGuire was finally coming to the end of his remarks and smiling affably at the jury now, a humble smile meant to beguile those I prayed would not be swayed.

"Now, I've taken a lot of your time. You've been very patient. All of you have come from your jobs and other experiences to spend over four weeks here so far. Mr. Shore and I and my client thank you very much for volunteering your time. Mr. Shore, probably after a little break, will have an opportunity to give the final, final closing, because he has the burden of proof. I do not get to respond to his final statement. But, again, I just want to thank you for your patience.

"My client, Richard Carrasco, is coming to you as the ministers of justice in this courtroom. You are the jury, and he's hoping that you will fulfill your duty. And I'm not going to tell you how to decide each of the counts. I'm just going to say, please do your duty. Thank you very much."

Shore did not meet McGuire's smile. His eyes blazing with the injustice of the situation, he rose to rebut the defense attorney's argument.

"Mr. McGuire says that he doesn't have to prove anything to you, and that is true. But we come back to something that he never touched upon, which is reasonable interpretations of the evidence. Specifically, what or when was the fatal blow that was struck? I told you yesterday that whether it was a foreign object or not really doesn't matter as to the analysis. Certainly, the laceration that Mrs. Rothwell suffered—this is the only reasonable explanation—occurred during the attempted commission or the commission of the rape.

"Let's think about the possibilities otherwise. Otherwise, we would have to believe Mr. McGuire sort of inferred this. He didn't go very far with it, because it is absolutely so ridiculous, but I guess it's possible that Mr. Carrasco came and raped Mrs. Rothwell, left her there, and along came someone else who inflicted the fatal wound . . . I'm not saying it's not possible. I'm saying it's unreasonable.

"The only reasonable explanation, ladies and gentlemen, of how that crime was committed, of how Mrs. Rothwell suffered those injuries, is that Mr. Carrasco, who was in the course and scope of raping her, perpetrated that fatal blow on her."

Shore strode to his seat with the righteousness of a crusader. As he sat down, his eyes met mine in a form of silent but intimate communication. For one moment, it seemed as if we were alone in the courtroom. Then I nodded, and he understood.

With the closing statements completed, Judge Ball went over the law for the jury and read the charges aloud again. It felt different hearing the charges read again after sitting through the trial. I felt the weight of them drop down on me. Finally, the case was given to the jury who, in two silent lines, heads down, filed out. After eight years of waiting, eight years that seemed like an eternity, there was nothing for me to do but go home and wait some more.

Time was on hold.

At ten o'clock in the morning on February 5, Detective

Brown called. "The jury is going to deliver their verdict this afternoon."

"What do you mean, they're back?" I asked shocked. "Is that good?"

"I don't know," he said, "it just is. Paula, it is difficult to read these things, but Jim made a strong case."

I didn't have to be at the courthouse until one o'clock, but I was there by noon. Carrasco's family was there also. The first official person to arrive was Detective Brown. At twelve-fifteen he got off the elevator and walked down the hallway towards me.

"You must have been worried about me," I said when he reached me.

"Yep," he said, and we sat side by side without saying a word.

At a quarter to one the jury began arriving. They didn't look at me. They didn't look at Carrasco's family either, but I was still unnerved. When the courtroom doors opened promptly at one o'clock, all I could think was, *Thank God we're on time.* The pounding in my ears was so loud that I could barely make out the conversations around me. I was afraid that I would not be able to hear the verdict.

I began to imagine everything that could go wrong, all the different ways in which twelve intelligent people could find Carrasco not guilty. I needed a guilty verdict. Even if he was convicted of the other two rapes, it would not be enough. I needed Richard Carrasco to get out from in between my mother and me. I needed him to be convicted. Something about the act of murder stalls the mourning process. You can't get around the fact of the murder and back to your loss. The crime keeps getting bigger until it overwhelms you.

Finally, it was officially announced in the courtroom that the jury had reached a verdict. The jury's presentation of the verdict was solemn, drawn-out, seeming to last longer than the fifteen minutes that, in reality, it took. First, the judge sent the bailiff to the deliberating room to escort the jurors back to the courtroom. After some time, the bailiff returned leading the jury to their prescribed daily seats. Through most of the trial the bailiff had been jovial, telling bad jokes, and talking to the court clerk and court reporter about normal things not connected to the trial. Often, I wondered if he'd recognize me a year from now, if he were to see me on the streets. Today, he was obviously nervous, glancing often around the courtroom and hitching up his pants as if his belt was failing in its duty to keep them up. Though the clock was silent, I wished for a tick-tock sound that might match the beating of my heart, thereby calming it.

Finally, Judge Ball asked the members of the jury, "Have you reached a verdict?"

The foreman of the jury was a blond-haired, fiftyish woman. She stood up and read from a piece of paper: "Regarding count one: We the people of the State of California find the defendant, Richard Carrasco, guilty of murder in the first degree in the case of Elaine Rothwell. Regarding count two: We the people of the State of California find the defendant, Richard Carrasco, guilty of rape in the first degree in the case of Elaine Rothwell."

I felt a great welling up inside my throat, and my eyes grew warm and moist. I gasped and looked up at the ceiling and whispered, "Thank God." When I finally looked over at the jury, they were looking at me, and every juror was smiling.

Count 1, 187: Murder of Elaine Rothwell, a human being: Guilty

Count 2, 261: Rape of Elaine Rothwell with the intent to commit great bodily harm: Guilty

CHAPTER 17

Elaine Rothwell, Human Being

After the jury announced their verdict, nervousness reigned in the courtroom. I did not make a sound, but inside my head was a loud whirring, as if helicopter blades were spinning around in my brain. It's possible that it wasn't as soundless as I thought.

I heard gasps from the side of the courtroom where Carrasco's family sat, but I didn't look over at them. The bailiff, like an alert Doberman, hitched up his gun belt and demanded silence in the courtroom. His eyes bounced around the spectators, attaching themselves to the faces with which he was familiar, looking for signs of a situation that he would need to handle. None came. Richard Carrasco was led away. His family filed quietly out of the courtroom immediately after.

I stayed long enough to give each juror a hug.

When I got home, I lay down on the couch without even changing my clothes, just lay there in my suit, staring up at the ceiling. Tom wasn't home from work yet.

My cat respected my privacy and left me alone. Cats are great respecters of one's right to be left alone, and with everyone I knew wanting to congratulate me on the verdict, what I wanted most right now was quiet. I lay on the couch, listened to the sound of my breathing, and stared at a point on the wall until the wall itself became fuzzy and my eyes stung like when you are very tired or have been crying.

"I should call Aunt Gayle and my brother," I said to the cat, but I didn't move from the couch. The telephone rang several times, but the effort to get off the couch and answer it seemed overwhelming. So, I stayed put on the couch, hypnotized by that certain point on the wall. Eventually, Tom came home. He walked in carrying a pile of mail. Tom had a system for going through the mail: first, he looked at the front of the letter, then the back of the letter, then he shuffled the letter to the bottom of the pile. After he shuffled through the entire stack, he chose a letter to open. I watched him at his mail ritual. Finally, he noticed me.

"I didn't see you," he said. "How long have you been there?"

"A bit," I answered.

"Oh." Tom looked at the mail. "Here's something from your Aunt Gayle." He walked over to where I lay and handed me the letter. "What was the verdict?" he asked softly.

"Richard Carrasco was convicted," I answered, my voice sounding flat and inadequate.

"That's great," Tom said. "That's what you've been waiting for. How does it feel to have it over with finally?" He sat down on the edge of the couch and waited for me to answer.

I thought about that for a minute. "I don't know," I said. "I guess it still feels kind of undone."

"Oh," Tom said. He looked at me with understanding. "Maybe now you can put it all behind you," he said gently.

"I'm not sure this is something I can ever put behind me. I think I may have to settle for letting it become part of me," I said. "Right now I feel numb."

"I can understand that," Tom said. "Since the trial began you've been so focused on every bit of testimony. Every night, I've watched you go over your notes from the trial, and sometimes I catch a look on your face. I don't know how to describe it."

"Try," I said.

"Sad. You just looked so sad, and I didn't know how to comfort you. I have sensed from the beginning this was something you felt you wanted to bear alone."

"Thank you for understanding that," I said quietly, looking back at my spot on the wall for comfort and direction. "And I think I needed to be sad, so that someday I can be less sad."

Tom smiled and took my hand for a moment "I still love you, you know," he added softly, and got up and left the room.

I stared at the wall for another minute, then picked up my Aunt Gayle's letter and looked at the envelope. It was a greeting card type of envelope. I wondered if there were greeting cards appropriate for court verdicts and sentencings. Perhaps they were located on some undiscovered rack in stationery stores. One side of the rack could be for victims, one for criminals, and another rack for the innocent and guilty. I contemplated the possible profit margin in selling congratulation cards to people who had received probation instead of jail time.

I opened the envelope. The front of the card was covered with different colored daisies. In the middle of the daisies was printed: *To love and be loved is the greatest happiness of existence*. I opened the card.

My aunt wrote: "Dear Paula Jean, your mother's birthday, in case you have forgotten, is on February 24. I shall always say a prayer of love for her life on that day. She was my younger, gentle, kind sister who was much loved by her family. You, in time, may somehow overcome your grief, guilt, and anger over her death. During her visits with Gerald and me, she would say, 'I must go back to Paula and Michael.' She loved you both deeply and was proud of the years you sang in church. Your mother would be proud of your educational achievements, for she herself was a scholar."

I felt instantly angry and tense and believed myself judged once again as being unworthy of my mother's memory, proclaimed by my aunt as being somehow less scholarly and worthy than my mother. "Is nothing I ever do enough?" I said out loud. Then, suddenly I wasn't angry anymore. I reread my aunt's card. She was right. My mother was an educated woman, and she loved me very much. I realized that I had been looking at life through an angry lens for too long. It was time I altered my focus. I picked up the phone and dialed my brother's telephone number.

"Michael," I said when he answered.

"Is it over, Sister?" he asked.

"He's been convicted," I said. Neither of us spoke, and I could hear his breathing on the other side of the phone line.

"Good, Sister." He said, "Good night," and hung up.

I replaced the telephone receiver and almost immediately fell asleep. Sometime during the night I felt Tom gently cover me with a blanket and turn out the lights.

After the verdict I walked around for days with glazed eyes, answering everyone with an on-the-edge-of-rude "huh." Finally, I realized what was wrong with me. Everything had stopped, but nothing was really finished.

It wouldn't be over until February 27 when Richard Carrasco was sentenced.

I watched while other people were called before Judge Ball and sentenced to jail time or parole or fines. I listened to lectures from the bench. Prisoners waited in the jury box for their turn, but Carrasco wasn't among them. Finally, Jim entered the courtroom and sat next to me.

"I've got some news. Come out into the hall with me." He placed his hand briefly on my shoulder.

I followed him out into the hallway. Around us, people huddled in small groups talking and gesturing. I noticed Carrasco's mother sitting on the bench nearest the elevator. Francie held her hands up in front of her face as if in prayer. Next to her sat an anxious looking woman whom I took to be one of Carrasco's aunts. She'd been in the courtroom almost every day. Sometimes she was the only one there. Phillip McGuire stood talking to them, looking down as they stared up at him, expectant and unhappy.

"Here," Jim said, holding out a file to me. "I thought you might find this interesting. I'll be right back." He walked down the hall towards Phillip.

I opened the file. Inside was Richard Carrasco's probation report. I scanned the first few pages where the charges against him were listed. I glanced over the Supplemental Information section, which restated details of the crimes. From what I could see, the details matched the trial testimony. I flipped past the victims' statements and stopped at the defendant's statement. I sat down and started reading.

"Oh my God," I said. "I can't believe this." I looked up. Jim was standing in front of me.

"What can't you believe?" he asked.

"Carrasco got married while he was in jail. I can't believe it."

"Hey," Jim laughed, "believe it. Matter of fact, that's her." He pointed down the hall towards the group sitting by the elevator.

I looked at Carrasco's mother and his wife. They were standing now, waiting with Phillip McGuire for the elevator. "I thought that was his aunt," I said in Jim's direction, though I was really talking to the air. I stared at her. "She was at the trial every day. How can she stay married to him after listening to the evidence? How could she stand listening to those women testifying about being raped?"

"She doesn't believe he's guilty," Jim said and shrugged. He sighed. "Look, don't get upset, but there's going to be a delay."

I shook my head. "Now, there's a surprise," I said.

Jim sighed. "I know, I know." He rolled his eyes. "The sentencing is going to be put off until June twelfth. The judge wants the California Youth Authority to review the case."

"Well," I said, "what's three and a half more months after eight years?" I shrugged. "Really, I would have been more surprised if we'd moved ahead as planned."

"Judge Ball is being careful," Jim said. "When Carrasco was having his fun, there was a law requiring the California Youth Authority to review all juvenile convictions to ascertain whether the offenders could be successfully rehabilitated in a youth facility instead of the penitentiary."

"You're kidding, right?" I asked. "I thought he was convicted as an adult."

"He was." Jim held both hands out, palms up. Either he was placating me or warding me off. "Don't worry. Anyway, that law no longer applies, but since it did at the time of the crime, Judge Ball wants to lessen the possibility of appeal."

"Okay." I shrugged. "As I said, what's three and a half months compared to eight years?"

Jim patted me on the shoulder. "I'll give you a minute with the report."

I sat down and continued reading: "On February seven, two days after he was convicted, Carrasco shot a fellow inmate in the neck with a homemade blow gun dart. He'd prepared the dart by coating it with feces."

"Nice guy," I muttered. I looked up. Jim was standing in front of me again.

"Yeah, real nice guy. Well, that's our boy," Jim said. "I'll give you a copy after June twelfth, but I've got to take this one back now."

I put the report back into its folder and handed it to Jim.

"I'll see you on June twelfth," I said, then I turned and walked down the hall.

Waiting a few months for the sentencing was difficult, but I just took it a day at a time. I knew the end was near, and that sustained me. My friends thought me very brave, and I accepted their compliments on my courage with a self-deprecating, "No, not at all. Just one more thing to go through."

However brave I appeared on the surface, this new round of waiting made me weary. Simple activities exhausted me. I wore myself out walking across rooms. Halfway through my morning jog, I found myself panting, unable to catch my breath or continue running. I became winded riding the escalator. Concerned, I had a physical examination. I was healthy. Afterward, I realized that I had nothing to blame for my exhaustion but this period of pausing and waiting for it all to be over.

Despite my weariness, I couldn't really allow myself to

give in to exhaustion. I was in the middle of my second semester as an MBA student at San Jose State University, and studying took up a lot of my time. I was also working full time as a freelance writer. So, I couldn't let myself cave in. I needed to keep my mind clear and focused. I needed to remain determined.

All my life, being determined presented a problem for me. I had quit high school, because I didn't want to try to succeed and be disappointed. I quit college the first time I'd tried it, for the same reason. Before I quit both high school and college, I made sure my grades were poor so that my quitting would be more acceptable, and even expected. It was my mother's death that made me as determined to succeed as I had formerly been determined to fail. My mother's final gift to me was perseverance. If she could survive the last years of her life sleeping in a cardboard box under a freeway underpass, I told myself, I could make a success of my life. I fought hard for my opportunities; I didn't want to let my mother's memory down. In this interim period, I realized I hadn't just found my mother at the trial. In every bit of painful testimony I'd found a reason to grow stronger. I'd rediscovered myself.

One warm May morning as the waiting period dragged on, I woke up feeling determined to do something, but not knowing what or why. After my second cup of coffee I knew what I wanted to do. I wanted to go home, back to Hayward and my old neighborhood. I wanted to look at my life from the outside and then turn it inside and take another look.

My father, of course, didn't understand my need. When I called him to get our old address, he was annoyed.

"I don't remember," he said. "What do you want to do that for, anyway?"

"I want to see how it feels," I replied.

"It doesn't feel like anything," he said. "It's a house. It's just sitting there on a plot of land in a neighborhood. Don't waste your time."

"I don't consider it a waste of time," I said. "And why does this bother you so much?" I asked, curious and half dreading his answer. He was quiet for a while, but I was patient. During our silence I began feeling sorry for him. It has to be a painful thing to have a daughter intent on digging up all the secrets and sufferings you've taken such care to bury.

"Thirteen seventy-five Regal Avenue," my father muttered into the phone.

"What?" I said. "Dad, I didn't hear you."

"Yes, you did."

"No, Dad. Could you say it again?" Silence. I imagined his face. The puckered look his mouth got when he was on the verge of getting really angry. "Dad?" I said again.

"Thirteen seventy-five Regal Avenue," he said.

"Thank you," I replied, but he had already hung up.

I found the house with no problem, but seeing the old neighborhood gave me a queasy, disoriented feeling. I'd successfully erased my memories to the point that nothing looked familiar to me. Even the curve of the neighborhood streets seemed odd. Not only that, everything seemed to have shrunk. The grocery store where my mother shopped was dirty and the shelves understocked. The rich area of the neighborhood with the big houses was badly kept up, and the houses were smaller than I remembered. I drove by our old house three times before I allowed myself to believe I'd once lived there. It was small and shabby and certainly not worthy of holding all the painful memories of my growing up plus the weight of my mother's schizophrenia. I parked across the street and sat for a while looking at my old home.

In this house I decorated Christmas trees, watched

television, and argued with my father over how much time I could reasonably expect to spend in the bathroom.

And in the bathroom I cut my wrists with my father's razor, determined to erase my childhood and my future.

In this house my mother washed dishes and sang "Moon River" over the sink, while I sat at the table trying to overdose by swallowing an entire bottle of aspirin.

And in this house my mother made lists of things people stole from her and listened to voices only she could hear.

In this house my brother and I, to avoid eating my mother's inedible dinners, encouraged my father to talk at mealtimes, telling stories of his childhood experiences. We laughed, I recall, as he talked, while both our parents ignored the fact that we were stuffing food like my mother's football-textured meatloaf into our napkins or spreading it out on our plates, distributing it to create the illusion that we'd actually eaten some.

And from this house we all fled, my mother, father, brother and myself, sick to death of the silence and the screams and of being different from everyone else.

As I sat in my car, a little girl rode a bicycle onto the lawn of my old home. She got off her bike and, dropping it casually on the lawn, went into the house, calling "Mom" as she went. I smiled. My father was right. It was just a house. Not a ghost house stuck somewhere between heaven and hell, just a house after all, with another family making memories in its rooms and hallways.

I started my car and drove through my old neighborhood, down the skinny streets where I'd played tag and touch football. Past the corners I careened around on my skateboard, feeling as if I were flying and certain nothing would ever catch me. Past my grammar school where I'd broken my foot once, falling off the jungle gym. I'd been dared to stand on the top with no hands and so had tried to do just that. For just a moment, before I came crashing down, I'd stood with arms outstretched and felt on top of the world. I continued driving and eventually came out at the other end of the neighborhood near the library. As a child, my fines for overdue books exceeded my father's patience for paying them. I parked by the library for a while and finally drove home to San Jose.

When I got home, I didn't immediately get out of my car. Instead, I looked at my own house for a while. I watched children walk by with their parents and a neighbor's tabby cat settle onto my lawn for a nap. When I was a little girl, I used to lie on the lawn in my backyard, dig my toes into the grass and wait for the sky to swoop down and carry me away. Remembering this made me smile, and I could see the barefoot girl I was, riding her bike with her long hair flying. I closed my eyes and thought of the barefoot girl my mother had been. I sat in my car for a while with my eyes closed and my head back against the seat, imagining my mother lying on her childhood lawn, digging her toes into the soft Tennessee grass and waiting for the sky to take her away to a different life, where crazy little girls can be crazy in peace.

The morning of June 12, the date on which the sentencing was scheduled, I woke up at 5:00 A.M. and wrote in my journal until it was time to leave for court. The pause in my life was ending. For the first time, I felt a surge of energy pass through me as if a great weight was being lifted from my shoulders. This was the day I'd been waiting eight years for: *my day in court.*

All my life I blamed myself for my mother's insanity. I grew up telling everyone that my mother had been fine until she gave birth to me. My father told me that she was given "twilight sleep" in the hospital and never quite came out of it. This lie allowed me to explain and take blame for my mother's insanity. It also allowed me to stay angry with her for abandoning me.

When I was ten years old, I overheard my father on the phone late at night telling someone that my mother had been perfectly fine until "Paula Jean" was born. Then his voice lowered to a whisper, and I couldn't risk getting closer in order to hear more.

I understood my father now. He was scared. Together, my parents were a catastrophe. Yet I can't say that they shouldn't have married. My brother and I came from these two people: one stuck in a constant state of denial and one insane. We all did our best. We were as normal as an abnormal family could be, and who is to say that anyone, anywhere, has a perfect and safe life?

Even homeless and insane, my mother chose to live her last years as close to me as she could get. Ours was not the relationship for which I so long had searched, but I knew now it was a binding type of love nevertheless.

Once again, I sat in the courtroom.

The bailiff said stiffly, "I'll call the case of the People of the State of California versus Richard Carrasco."

"Jim Shore on behalf of the People."

"Phillip McGuire appearing for Mr. Carrasco. He is present and in custody."

Judge Ball nodded to the two attorneys and said, "All right. Now is the time and place set for hearing on probation report and sentencing.

"The Court has read and reviewed the original probation officer report and recommendation, together with the amenability termination filed by the California Department of Youth Authority. The Court further has discussed the matter with counsel in chambers.

"Is cause, arraignment, and time waived in this matter, Mr. McGuire?"

"Yes, Your Honor."

"All right," said Judge Ball. "We're ready then to proceed. I will state initially that I have, as I've indicated, received the amenability study. Does either counsel wish to comment upon the issue as to whether the Court should proceed under the California Youth Authority or the Department of Corrections commitment?"

"I'll submit the matter," Shore said.

McGuire echoed him. "I'll submit the matter, Your Honor."

The judge nodded. "All right. Court, under Welfare and Institutions Code Seven-Zero-Seventy-two and *People versus Jones*, has considered the report submitted by the Youth Authority, the probation report, and such other attached documents.

"I find that the primary considerations as set forth in the Code, and I find that these sentence offenses, when compared with the nature and seriousness of other or similar offenses, has grave or far more greater interest of justice, including the needs to protect society, suggesting that the minor cannot be suitable to training and treatment offered by the Youth Authority, the determination of the unamenability by the Department of the Youth Authority, the defendant is criminally sophisticated, he does have a history of prior criminal behavior. Prior efforts to change the defendant's behavior have not been successful.

"I considered the likelihood that his criminal behavior cannot be significantly reduced or eliminated by a commitment to the Youth Authority, nor do I find that the criminal behavior of the defendant would be exacerbated by a commitment to prison. Therefore, the Court is going to proceed to sentence the defendant to the California

Department of Corrections pursuant to the reasons as set forth previously.

"Having made that determination, I will now proceed to the sentencing under that determination.

"I'll allow you first, Mr. McGuire. Is there anything you wish to bring to my attention?"

McGuire responded, "Just briefly, Your Honor," and spoke for a few minutes of why a full sentence should not be imposed.

"Thank you," Judge Ball said. "Anything on behalf of the People, Mr. Shore?"

"Your Honor, before I make my comments to the Court, there's someone that would like to address the Court. That's Paula Mints, the daughter of Mrs. Rothwell. May she come forward?"

I stood up. My palms were sweaty, and in one hand I clutched the statement I had prepared. It began: *"A long line of cases shows that it is not merely of some importance, but it is of fundamental importance that justice should not only be done, but should manifestly and undoubtedly be seen to be done." Gordon Stewart, 1923, Law Reports, King's Bench Division."* I intended my statement to be an indictment of everything that was wrong with justice and victimhood in America.

"You can come forward, Ms. Mints," Judge Ball said. "Now, you don't have to be sworn, just state your name loudly and clearly." The judge looked, in that moment, like everyone's favorite grandfather.

Everyone waited for me to speak. The courtroom was filled with strangers, both the guilty waiting to be sentenced and spectators watching.

Of course, there was also Richard Carrasco's family.

And Carrasco.

I looked at my paper for a minute. Finally, I turned it over, face down on the table. "My name," I began, "is

Paula Rothwell Mints." I looked up at the judge. "My mother was Lucia Elaine Rothwell." I paused.

"Go on, Ms. Mints," Judge Ball said.

"I came here today," I continued, "with a prepared statement. I knew when I walked in here just what I was going to say. But this piece of paper doesn't mean anything to me. The only thing I can think to say right now is how much I miss my mother." I stopped again and couldn't speak for a moment because I was crying. "Richard Carrasco," I continued, "raped and murdered my mother, a helpless, homeless, schizophrenic woman. She would have been completely defenseless against his attack." I wiped my tear-streaked cheeks and noticed my hands were shaking, but I wasn't nervous. Indeed, I'd never felt stronger.

As I continued, I heard my voice gathering force. "When I first met District Attorney Jim Shore, I didn't think of myself as a victim—I described myself as my mother's victim in proxy. But I have since changed my mind and my definition of what it means to be a victim." I paused and looked Judge Ball directly in the eyes.

"I am a victim," I said. "And being a victim doesn't mean the same thing as being helpless. It means that I lost my mother. She never saw me graduate from college. She won't see me earn my MBA. She won't see her granddaughter, my brother's daughter, grow up. Richard Carrasco took my mother away from all of us. In the eight years since he killed her, I have wished every day to see my mother again and to have a chance to tell her I love her. Mr. Carrasco took away my mother's life violently. I do not know what she suffered that day, but I have a pretty good idea from seeing the videotape of the crime scene.

"I'm not a proponent of the death penalty, so I never would have asked for that, but I—I don't think Richard

Carrasco should be on the streets again and have the opportunity to cause this much pain.

"The day that the coroner's office called and asked me to identify my mother, I hadn't seen her for three years. The last time I saw her, I put her on a plane to live with my aunt who was in the medical field and could take care of her, or so I thought. That point is moot.

"The day that I was called by the coroner's office, I dropped the phone. I was at work, and I screamed for five minutes. And I can still shut my eyes and hear those screams. And I can shut my eyes, and I can see my mother's face on that metal table."

I stopped again and couldn't speak for a minute. "I'm sorry, Your Honor," I said. "I came here today with the best of intentions to read what was on this piece of paper, but all I can think of to say is, please, Your Honor, don't let Richard Carrasco out of jail to cause anyone else this much pain again."

"Thank you, Ms. Mints," Judge Ball said.

I returned to my seat.

After I was seated, Judge Ball looked across the courtroom at me. "Ms. Mints, I want you to know that your presence in this courtroom, every day of the trial and today, will not be forgotten by me. Your mother, Lucia Elaine Rothwell, has made an impact. I will not forget her."

Judge Ball looked down for a moment He folded his hands and said, "Mr. Shore, have you anything further? No?" It seemed as if a lot of time passed before he looked over at Richard Carrasco. Finally, he spoke. "Mr. Carrasco, before I pass sentence I want to tell you that you are the most despicable person ever to pass through my courtroom. The pain you have caused, the rape of a sixty-three-year-old woman and the young woman whose life you ruined, shows the sophisticated mind of a serial rapist. As for Mrs. Rothwell, I can't imagine a more helpless victim.

Do you have anything to say for yourself?" He glanced toward Richard Carrasco.

"Yes, Your Honor," Carrasco said. "I dispute your jurisdiction in this matter."

"Very well," Judge Ball said, and I watched his back stiffen and that intense look I'd come to know come back. "All right. Matter being submitted, the Court has heard the evidence in his case, and there is very little that I can add to what has been said. Clearly, this one would be one of the most tragic and despicable crimes this Court has heard.

"Probation in this matter is denied. Based upon the nature and seriousness of all of these offenses, criminality, sophistication, use of weapons, active participation, prior criminal activity, determination that defendant is a threat to society.

"As to Count One, the term as prescribed by law, defendant will be sentenced to serve a period of twenty-five years to life for the murder of the victim, Elaine Rothwell.

"And, unfortunately, I have nothing more to say, Ms. Mints, that will in any way balm your loss or in any way make up for the suffering that you have. All I can say is that this hopefully will be a closure for you and that you can rest assured that the interests of justice have been served."

I stood up. "Thank you."

Ball continued, "As to Count Two, rape of this victim, I will imply as maximum a term as I can, which is eight years of the aggravated term due to the nature and circumstances of that act. I'll pose the enhancement of five years, a total of thirteen years, but since this act was done at the time of the loss, that sentence is stayed.

"Regarding the remaining counts, I have considered the appropriateness of sentencing in those matters. I concur with the recommendation of the probation department and that of the district attorney.

"I have considered the appropriate terms in regard to each of those counts. The factors in aggravation are clearly predominant. The defendant showed evidence of planning and sophistication.

"Further evidence that his sophistication, his cruelty, and vicious influence that he ignored the victims' pleas regarding their pain, insisting on continuing on until he was satiated. He queried them after the rape for money or valuables, further evidence of callousness.

"The victims were all particularly vulnerable. It's difficult to imagine a more vulnerable victim than Mrs. Rothwell.

"It is the wish of all victims that this defendant never be afforded the opportunity to prey upon single, virtually defenseless senior citizens and ruining the life of the young woman that's been referred to. So, I'm going to impose the maximum allowable period of confinement to insure this defendant serve the balance of his lifetime in a setting as secure as possible."

Richard Carrasco was sentenced to a consecutive 141 years in jail. He must serve a minimum of seventy-seven years before he comes up for parole.

On the way out of the courtroom, I noticed some spectators in the back row, a man and woman with two children. The man smiled at me and gave me the thumbs-up sign. I returned it.

Jim and I waited until Richard Carrasco's family had gotten into the elevator. "A sheriff will meet you downstairs and walk you to your car," Jim said. We walked down the hall without saying a word. Near the elevator, Jim turned to me. "Well," he said.

"Jim, thank you. That's the only thing I can think of to say. Thank you." I reached out to shake his hand, thought better of it, and hugged him. "Thank you," I said into his coat before he left.

On the wall were telephones. I called Tom. "It's over," I said. "Now I can come home."

"I'll be here," he said gently.

I rode down in the elevator staring straight ahead at the doors. When they opened, the sheriff was waiting for me. I walked ahead of him towards the door.

When we got there, I stopped and peered outside. For a few moments, I could not seem to move forward. I felt rooted to the spot.

"Are you okay, ma'am?" the sheriff asked, but it was another voice I heard. A voice that came over the telephone line eight years before and said:

"Mrs. Mints, we believe we have the body of your mother at the coroner's office, and we need you to come down and make an identification."

I put that memory back to sleep, returning it to the nether world from which it had come. Then I turned and smiled at the sheriff. Eight years, I thought, of struggle and waiting were over. Just like the day at work when I found out my mother was dead, I felt my whole life catch up with me. This time I was ready for it.

"I'm fine," I said. "You can go now." Then I opened the door and walked outside. It was a sunny day. I looked up and noticed that the sky was the same clear bright blue as my mother's eyes.

EPILOGUE

Once upon a time, there was a little girl who didn't believe that anyone loved her. Because of this, she lived most of her life both angry and scared.

Mother, you died on April 2, 1990, and I didn't know you. All I saw was the crazy woman that you sometimes were, and I was embarrassed by our mother/daughter connection. Most of my life I was afraid that I was like you, so I worked at being as different as possible.

When you died, I realized that you'd been inside me all the time. It took your death for me to discover you. At your trial I learned what you suffered because of the ignorance and prejudice of others, including myself. I also learned you were brave, and in discovering your courage I became brave too.

I didn't really get to know you until I wrote this book. In writing about you, I was forced to look at your entire life, not just the painful bits that are the easiest to remember. I saw you as a child, filled with hope, and as a young woman with plans and dreams. I imagined you in love for the first time and standing in front of a classroom teaching.

Finally, I remembered you as a mother, probably your

favorite role. Writing this book and reliving our lives and the struggle to bring your murderer to justice helped me realize that I'd loved you all along, and that you'd always loved me.

Thank you, Mother, for the legacy of your courage. It has set me free. Thank you also for your kindness and even your craziness. I miss you now and will miss you always. Everything I do from now on I do partly for you.

> *Mama, your life makes me humble*
> *Your courage makes me proud*
> *And your death made me strong.*

SPECIAL UPDATE
FOR THE
PAPERBACK EDITION

And After That

In November 1998, after the trial ended, I started work as an analyst at a small market research company called Strategies Unlimited, located in Mountain View, California. I was interested in research and had been looking for a subject to focus on for a couple of years. Truthfully, I wanted to be good at something other than surviving my mother's death. A friend of mine knew the vice president of the photovoltaic technology division (solar electric energy) and offered to introduce me. Luckily, we clicked, and I began what would become my life's work.

Having bounced from job to job, I had not thought much about finding joy and fulfillment in work. Certainly when I walked into Strategies Unlimited's small offices, I never thought I would end up staying. I had no knowledge or understanding of solar electricity. And though I was concerned about the environment and believed in doing my part by recycling and conserving energy, I had not sought out work that would get me directly involved with renewable energy.

To analyze an industry, and to do a good job of it, you have to be a general expert from its raw material through to the end user. My job involves constant learning and touches on aspects of the world that are now very important to me. It was only after taking this job that I realized how important these aspects—global warming and the alleviation of worldwide poverty—were to me.

Solar electric energy is a clean distributed generation source of electricity, providing power at the point of use, and a renewable technology that is crucial in the struggle to reverse the effects of global warming. The technology is the best chance that the almost 2 billion people living in the developing world without electricity have to experience its life-altering effects. In the developing world solar provides electricity for refrigeration, for community centers and rural schools, and also provides a nonpolluting source of lighting for households. For people in the world who will never have access to utility electricity, solar profoundly changes lives.

My new boss, Bob Johnson, is one of the experts in the solar industry, and is internationally respected for his knowledge. Upon meeting him, he reminded me almost immediately of my father, and like my father, he expected more from me on a daily basis than I thought possible. Bob was a tough but fair taskmaster. He made me rethink my analyses until I had factored in every nuance. Then he made me rethink them, again. Though I had no experience with the photovoltaic industry, he gave me enormous responsibility and believed that I would succeed.

During my first year at Strategies, I was also finishing this book and working toward my MBA. So, in a sense, I had three full-time jobs and was entering the most productive phase of my life. I started work at eight-thirty in the morning, went from work to school in the evening, and came home at ten o'clock at night to work on the book.

After six months on the job I was certain that I would never be an expert in anything, let alone solar electric energy. However, I persevered. In late 1999, this book was accepted for publication. I also earned my MBA in 1999. Around this same time I realized that I loved my work and did it well. I had finally found work that I was ideally suited for and that used my writing talent, analytical skills—which I had not known I possessed—made good use of my innate curiosity and talent for research, and introduced me to a subject about which I was now passionate. My mother, I knew, would have been proud of me.

On June 12, 1999, I walked out of the courthouse after Richard Carrasco had been sentenced, looked up at the blue sky, and drank in a feeling of freedom that had not been my experience for years. The trial had given me a purpose, but the focus it required of me was relentless. I had to sit in court every day with the person who killed my mother, holding on tight to my desire to see him punished. This sort of focus has a cost, and it is lonely because very few people understand the emotions. I didn't want revenge, I wanted my mother back. I didn't want justice, I wanted an answer. I wanted to know why my mother had lived only a few miles from my house and not contacted me. I wanted to know how she had survived. I wanted to know how Richard Carrasco could hurt her.

I learned how she had lived, how she had survived, how she had died. I knew that she lived close to me because she loved me but that she was also afraid that I would have her committed and so did not contact me. I was not close to understanding why Carrasco had murdered her. At the sentencing I realized that I did not need to understand why and that it was enough to know he would never hurt anyone else.

Now that Carrasco was sentenced, I could let go of the anger and pain that had fed my focus. Walking down the steps of the courthouse, I passed small groups of people and wanted to tell them all, "It's over," even though none of these people would know what I was talking about. On the way to my car I called friends on my cell phone to tell them that Carrasco would never hurt anyone again.

The main courthouse is in North San Jose, near where my mother lived as a homeless woman, and also where she died. During the trial I had mistakenly sat on the wrong side of the courtroom, behind the defendant. Apparently, unwritten court protocol is that the victims and survivors sit on the prosecution side of the courtroom. For a time this courthouse had been a second home, and all along I had gotten it wrong. Even at the sentencing I sat on the wrong side. None of this mattered to me now. That day, leaving the tall cement block that is the courthouse, I thought that nothing would be this hard again, and I wanted to celebrate. Instead, I went back to work.

I was in my office at work one afternoon in January 2001 when the phone rang. I was working on the industry newsletter that I was responsible for writing. "Hello," I answered as I typed a sentence about the use of solar electricity in China.

"Happy New Year!" It was Jim Shore, the assistant DA who tried Richard Carrasco for my mother's murder.

"Jim, how are you?" I turned from my computer to my desk. My office was small and crammed with piles of papers, files, and filing cabinets. It resembled the inside of my car, which is also filled with piles of books, papers, and magazines. I am not a hoarder by nature, I'm just always reading. Looking out my doorway, I could see the office manager's desk. Joy, who was also a good friend, was bent over her work.

"I'm fine." Jim was silent for a minute. I'd like to write that my instincts told me that something was up, but, unfortunately, we usually do not know when our life is about to change, again.

Jim cleared his throat, then plunged in with the point of his call. "I'm sorry, Paula, the case was reversed on appeal. I knew in November, but I chose not to tell you. I wanted you to have a nice Christmas—"

"Excuse me?" I interrupted him. "What do you mean 'reversed on appeal'?" One of my hands gripped the phone, and the other slammed down on the desktop. Joy looked up from her desk. "Excuse me," I said again. I put the telephone receiver down, got up, and shut the door. "Okay," I said, picking the receiver back up, "what do you mean?"

Jim sighed. "The conviction was reversed on a technicality, and unless the California Supreme Court agrees to hear the case, it will go back for trial. All cases go through the appeals process."

I sat at my desk, stunned. My throat closed, and I began very quietly to cry. Every part of me felt as if it were melting into the desktop. "Why?" I finally asked.

Jim sighed again. "The appeals court agreed that Carrasco had been denied his right to defend himself." Jim went on to describe the situation, but he didn't have to, I remembered. I was present in court the day for the trial setting, only to find out that Carrasco, in a delaying tactic, had fired his court-appointed attorney and requested *pro se* status, meaning that he asked to represent himself. Carrasco also asked for a delay so that he could learn more

about DNA evidence. The court denied his request, and
Carrasco thought better of representing himself. All of this
scrambling around, negotiating and changing of minds,
took just a couple of hours. Even though I did not know it
at the time, this couple of hours would impact me in the
future. The appeals court had ruled that since Carrasco
had been denied his delay, he had been denied his right
to represent himself, and they reversed the conviction.

"I don't understand," I said. "What does this mean?"

"It means that there is a high likelihood that the case
will be retried unless the state supreme court agrees to
hear the case and reinstates the verdict. If they decide
not to hear the case, then it will be retried."

"He won't get out of jail?" I asked. I felt cold all over
and began to shiver, even though the heating in our
office tended to make every room feel tropical.

"No, don't worry, no one wants him out of jail."

I asked if there was anything I could do, and Jim assured me that he would keep in touch. After we finished
the call, I sat at my desk, palms down on the desktop,
and felt exactly as I did when I found out my mother was
murdered. Every emotion was just as raw as the day I got
the phone call from the coroner—maybe even more
so—because this time I knew what the stakes were and
what I was in for. For one thing I had to call my brother
and give him the news.

My brother and a girlfriend had a daughter in 1986.
Though the relationship had not worked out, he was a devoted father. He was recently married to a longtime friend,
a beautiful Hispanic woman he'd loved for a long time. I
looked at my watch; it was three o'clock in the afternoon.
My brother worked the evening shift at the Santa Clarita
post office, so he was at work now. I could put the call off
for another day at least. I sat in my office for over an hour,

staring at the door. Finally I gathered my things and went home for the day.

I woke up the next morning very early, and very angry. I decided that I would do everything I could to influence the California Supreme Court to hear my mother's case. I got out of bed at 4:00 A.M. and began writing letters. I wrote to all of my state and federal representatives and to the chief justice of the California Supreme Court. Over the next few weeks I received a number of form letters in return and finally a call from Jim Shore telling me that the supreme court had declined to hear the case. We were going back for a second trial. The waiting began again.

It felt as if my mother had been murdered a second time, and I thought that nothing could be harder than doing this again.

I waited a few months after I got the news from Jim to tell my father about the retrial. At first, he was shocked and angry, and then he pushed the news away and refused to discuss it. Every month he became more frail and helpless. After a while he rarely left the house and could not walk without support.

I drove to Hayward from San Jose every other Sunday to take my father to lunch, just as I had once driven, years ago, to bring my mother groceries. On the way to his house I passed the motel where I had picked up my mother before putting her on a plane to her sister in Florida. I did not look at the motel as I drove by it. If I glanced at it, I remembered seeing my mother in the window looking down at me when I came to pick her up. I remembered how happy she was to see me, and how terrified of her schizophrenia I had once been. Every time I drove to Hayward, my insides hurt.

In May 2002, my father had his seventy-sixth birthday, and I gave him a party. My father's birthday party was the last time I saw my father smile. His diabetes was not controlled, and he could no longer focus his eyes to read. He was so frail that when I held his arm, he seemed to have no solid bones left. His twin brother had died the previous December, we had the second trial ahead of us, and my new sister-in-law had been diagnosed with lung cancer. But at his party my father sat at the head of the table and beamed, unable to eat his food, because he could not stop smiling.

One Friday morning that August, the phone rang at four o'clock. My stepmother was calling to tell me that my father had been rushed to the hospital. "The doctor told me that it was time to call his children," she said. Apparently, my father had been suffering from pneumonia, but he had not complained. Now he was so weak that my stepmother had taken him to the hospital. Once there he had a heart attack and was now in a coma.

I called my brother on the ride to the hospital in Hayward from my house in San Jose. He told me that he would leave immediately from southern California. Around noon I looked through the window in my father's hospital room to see my brother walking from the parking garage to the hospital. No matter what, my brother and I always reached out to each other when life went wrong, just like when we were children and our mother was sick. I knew that I could be strong with my brother there. We stayed at the hospital for the better part of twenty-four hours. The next afternoon it became obvious that our father was failing, and we asked the hospital to disconnect all of his tubes. I held my father's hand until he died.

The retrial began in October 2002. Carrasco had a private attorney for this trial, and we had a different assistant DA. Right before the trial began, my company restructured and I was laid off. I did not, of course, have much time to think about being out of work, as I was focused on the retrial. Seeing Carrasco again after these few years was a shock of recognition and disgust. In front of me every day, again, was a person who had killed my mother and wrecked many other lives. My focus on his conviction was back, stuck to me as indelibly as a tattoo.

During the first trial I had avoided the press, but this time I gave an interview as a survivor of homicide, speaking for the victim that my mother was, and that I was not. This trial had more visual evidence—pictures of my mother on the autopsy table—which I tried not to look at. This time I sat through the entire crime scene videotape. I saw where my mother had lived and died. I saw her body at the crime scene, which was also her last home. Every day my heart broke a little more, until I didn't think there was anything left to break. I let myself cry openly in court, no longer just a witness, but inside my mother's skin, mourning her openly. When the trial was over, the verdict took two hours. Carrasco was found guilty again, sentenced to a long enough term that he will never get out of jail. Of course he appealed, and this time his appeal was rejected. This time it was really over.

On December 15, 2002, my brother called to tell me that his wife had died. He was left with two stepchildren and his own child, my niece. I realized anew how much pain there is in the world, and how little control we seem to have over any of it. But also, watching my brother pick up his responsibilities and continue caring for his family, I realized that courage is often quiet, leaving few footprints, so it can easily go unnoticed.

I decided that I wanted to use my off-work time to do something more than look for a job. I had been serving once a month at a soup kitchen, but I wanted to work with people who were grieving. Grief is an emotion that overtakes you, overwhelms you, and changes you forever. It takes courage to walk through your own aching heart, and it is very hard to do alone. The weight of so much pain is difficult to witness, and so often the grieving are left alone by their friends and family. I began volunteering as a grief counselor at the Centre for Living with Dying. The center is filled with volunteers who know grief well, and who can open their hearts, listen completely, and be truly present for others. In particular, I wanted to sit with people who had lost someone to violent death.

In late 2003, Bob Johnson retired and I was called back to work as the director of the photovoltaic practice. I had missed my work and was very happy to be back. I knew that I was lucky to have work that I both loved and for which I was ideally suited. Also, I was recognized in my own right as an expert in the solar electric industry. I had the great good fortune of being able to carry forward the work of my former boss and mentor.

On August 13, 2004, at 2:00 A.M., the phone rang. It was my niece. My brother had been killed in an accident. He had been coming back from a friend's house late at night, and an abandoned car had rolled onto the freeway as he passed by on his motorcycle. At first, I did not understand what my niece was telling me. Once I did, I felt very stiff and still, as if I'd been turned into a mechanical doll that could not move without help. I forced myself to be calm and find out where my niece was, to make certain that she was okay. I asked all of the correct questions, and then hung up the phone. She had turned eighteen that June. She had just graduated from high school. After I made certain that she was not alone, and that someone would stay with her until I could get a flight to southern California, I sank down on my knees and cried. I cried for all of them—my mother, my father, and my brother. All of the people who knew where I came from were gone.

The month before his accident, my brother had spent the Fourth of July with my husband and me at our cabin in South Lake Tahoe. He'd come up alone on his motorcycle, and was late arriving. When he arrived, I yelled at him for worrying me. Instead of joking me out of my mood, my brother turned serious.

"We should talk about this," he'd said.

"No," I answered, "I don't want to talk about it, nothing is going to happen to either of us." The conversation made me nervous and I remember standing up and pacing. I didn't want to talk about death.

"Sister," he said, "if something happens to me, I want you to promise to look after my daughter. She is pretty naïve, and I need you to teach her how to be an adult."

I said I would, but told him that nothing was going to happen to him. On the night of the Fourth, we walked across the street to the beach and watched the fireworks. They burst across the clear sky, dancing to the music, as my brother, husband, and I leaned against the pier and stared up at the spectacle.

Two days before my brother died, he rode up from Los Angeles on his motorcycle for a quick visit. I was busy; I had a report and a newsletter to get out, but my brother was not a "call first" kind of guy. When he was in the U.S. Marines, he'd drop in unexpectedly with twenty of his marine friends and eat me out of house and home. By the time he and his friends left, the cupboard and refrigerator were usually picked clean as a chicken bone.

This time I yelled at him for dropping in, and then hugged him and told him to be careful. I told him that I did not know what I would do without him, and that he was the person I loved most in the world. Two days later he was dead.

I did not have time to fall apart. I had to book a flight and head to southern California to help my eighteen-year-old niece. My brother had died without a will, and someone had to handle his estate. Someone had to support his daughter until his life insurance became available. He had counted on me, and I needed to be the person he expected me to be.

I arrived at my brother's house in the morning, and my niece, looking about twelve years old, and with my mother's eyes, answered the door. I knew the moment she opened the door that no matter how alone I felt, it wasn't the truth. In front of me was a living extension of my mother and my brother, and I would always need to be strong for her.

A great deal has happened in my life since the first trial ended. I have lost, in painful and harsh ways, people I love. For a while after my brother died, I did not understand how so much could happen in one life, and I wondered what I was supposed to take away from it all.

I learned through my volunteer work with the homeless and grief counseling to open my heart completely to others, and that though a heart can break, it can mend, and then expand again. I learned a small and important truth, to tell people how you feel now, when you have the chance to be heard.

In mid-2005, I moved my practice to Navigant Consulting, where I am an associate director in charge of the PV Service Market Research Program. I am internationally known and respected for my analysis of the solar electric industry. I have been published in several respected industry magazines and am asked to speak at conferences. When I was a little girl, I wanted to know everything and make my living writing. Now I make my living from my expertise, and I am a respected writer in my field.

As a grief counselor I learned that we carry those we love in our hearts forever. I have a heart that has been broken many times now, but it has been restitched, and it is stronger, though there is a poignancy that follows me everywhere I go. I stopped grief counseling after my brother died, but it remains one of the most rewarding periods of my life. My husband and I divorced in 2006 and we remain good friends. I have wonderful friendships, and a whole new family of people I love and carry with me in this world.

I still carry the best parts of my mother forward, in the eyes that I inherited from her, in her quick intelligence which I hope I have a little of, and in all the best parts of her that I hope to continue bringing to the world. In the end I am stronger for being a part of my mother, her craziness, her love, her expectations, and her tragedies. I can look up at the blue sky—the color of my mother's, my father's, and my brother's eyes—and be grateful for the chance to love them and have them in my heart. All of their hopes live on in me.

—Paula Mints